Feminism³

Feminism³

The Third Generation in Fiction

edited by

Irene Zahava

WestviewPress

A Division of HarperCollins*Publishers*

Copyright © 1996 by Westview Press, Inc., A Division of HarperCollins Publishers, Inc.

Published in 1996 in the United States of America by Westview Press, Inc., 5500 Central Avenue, Boulder, Colorado 80301-2877, and in the United Kingdom by Westview Press, 12 Hid's Copse Road, Cumnor Hill, Oxford OX2 9JJ

Library of Congress Cataloging-in-Publication Data
Feminism 3 : the third generation in fiction / edited by Irene Zahava.
     p.   cm.
   ISBN 0-8133-2550-1. — ISBN 0-8133-2551-X (pbk.)
   1. Short stories—Women authors.   2. Feminism—Fiction.
3. Immigrants—Fiction.   I. Zahava, Irene.
PN6120.92.W65F46   1996
813'. 0108355—dc20   95-33663
                                                                              CIP

The paper used in this publication meets the requirements of the American National Standard for Permanence of Paper for Printed Library Materials Z39.48-1984.

10   9   8   7   6   5   4   3   2

Contents

Credits

SARAH SCHULMAN

Introduction

For the most part, First Wave feminists could read and write, even though they did not have the vote. Our Second Wave foremothers benefited from a rich radical tradition of revolution—international and domestic, social, political, and internal. Most of us included in this collection are descended from slaves, peasants, illiterate or undereducated miners, factory workers, farmers, sharecroppers, as well as educated warriors from all social and economic classes. Our legacies reflect the native born, immigrants, and war refugees of all stripes. We are also descended from passive bypassers, collaborators, turncoats, and lackeys. We have survived a collapsing economy to still find time to write. We have managed to learn despite an ineffectual school system, lived to adulthood without national health care. Some of us have done this through will and luck, others through protection and support. But most amazingly, we still have enough hope to make art, even as the nation plummets into incalculable depths of reaction.

So given all this historical baggage, what do we ask of a mature feminist literature? How do we take our place in the literary life of the nation? This collection is an excellent place to investigate those questions because the work covers all the bases. There are writers who have been laboring at their craft for years, some in obscurity, others as flavor of the month. There are bright young bucks from the plains. There are familiar old favorites and startling new voices. Experimentalists, social realists, recorders, and inventors. Rural adventurers, upper-class suburbanites, prisoners of small towns, exiles in the rough. One necessary component is that our work is moving from the functional writing of documentation to the expressive power of writing as an art form. From simply telling the facts of your life to actually transforming them.

For example, Rebecca Brown's story "The Death of Napoleon: Its Influence on History" avoids the trap of simply stating, "I felt powerless." Instead, she evokes the feeling in all its complex imagery in the way that a straight-ahead declaration never can. Brown achieves a virtuosic level of discovery *in* the writing, instead of simply reportorial writing *about* her discovery.

So many of us—Edwidge Danticat, Amy Bloom, Lisa Harris, Rebecca Wells, Esmeralda Santiago—are writing in the voices of young girls. Girls who don't want to grow up to be like their mothers, who have to mourn their mothers' lives. Our mothers' humiliations. Will we be able to avenge their diminishment? Will we be the first generation to not have to be mothers—the first generation whose daughters won't have to mourn? As the social climate leaves older women's hopes and expectations on the garbage heap of history, how will we cling to the power of their dream?

This combination is our generation's challenge: to take what we have learned about the art of writing, a more sophisticated and revealing approach to our subject matter, perspectives, and formal possibilities than freedom movements often produce. Then we must apply it to a retrogressive political climate. For we are in the unusual historical position of having come so far while the rest of the society has been unable to move. It is that tension, between our heightened level of demand and their virulent refusal, that sets the stage for our work.

"What means switch?" asks a character by Gish Jen, as a young Chinese girl moves into a Jewish neighborhood. She has to spend her life explaining herself. But eventually she learns that the others can never get it right, so she starts describing herself in a way that they can understand, that is not too upsetting for them, that does not disturb. And she goes through the same process with their lives, although with less awareness of the translation. The time has come for our switch. Our generation of feminist writers should no longer be required to simply explain our marginalized lives, to describe them, to "break the silence." Instead it is time for us to move on to describe the whole world, not just our world. To describe what the father-son bond really means, what going to the movies with your lover without risking your life is really like. Cris Mazza takes this on in her story "Is It Sexual Harassment Yet?" Trying through both character work and formal invention to convey the complexity of sexuality in a workplace environment.

We're being told in the newspaper every day that gay people have "special rights and special privileges," that women and people of color have unfair advantages. We are being told that we practice "reverse discrimination," that oppression and resistance are the same act. Obviously dominant people have no idea of how *they* really live. And until their lives are part of our subject matter, this false representation will be left in their hands.

So, once again, we must be devilish, brilliant, destructive, rash, thrashing, subtle, and sweet. We have to forge new subjects of inquiry. At the same time that there is an enormous amount left to be said about our favorite territorial subjects (motherhood, daughterhood, coming out, all forms of love and romance), there are thematic mountain ranges and topical deep seas that have not yet been articulated. We have to challenge ourselves not to run over the same, staked-out property. This can also be said for point of view. While we are struggling to articulate a vision of freedom in a society gone awry, we still have to re-think and re-articulate and re-imagine even our most dearly held beliefs, our most comfortable vocabularies. We have to speak for the whole world. "Madame Bovary c'est moi," said Flaubert without a blink. The time has come for us to dare to speak for him.

As Sigrid Nunez writes in "A Feather on the Breath of God," "Her father does not look at her. Her father does not know one daughter from another. But the world is full of fathers, and she can't be invisible to all of them. She cannot remember a time when the temptation did not exist for her. She was forever looking back. Her eyes grew huge with looking back."

It is an irony of history that those who make change often do not profit from it—that reward goes to the more palatable ones, to the ones best positioned to take advantage of change, or to the next generation. If we see ourselves as inheritors and progenitors of the feminist literature of freedom, we owe it to our descendants to fail to assimilate, to refuse to be contained, to insist on not repeating ourselves. The women in this volume will continue to write for many years. Compare this collection to their future collective works. If we do our jobs, you will soon read the work of the Fourth Wave—more troublemakers, misbehaved, erratic thinkers and pleasure seekers. But in the meantime thanks for checking in midstream.

Feminism³

DOROTHY ALLISON

Steal Away

Mʏ ʜᴀɴᴅs sʜᴀᴋᴇ when I am hungry, and I have always been hungry. Not for food; I have always had enough biscuit-fat to last me. In college I got breakfast, lunch, and dinner with my dormitory fees, but my restless hunger didn't abate. It was having only four dollars till the end of the month and not enough coming in then. I sat at a lunch table with the girls who planned to go to the movies for the afternoon, counting three dollars in worn bills, the rest in coins, over and over in my pocket. I couldn't go see any movies.

I went, instead, downtown to steal. I became what had always been expected of me—a thief. Dangerous, but careful. Wanting everything, I tamed my anger, smiling wide and innocent. With the help of that smile I stole toilet paper from the Burger King restroom, magazines from the lower shelves at 7-11, and sardines from the deli—sliding those little cans down my jeans to where I had drawn the cuffs tight with rubber bands. I lined my pockets with plastic bags for a trip to the local Winn Dixie, where I could collect smoked oysters from the gourmet section and fresh grapes from the open bins of produce. From the hobby shop in the same shopping center, I pocketed metal snaps to replace the rubber bands on my pant leg cuffs and metal guitar picks I could use to pry loose and switch price tags on items too big to carry away. Anything small enough to fit a palm walked out with me, anything round to fit an armpit, anything thin enough to carry between my belly and belt. The smallest, sharpest, most expensive items rested behind my teeth, behind that smile that remained my ultimate shield.

On the day that I was turned away from registration because my scholarship check was late, I dressed myself in my Sunday best and went downtown to the Hilton Hotel. There was a Methodist Outreach Convention with meetings in all the ballrooms, and a hospitality suite. I walked from room to room filling a JC Penney's shopping bag with cut glass ashtrays showing the

1

Hilton logo and faceted wine glasses marked only with the dregs of grape juice. I dragged the bag out to St. Pete beach and sailed those ashtrays off the pier like frisbees. Then I waited for sunset to toss the wine glasses high enough to see the red and purple reflections as they flipped end over end. Each piece shattered ecstatically on the tar black rocks under the pier, throwing up glass fragments into the spray. Sight and sound, it was better than a movie.

The president of the college invited all of the scholarship students over for tea or wine. He served cheese that had to be cut from a great block with delicate little knives. I sipped wine, toothed cheese, talked politely, and used my smile. The president's wife nodded at me and put her pink fleshy hand on my shoulder. I put my own hand on hers and gave one short squeeze. She started but didn't back away, and I found myself giggling at her attempts to tell us all a funny story. She flushed and told us how happy she was to have us in her home. I smiled and told her how happy I was to have come, my jacket draped loosely over the wine glasses I had hooked in my belt. Walking back to the dorm, I slipped one hand into my pocket, carefully fingering two delicate little knives.

Junior year my scholarship was cut yet again, and I became nervous that working in the mailroom wouldn't pay for all I needed. St. Vincent De Paul offered me a ransom, paying a dime apiece for plates and trays carted off from the cafeteria. Glasses were only good for three cents and hard to carry down on the bus without breaking, but sheets from the alumni guest room provided the necessary padding. My roommate complained that I made her nervous, always carrying boxes in and out. She moved out shortly after Christmas, and I chewed my nails trying to come up with a way to carry her mattress down to St. Vincent De Paul. I finally decided it was hopeless, and spent the rest of the holidays reading Jean Genet and walking through the art department hallways.

They had hardwood stools in the studios, and stacking fileboxes no one had opened in years. I wore a cloth cap when I took them, and my no-nonsense expression. I was so calm that one of the professors helped me clear paper off the third one. He was distracted, discussing Jackson Pollock with a very pale woman whose hands were marked with artist's tush. "Glad they finally decided to get these out of here," was all he said to me, never once looking up into my face. My anger came up from my stomach with an acid taste. I went back for his clipboard and papers, but his desk was locked and my file broke on the rim. In compensation I took the silk lining out of the pockets of the corduroy coat he'd left thrown over a stool. The silk made a lemongrass sachet I gave my mother for her birthday, and every time I saw him in that jacket I smiled.

My sociology professor had red hair, forty shelves of books, four children, and an entirely cordial relationship with her ex-husband. When she invited me to dinner, I did not understand what she wanted with me. I watched her closely and kept my hands in my pockets. She talked about her divorce and the politics in the department, how she had worked for John F. Kennedy in 1960 and demonstrated for civil rights in Little Rock in '65. There were lots of books she could lend me, she insisted, but didn't say exactly which ones. She poured me Harvey's Bristol Cream, trailing her fingers across my wrist when I took the glass. Then she shook her head nervously and tried to persuade me to talk about myself, interrupting only to get me to switch topics as she moved restlessly from her rocking chair to a bolster to the couch beside me. She did not want to hear about my summers working in the mop factory, but she loved my lies about hitchhiking cross-country.

"Meet me for lunch on Monday," she insisted, while her eyes behind her glasses kept glancing at me, turning away and turning back. My palms were sweaty, but I nodded yes. At the door she stopped me, and put her hand out to touch my face.

"Your family is very poor, aren't they?"

My face froze and burned at the same time. "Not really," I told her, "not anymore." She nodded and smiled, and the heat in my face went down my body in waves.

I didn't want to go on Monday but made myself. Her secretary was confused when I asked about lunch. "I don't have anything written down about it," she said, without looking up from her calendar.

After class that afternoon the sociology professor explained her absence with a story about one of her children who had been bitten by a dog, "but not seriously. Come on Thursday," she insisted, but on Thursday neither she nor her secretary was there. I stood in the doorway to her office and tilted my head back to take in her shelves of books. I wanted to pocket them all, but at the same time I didn't want anything of hers. Trembling, I reached and pulled out the fattest book on the closest shelf. It was a hardbound edition of *Sadism in the Movies,* with a third of the pages underlined in red. It fit easily in my backpack, and I stopped in the Student Union bookstore on the way back to the dorm to buy a Hershey's bar and steal a bright blue pen.

On the next Monday, she apologized again, and again invited me to go to lunch the next day. I skipped lunch but slipped in that afternoon to return her book, now full of my bright blue comments. In its spot on the shelf there was now a collection of the essays of Georges Bataille, still unmarked. By the time I returned it on Friday, heavy blue ink stains showed on the binding itself.

Eventually we did have lunch. She talked to me about how hard it was to be a woman alone in a college town, about how all the male professors treated her like a fool, and yet how hard she worked. I nodded.

"You read so much," I whispered.

"I keep up," she agreed with me.

"So do I," I smiled.

She looked nervous and changed the subject but let me walk her back to her office. On her desk, there was a new edition of Malinowski's *The Sexual Life of Savages*. I laid my notebook down on top of it, and took them both when I left. Malinowski was a fast read. I had that one back a day later. She was going through her datebook looking for a free evening we could have dinner. But exams were coming up so soon. I smiled and nodded and backed out the door. The secretary, used to seeing me come and go, didn't even look up.

I took no other meals with professors; didn't trust myself in their houses. But I studied their words, gestures, jokes, and quarrels to see just how they were different from me. I limited my outrage to their office shelves, working my way through their books one at a time, carefully underlining my favorite passages in dark blue ink—occasionally covering over their own faded marks. I continued to take the sociology professor's classes but refused to stay after to talk, and when she called my name in the halls, I would just smile and keep walking. Once she sat beside me in a seminar and put her hand on the back of my neck where I was leaning back in my chair. I turned and saw she was biting her lips. I remembered her saying, "Your family is very poor, aren't they?" I kept my face expressionless and looked forward again. That was the afternoon I made myself a pair of harem pants out of the gauze curtains from the infirmary.

My parents came for graduation, Mama taking the day off from the diner, my stepfather walking slow in his backbrace. They both were bored at the lunch, uncomfortable and impatient to have the ceremony be over so we could pack my boxes in the car and leave. Mama kept pulling at the collar of my robe while waiting for the call for me to join my class. She was so nervous she kept rocking back on her heels and poked my statistics professor with her elbow as he tried to pass.

"Quite something, your daughter," he grinned, as he shook my mama's hand. Mama and I could both tell he was uncomfortable so she just nodded, not knowing what to say. "We're expecting great things of her," he added, and quickly joined the other professors on the platform, their eyes roaming over the parents headed for the elevated rows at the sides and back of the hall. I saw my sociology professor sharing a quick sip from the Dean's pocket flask. She caught me watching, and her face flushed a dull reddish grey. I smiled as widely as ever I had, and held that smile through the long slow ceremony that followed, the walk up to get my diploma, and the confused milling around that followed the moment when we were all supposed to throw our tassels over to the other side. Some of the students threw their mortarboards drunkenly into the air, but I tucked mine under my arm and found my parents before they had finished shaking the cramps out of their legs.

"Sure went on forever," Mama whispered, as we walked toward the exit.

The statistics professor was standing near the door telling a tall Black woman, "Quite something, your son. We're expecting great things of him."

I laughed and tucked my diploma in Mama's bag for the walk back to the dormitory. People were packing station wagons, U-Haul trailers, and bulging little sedans. Our Pontiac was almost full and my face was starting to ache from smiling, but I made a quick trip down into the dormitory basement anyway. There was a vacuum cleaner and two wooden picture frames I'd stashed behind the laundry room doors that I knew would fit perfectly in the Pontiac's trunk. Mama watched me carry them up but said nothing. Daddy only laughed and revved the engine while we swung past the auditorium. At the entrance to the campus I got them to pull over and look back at the scattered buildings. It was a rare moment, and for a change my hunger wasn't bothering me at all. But while my parents waited, I climbed out and pulled the commemorative roses off the welcome sign. I got back in the car and piled them into my mama's lap.

"Quite something, my daughter," she laughed, and hugged the flowers to her breast. She rocked in her seat as my stepfather gunned the engine and spun the tires pulling out. I grinned while she laughed.

"Quite something."

It was the best moment I'd had in four years.

KAREN E. BENDER

Talk to Me Jenny

Someone had seen her wearing a yellow halter top and eating a Fudgesicle at Knott's Berry Farm. Someone had seen her walking beside a man with a feathered haircut. Someone had seen her sitting on his lap, his hands firmly holding her bare, tanned waist. Someone had seen her begin to cry. Someone had seen them sitting side by side on the corkscrew roller coaster, Jenny Foley's blond hair flaming around the back of her neck.

Shelley was fourteen the summer that everyone was looking for Jenny Foley. On Saturday, the girl disappeared from Knott's Berry Farm; by the time Camp Olympia resumed on Monday, Jenny Foley's face was in the bottom right corner of the Los Angeles *Times*. When Shelley rode the bus to camp that morning, she stared at Jenny Foley's face in the paper. Jenny had almost been a counselor at Camp Olympia, where Shelley was a counselor for a group of six-year-olds who called themselves the Funny Bunnies. Jenny Foley was also fourteen. She had walked through the camp one afternoon with Merri, the camp director, talking about how Jenny might be able to teach gymnastics. As she stood with Merri beside the Funny Bunnies, Shelley tried to categorize her quickly, as she did everyone: would Jenny Foley be her friend or not? Shelley remembered how Jenny walked across the baseball diamond. She tossed a baseball back to a camper in thirteen-year-old boys. She bent over and took a drink from the drinking fountain.

Now Jenny Foley had disappeared. She was somehow different from Shelley. Shelley looked carefully at Jenny Foley's picture. The photo was carefully posed, Jenny Foley's teeth bright and eyes glowing. Shelley had a theory that people who were victims of strange crimes somehow—intuitively—knew it before it happened. Jenny Foley, for example, had to know

6

as she sat before the yearbook photographer that this photo would be the one in all the papers. Shelley looked at the photo of Jenny Foley, at her smile, and tried to find some knowledge, some difference in her expression. But in the photo, the girl looked as though she knew she was safe.

Shelley dropped off the bus at Wilshire Boulevard and walked down the street to Camp Olympia. The sports day camp was held on the empty grounds of a local high school. She was proud about working for Camp Olympia, though she knew she was probably the only girl there who had never even kissed a boy. From the first day Shelley walked into the camp, she knew the other girls knew what she didn't—it was the way they walked, slowly, as though something had died inside them. Shelley almost didn't want to kiss a boy—she thought she'd be like the rest of them then, combing their hair endlessly in the locker room, complaining that Todd was flirting with someone else, or that Evan never called back. They stood, their breasts huge and relentless, while Shelley stood at the back of the locker room and figured out how to change from her shirt to her swimsuit so no one could see her naked body. The other counselors rarely said a word to her. Her locker was adorned with the gigantically smiling face of Tom Cruise. Why are you here? she thought. Shelley didn't really like Tom Cruise, but the other counselors' lockers were covered with pictures carefully cut out of *GQ*, so without any pictures it looked as though she did not have a life at all.

Shelley imagined she would run into Jenny on Wilshire Boulevard. The girl would be strolling out of a 7-Eleven, drinking a Slurpee. Or she would be looking into a store window, sunglasses pushed up on her head. Jenny Foley would want to be her friend. She would be done with the feathered hair man from Knott's Berry Farm. "Oh, that guy," she would say, giggling, to Shelley. "He got boring. Forget him." Shelley imagined how proud everyone would be of her for finding Jenny. Their pictures would be together in the Los Angeles *Times*.

She pushed open the wire fence to Camp Olympia. The 237 campers and their counselors were sitting in crooked rows on the baseball diamond. Merri, the director, stood on a chair in front of them, holding a megaphone.

"Olympians," Merri said, "welcome back to camp this week." The microphone squawked; she shook it. "We know you're rarin' to go to slam some baseballs and kick those soccer balls, but first we want to go over a subject that you should all know about . . . camp security."

The campers rumbled, tiredly.

The thirteen-year-old boys, who had voted to call their group Acidheads, passed around that day's newspaper.

Gary was the shortest Acidhead. He wore the sleeves of his Camp Olympia T-shirt rolled all the way up his arms. He had attached himself to Roy, the most sunburned Acidhead. Roy stared at his very pink arm and peeled off clear pieces of skin. Gary leaned against him, watching.

"Hey," Gary said. "What do Santa Monica, Tarzana, Inglewood, and Downey have in common?"

"What."

"Jenny Foley!" Gary grinned.

Roy laughed, Gary sat up, encouraged.

"Listen. How does Jenny Foley blow-dry her hair?"

"How?" said Roy.

"Mole farts!"

Another Acidhead passed a newspaper to Roy. A large picture of Jenny Foley was on page one. The newspaper lay on Roy's knees.

Roy stared at the picture of Jenny Foley. "Wait. She was here," said Roy.

Gary looked at him, puzzled. "Where, here?"

"Here," said Roy. "She threw me a baseball." He stood up and ran to the baseball diamond. "I know her."

Gary followed him. Roy knelt and touched the dirt on the baseball diamond.

"She was right here," he said.

Roy stood up, clutching a handful of dirt. "He's gonna come get me," said Roy. "I know it."

"Who?"

"That dude," said Roy. "She looked at me. She knew."

Gary picked up his own fistful of dirt. He looked at it and then prepared to throw it.

Dana, in the group of nine-year-olds called Fonzie's Girls, sat between her friend Patrice's legs so Patrice could french braid her hair.

"I would have stepped on his foot and run," said Dana.

"From who?" asked Patrice.

"That man," said Dana.

"Right," said Patrice.

"I would have jumped on the Log Jammer and swum away," said Dana.

"Yeah," said Patrice.

"Or," said Dana. "I would have screamed in his ear and smushed a cotton candy in his face."

"Right," said Patrice, biting a fingernail.

"Couldn't she tell he was a weirdo?"

"I can tell a weirdo a mile away," said Patrice.

"She was an idiot," said Dana, softly.

Shelly reached her group as her co-counselor was reciting the new rules of the camp. Funny Bunnies held hands as though they were trying to yank something important from one another. They nodded fiercely before the counselor finished her sentences. "Stick with the group at all times," the counselor said. "Get with a counselor if you need to go anywhere far. Find buddies for short distances." At the word "buddies," the campers looked at each other frantically, reaching out their arms as though each one had suddenly begun to drown. The circle dissolved as they claimed each other, furiously grabbing hands and knees. They reassembled and gazed solemnly at the counselors.

Shelley thought, I have no buddy. She was embarrassed by this thought almost as soon as she had it. She looked at her campers' hands, the safe knots they made.

Wendy, a Funny Bunny who had glued herself to Diane, raised her hand—and Diane's—carefully.

"Yes?" asked Shelley.

"If I need to get my jacket—" she pointed to a red windbreaker lying five feet from her—"do I need to bring Diane with me?"

Shelley stared at Wendy's face, blank and eager. She realized, slightly horrified, that she was supposed to give her an answer. "Uh, sure, Wendy, you can get that yourself," she said.

Wendy leaned her head on Diane's shoulder. "OK," she said.

Noreen was co-counselor of eight-year-olds. When the campers got up from the meeting to go to their activities, she left her troop with her assistant and walked by the boy counselors. Shelley watched her. Noreen wore low-cut tank tops to camp, the way Shelley did; but Noreen's breasts were huge. It looked to Shelley as though there were two large animals under her T-shirt, struggling to escape. Noreen smiled at Shelley when she passed her, and Shelley looked away. She was afraid of Noreen. She believed that Noreen knew what she didn't about everything; she admired the hard, sure way she walked by the boys. Noreen made a circle around the boy counselors, patting them on the rear. "Hey, miss me, don't you?" she giggled. "No use pretending. I know you do." The boys whirled, gave her a high five, looked away. Shelley shoved closer to look at the newspaper's police sketch of the man who disappeared with Jenny Foley. The man was good-looking in a bland way; he had features that looked as though they had come out of a can.

The Funny Bunnies hugged Shelley, pulling her to their first activity. As Shelley walked with them, she watched Noreen move smoothly into the crowd of boys. Shelley quickly looked away again.

Shelley wore low-cut camisoles to camp. She told herself it was to keep up her tan. Her arms were getting darker each day, and every night she slowly took her top off over her head and admired her new tan lines, at the way her skin stopped white when it got to her breasts.

Every afternoon after camp, it was part of her job to stand in the parking lot, getting kids into the right cars. Heavy, expensive cars pulled into the parking lot; the campers ignored them as long as they could. Pushing the campers to the right cars was complicated. Shelley held a camper by the hand and peered into the window carefully, making sure the mother was not an ax murderer. While she was doing this, a boy, Phil, kept coming over and trying to talk to her. Phil was co-counselor for six-year-old boys. Shelley had seen him watching her during lunchtime, while she sat surrounded by campers playing White Duck Yellow Duck. When she saw him watching her, she began to play White Duck Yellow Duck with renewed, intense concentration, speaking in a brighter, happier voice.

Phil was standing in front of her. He was not cute. This was just a fact. It did not seem like a fact that could be twisted or handled in a better way. She herded two small girls to a Volvo station wagon, ducked her head into a window and saw that it was being driven by Inez, the girls' housekeeper. "*Hola*, Inez!" she called, loudly. She turned and headed for the next carpool. Phil followed.

"So, can you teach White Duck Yellow Duck to my group?" he asked.

"What?" She tried to look extremely busy with her campers. They kept running out to the yellow line where the cars stopped, standing there until they saw a car coming and then barreling back, shrieking and hurling themselves against the fence. "Funny Bunnies, shut up!" she called.

"Or maybe Red Light Green Light," he said. He followed her the way dust would if she were running, kicked up behind her heels. A silver Mercedes drove up. "Mommy!" cried a gaggle of seven-year-olds.

"Wait," said Shelley. She knocked on the window of the Mercedes. A mother, ponytailed, smooth-faced, leaned over. "Hi, I'm here for Penny and Alan Smith," she said.

Shelley nodded. The mothers leaned over the seat to her, smiling, assuring her they were there for their children. She had to decide, quickly, if it was safe, if the mother was a mother, if she had an ax in her backseat. It was just a feeling. You just knew. She took Penny and Alan Smith to the rear doors. "Mommy!" they yelled. Knott's Berry Farm denied anyone could be kidnapped on its grounds.

Phil stood beside her. "Do you think you can?" he asked.

"I don't know," said Shelley. She pushed up the straps of her camisole. She looked at Phil. She tried to imagine what he could do if a mother suddenly lunged at her with a steak knife. She stepped closer to him. She grabbed two more campers as they began to run toward their mother's Volvo. She checked out the driver and pushed them in the backseat. She left the door unlocked in case they had to get out.

After camp, Shelley walked up Wilshire Boulevard to the bus stop. She watched the cars, tops silver, move by, over and over. Shelley could see the dark shapes of men leaning back in their seats, one-handing the steering wheel. Sometimes they slowed their cars and looked at her. They seemed serious as they drove by the curb, their faces emptied of everything but her. Shelley touched the straps of her tank top. She kept her eyes down. She didn't mind them looking at her; she wore their gazes all the way up the street. The cars slowed. "Hey. You. Honey. Yeah. Smile. Don't be like that." Sometimes, men called who she didn't like—men thirty, forty, frighteningly old. They waved big, awkward hands at her, smiled. When she saw them, she walked faster. The cars broke away then and whizzed crooked up the street, slowing to a long bright line at the freeway entrance. The tops of the cars winked in the sun.

At lunch, Dana and Patrice met in the bathroom. They stood on top of closed toilet seats and looked at themselves in the smeary mirror. They piled their hair on top of their heads, sucked in their cheeks, tried to look sexy. "I'm so ugly," said Dana.

"No, you have really cute eyes," said Patrice.

Dana rolled up her shorts until it looked as though she were wearing a diaper. She hopped down from the toilet and looked at the picture of Jenny Foley that was taped to the mirror.

"That's why he got her," said Dana. "He said, 'Sweetie, you have really gross hair.'" She fell, giggling, onto the floor. Patrice collapsed on top of her.

"No way she's dead," said Patrice.

"She's not dead," said Dana.

"She's running around, trying to find someone to give her a normal haircut," said Patrice.

They stood up and looked at the picture again.

"She's sort of cute," said Patrice, solemnly.

"She looks snobby," said Dana.

Patrice was quiet.

"I bet she's a bitch," said Dana.

Patrice squinted.

"How do you know?" she asked.

"I just do," said Dana.

"I know someone who knew her in school," said Patrice. "She said she was really nice."

"No way," said Dana. "Total bitch. I know. Just look at her."

The girls leaned closer.

Two Funny Bunnies, Wendy and Diane, didn't want to go to the bathroom, even with a counselor. They began to walk, stiff-legged, by eleven in the morning. Shelley bent down to them and touched their faces. "You won't miss much Red Rover. We'll just take a second," she said. Diane and Wendy clung to each other and shook their heads. "No," said Diane.

"Why not?" asked Shelley.

"He's in there," said Diane.

Shelley tried to smile.

"Come on, I'll show you no one's in there."

She steered the two campers up to the bathroom. They stood at the entrance, holding each other around the waist. "Look," said Shelley. She swung each stall door. "Okay, go away, whoever you are," she said.

"I can hold it in," said Wendy.

"Honey," said Shelley. "There's nobody in here. Really." She walked toward the girls. Wendy ran, slowly, from the bathroom with Diane. "I'm not going in," she shrieked. A trickle ran down Wendy's leg.

Diane jumped away from Wendy. Wendy began to cry.

"Oh, Wendy," said Shelley.

Wendy sat on the step of the bathroom and a rush of urine went down her legs.

"I'm not," she said.

Shelley imagined that the man who took Jenny Foley was not a murderer. She imagined that he wanted someone to love. She imagined him sitting, lonely, in a chair. Jenny Foley would be at his side, reading magazines; she bored him. She would not be able to give him what he needed. Shelley imagined the man coming into her bedroom. She moved toward him, wearing a thin night-gown. "I've never done anything bad," he told her; "No one really knows who I am." He turned her face to his and kissed her. "Don't listen to them," he whispered. Gently, he slipped a hand into her nightgown.

Noreen had a locker next to Shelley's. She changed next to her when they took the campers swimming. Shelly pulled her swimsuit over her leg first; she did not want Noreen to see her completely naked. Noreen yanked her shorts off quickly and stood in front of her locker, breasts swinging. Shelley tried not to look at Noreen's breasts.

"How're you doing," said Noreen.

"OK," said Shelley.

"I keep burning," said Noreen, rubbing her shoulder. "Damn this sun-screen."

Shelley moved toward her, wondering if they'd have a conversation. Noreen smiled.

"Want a secret?" she asked.

"Sure," said Shelley.

"I've done Kevin," said Noreen.

"What?"

"He said I had the greatest ass he'd ever seen."

Shelley clasped her hands together.

"You don't believe me."

"I didn't say that."

"You don't," said Noreen. She trapped Shelley with her arms against a locker. "This is what we did. We walked behind Bungalow 11. He took off my shift. He sucked my boobs. They were the fourth best he had ever seen. They were so great he wanted them then. You should have seen him. I wanted to laugh. I said maybe. He said I was the greatest. So I pulled him. It dries like glue on your hands."

Shelley could smell Noreen, her skin, her breath too sweet from spearmint gum, on her neck.

"What about you?" asked Noreen. Shelley jerked her swimsuit over her hips. "How many have you done?" Her breast brushed against Shelley; it shook. Shelley thought it looked as though it were made of a different ma-terial than the rest of Noreen. Shelley could not stop looking at it. "Tell me how many," said Noreen. "And you can touch it."

Shelley stepped back. Noreen grabbed Shelley's hand and put it on her breast.

"How many?"

Shelley tried to pull her arm away but she could not; Noreen was holding her hand too tight.

"Don't," said Shelley.

"How many?" asked Noreen.

Noreen's breast shuddered. Shelley could feel Noreen's heart beating. "Tell me," said Noreen. She forced Shelley's hand on the nipple. It was small and solid. Shelley could hear the high voices of the campers playing outside. Give me that ball. No fair. She cheated. Shelley tried to tell them to come in. She tried to remember what she said when she was out with them: Grab a baseball. Go get your lunches.

No one was coming in. Her hand ached. Fear settled hard, high in her throat. She told herself she did not have a hand, Noreen was holding nothing, she was holding air.

"How many?"

"None," said Shelley.

"None?" asked Noreen. "Like zero?"

"None, none, none," said Shelley.

"Oh, please," said Noreen, and dropped Shelley's hand.

Shelley ran. She ran to a bathroom and held her hand under a faucet. She turned the water to hot so it would hurt, and held the hand that had touched Noreen under it as long as she could stand it. When she lifted it, dripping, she held it up to the mirror and stared. Her hand looked the same. She wanted it to show a blackened hand, or a bleeding one, something to show what Noreen had done. But the mirror showed her hand clean.

The counselors marched the campers out onto the beach. The younger campers held onto the rope with both hands, the older ones with a finger. Merri walked along beside them, watching to see that everyone was touching a part of the rope. When they got to the sand, the boys rushed out yelling, "Come on, Mr. Cutter-Upper!" Funny Bunnies unrolled their towels next to her.

Phil's back was getting sunburned, a hopeless burn that would never turn into anything. He was playing Frisbee and glancing at her. Shelley kept watching Phil because she imagined how glad he was to be watching her. This idea was astounding to her; she could not stop watching him.

She watched him walk over to her. The campers giggled into cupped hands. They scattered as though he were a wind.

"Hi," said Shelley.

Phil sat down. She watched the other boys walking by her, smiling but never stopping; that seemed the more normal way for them to be. She could smell Phil, salt and coconut, on her towel.

"How's it going?" he said.

"Okay," she said.

"Oh," he said. He saw a couple of the Acidheads running for a Frisbee. "Go, Roy, go!" he yelled. He stood up. Roy grabbed the Frisbee and rolled, over and over in the sand. "Way to go, Roy!" yelled Phil, running over to give him a high five.

"What a catch," said Phil, sitting down again.

Shelley smiled. She noticed him looking at her legs.

"Do you like Pat Benatar?" he asked.

"No," she said.

He nodded, as though he had expected this. "Well, I have two tickets to the Forum for next week."

She sat and listened to that.

"I mean do you really hate her or would you survive?" he asked.

"Uh, sure," she said. He smiled. She turned away from him, quickly. The Funny Bunnies were furiously digging a hole in the sand. "You girls need help?" asked Shelley.

"YES!" they chimed. "Start on this hole."

The Acidheads had arranged their towels on their own section of the beach. AC/DC was blasting from a huge silver box. They lay, belly-up on their towels. The littlest boys crawled through the sand and stared at them.

At the end of the day, everyone lined up—237 campers with their ropes. They looked as though they were going to begin a drill-team routine, fourteen lines standing on the sand. Merri counted. They waited to hear if anyone was missing.

Shelley was pulling softball equipment from a box. She looked at the drinking fountain that Jenny Foley had used. Shelley thought that people who were kidnapped or killed had one moment when they decided to do the wrong thing. She wondered if drinking from this fountain was the moment when Jenny made her mistake. This was where she thought it would be fun to go to Knott's Berry Farm. Or this was when she knew she was going to die. Shelley imagined that Jenny Foley became a different person then, a slower, dumber one. The problem was that she did not know how it would feel to know you were going to die, how to know if you were one of those people or not. I am not that dumb, she thought. I would not go to Knott's Berry Farm on that exact day. Jenny, you idiot, she thought. You should have known. She imagined Jenny Foley wandering around the park; she would walk like someone who knew she was going to die. Shelley turned on the water. Was this the thing that would make her end up like Jenny Foley? Or was not taking a drink the action that would make her like Jenny Foley? Tell me, she thought. She was afraid to do anything. The world sat, hot and lazy, in front of her, ready to destroy her if she made the wrong move. She wanted to cry, to kick the world, but the thing she kicked might be the exact thing that would save her. She leaned over and quickly drank from the fountain. This will save you, she tried to tell Jenny. I will drink from this fountain and that will make you live.

The Acidheads, Roy and Gary, ate their lunches in the parking lot. The girl counselors who were off sat nearby them. Their legs were dark against their bright nylon shorts. Roy and Gary leaned against cars, chewed on sandwiches, and watched them. "Gimme some ass, bitch," Gary said quietly to Roy. Roy laughed. "Lynn," Gary said. "Hot legs but totally titless. I don't know. She's do-able." The counselors bit into apples. The hair on their arms glinted gold in the heat. "Terri," continued Gary, "wants some. Bad." He pushed his hand through his hair. "She's not gonna get any from me."

They moved up to the fence. The camp bordered a busy boulevard, and office workers were hurrying out of big, mirrored buildings to lunch. Women on their lunch break rushed by, heels tapping the pavement. Gary pressed his face against the fence. "Let's meet some chicks," he said.

Roy gripped the fence and shook it, nervously. "How?" he asked.

"Hey, miss. Hey. My friend here thinks you're cute and wants to know . . . wants to know if you'll suck his dick," said Gary. The woman he was addressing pulled her purse closer to her and kept walking. Roy swung away from the fence with one arm and closed his eyes.

"Let's steal some extra Popsicles," Roy said.

"They love me," said Gary.

Roy turned away. Gary jumped on his back and they fell to the asphalt. Roy gagged on the black crumble. "Fuck you!" he yelled at Gary.

"Do it," said Gary.

"Fuck this," said Roy.

Gary grabbed his arm. "DO it," he said.

Roy pushed Gary so he flew off him, skidding along the asphalt. "Shit, man," said Gary. He pulled Roy up and flung him against the fence so he had to look at the sidewalk. Roy grabbed the fence and looked at what was out there.

"Hi," said Roy, gently, terrified, to anyone.

The woman he spoke to kept walking.

"I said, 'hi,'" said Roy, frantically.

"Hey Babe," said Gary, hopping beside him, "Try it. Hey Babe."

Roy shook Gary off his arm. He ran to a bungalow where no one could see him. He stood, alone, by the drinking fountain and kicked it. He kicked it again and again. He closed his eyes and kept kicking.

Dana sat on the bathroom sink and looked at a copy of that day's newspaper left in the trash can. Jenny Foley's face was still on the front page.

"Spare me," she said. She flipped through the paper. "I am so sick of her face," said Dana.

"Really," said Patrice.

"What did she do?" said Dana.

"Yeah," said Patrice.

"She's not that pretty."

"Right."

"She has weird hair."

"Yeah."

"Why aren't I in here?" said Dana, shaking the newspaper. "No one likes me as much as her."

Patrice took her hand. She examined Dana's face.

"Bangs," she said.

"What."

"I don't know. She has them."

"Are you sure?" said Dana, fiercely.

Patrice squinted. "Yes," she said.

Dana stared at herself in the mirror and sighed.

"OK," she said.

Shelley sat in bed at night and looked at her breasts. She would be reading a magazine and her nightgown would fall open to show her cleavage; it needed to be touched. She wished her family would leave the house so she could touch her breasts in different rooms. She imagined how they would look under the kitchen overhead, by the living-room lamp. She imagined herself walking through her house, looking down at her breasts. She slid under the under the covers. She wondered if Phil lay awake at night and thought of her breasts. It made her laugh, thinking of Phil digging his head into his pillow, imagining ways he could touch her breasts. She thought she would give him a gift; she would touch them for him. She lifted a hand and held it over her nipple. "I like your breasts, Shelley," she whispered in his voice and pinched her nipple the way she thought a boy might. She let him pinch her nipple twice.

Shelley tried to remember which hand Noreen had touched. Was it this hand or the other one? She rubbed her hand hard against the sheets. She tried to rub it to nothing.

Gary was chewing on a piece of apricot fruit roll and watching the women walk on the sidewalk. He looked blankly out at the figures moving in front of him, reached forward as though he wanted to explain something to them; they kept moving away.

"That one," he said.

Roy leaned hard against the fence. He spread his arms very wide and shook it so it rippled. "Cool it," he said.

Roy turned and ran to the equipment box. He pulled out the bag of baseballs. He poured them out onto the grass and began grabbing them, feeling them, trying to find something different about one. That girl had touched one of these balls.

"What's going on?" asked Gary.

Roy stood up, panicked, ran around the pile of balls.

"I'm in love," said Roy.

He stepped away from Gary, reached into his pocket and brought out a crumpled piece of newspaper. It showed another picture of Jenny Foley that had been in the paper—a smiling Jenny, standing beside a bicycle. Roy looked at the newspaper. "What a fox," he said.

"I know," said Gary.

"I'm serious," said Roy. "I love her."

Gary stood still, as though he were trying to hear something very quiet. "She's do-able," said Gary, agreeably.

"No," said Roy, waving the newspaper with relief, "I'm talking love. L-O-V-E."

The two of them looked at each other blankly. "You know," said Roy. He dived for a slightly torn baseball in the middle of the pile. He examined the baseball hopefully.

Gary moved closer.

"What?" said Gary.

Shelley went with Phil to the video arcade and watched him shoot moving cactus. He hunched over the rifle, trying to seem male. Shelley stood close to him and looked at the cactus. She looked at Phil's arms, his hair.

She imagined the taste of his mouth, full of cheap Mexican food. She imagined how that taste would fill hers, how their mouths could taste alike. She spun her hair around a finger. His car slowly glided toward her house.

She kept her hand on the door handle. The moment he stopped the car she smiled at him and said goodnight, hurtling the rest of the way up to her house.

She liked it this way, before he touched her. He did not know what she felt like. He could not say she was too thin or not curvy enough. All he could do was imagine how wonderful she could be.

Roy tucked the can of spray paint under his arm. He walked down to the parking lot and stood in front of a blank bungalow wall. He shook the can of spray paint a couple times and then stepped forward. He did all four sides of the bungalow: I LOVE YOU JENNY I LOVE YOU JENNY I LOVE YOU JENNY I LOVE YOU JENNY, using the leftover spray paint to make a huge black dot. Roy walked around the bungalow three times, looking at what he had written.

"Hey!" called Gary. "What's going on?"

Roy looked at Gary cautiously. "Nothing," he said.

Gary saw the graffiti. "No way, man, no WAY." He ran around the bungalow, then slapped Roy on the back. "It's beautiful. Beautiful."

"Do you think she'll see it?" asked Roy.

"Merri? Hopefully."

"No, that girl."

"What girl."

"That Jenny girl," said Roy, fiercely.

Gary contemplated this. "Isn't she wasted?"

"No," said Roy.

"Didn't they think they found her legs at some mini mall?"

"NO," said Roy, nervously stepping away.

"I think she's wasted," said Gary, gleefully. "I think she's gone. Dead. A major worm-meal. A feast . . ."

Roy stepped forward and glared at Gary. "Look," he said to Gary. "She threw me that damn baseball. She can tell him not to find me. So fuck off, will you?"

Gary's eyes were small and puzzled. "Oh, thanks. Thanks. I tell you what a gorgeous thing you've done and you tell me to fuck off. Well fuck you, fuck YOU, Roy." He turned around and ran back up to the lunch area.

Roy stood by himself in the parking lot. He walked to the farthest point of the lot. He examined the letters. It was all he knew how to do.

Wendy began to hide. She did this while the group was walking to different activities; slipped behind a bush or crawled into a burned-out tree stump or zoomed, frantically, up to the locker room. When Shelley counted only eleven Funny Bunnies, she knew who would be missing; she let her co-counselor take over the group while she ran through the camp, looking for Wendy. The girl usually picked ridiculously obvious hiding places, a sleeve of her bright red Camp Olympia T-shirt peeking out. She would be curled up tightly in a ball, the wind gently lifting her hair.

Shelley touched Wendy gently. "Hey, we need you for Red Rover," she said.

Wendy kept her face in her arms. "No," she said.

"Why?"

Wendy rolled her eyes. "He won't find me here," she whispered.

"Who?"

Wendy lifted her head and sighed. "You know," she said.

Shelley was sitting beside Phil in the car. He was fiddling with the knobs on the radio. His leg was pressed against hers. She wondered if he noticed this. She liked the slight pressure of his leg against hers. She didn't know how to keep it this way, their legs pressed together. That was all.

"That is the most horrible song in the world," she said, as Phil flicked by a disco song.

"I know," he said, nodding as though his hatred of the song were the key to himself and his theory of life. "It's almost as bad as Donna Summer."

"You are so right," said Shelley.

They sat, agreeing. Shelley noticed an odd look in Phil's eyes, a determination.

"Shelley," he said, softly.

She saw his hand, a blur, move toward her face, and he was holding her, his face close. He looked different close up. His nose looked large, his eyes very small; he looked like someone else. His hand was on her shoulder, and she sat there under his hand, not moving. She thought she understood why Jenny did not run. Maybe she did not think anything could happen; maybe she wanted to see what would happen. Phil's mouth was wet on hers, his tongue a strange animal; his hand gripped her shoulder. She thought he liked her, that was why he was holding her this way; maybe Jenny thought this, too; maybe she thought the murderer loved her. Fear began to gather inside her; she tried to get herself to move, to run. She didn't. She held still for him because she did not know what else there was for her to do.

Phil moved back and rubbed his hand over his mouth. He was just Phil. "I like you," he said.

Shelley rubbed her arms. She did not know what part of her Phil had touched. It seemed more delicate than skin. It did not hurt, but she waited to begin to hurt.

She wanted to be big, bigger than she was; she wanted to find Jenny's small, shaking hand and bring her home.

Phil pulled at his watch.

"Is that OK?" he asked.

Dana was getting her hair cut. That was how she found out. She was dropped off at noon at the parking lot and rushed up to the lunch area. She slowed down and walked, hair damp, toward the rest of the campers. She touched her bangs and took a deep breath.

Shelley saw her standing quietly by the Funny Bunnies. "Hey, Dana, what's up?" she asked.

Dana touched her hair. Shelley smiled. She did not say anything. Dana looked at the ground.

"Nothing," she said.

Shelley nodded and turned back to the Funny Bunnies.

"They found that girl," said Dana.

"What?"

"She's totally dead," said Dana.

The Funny Bunnies stopped eating their sandwiches. They watched Shelley carefully.

"How do you know?" asked Shelley.

"I heard it with my mom on the radio," said Dana.

"Well, what?" she said. She wanted to shake Dana. "How do they know?"

Dana touched her hair again. "They found her head in a trash can," said Dana. "At the beach."

Roy and Gary walked by, carrying their lunches, and stopped.

"Who, that chick?" asked Gary.

"Yeah," said Dana.

Diane ran back to Shelley and wrapped her arms around her leg.

Shelley sat down amid the Funny Bunnies. She felt their spit, their stringy hair. They watched her. She had nothing to tell them. She wanted to say something good, but she could think of nothing to say.

The Funny Bunnies saw this; they clutched her legs, her arms, harder, harder. The Funny Bunnies pushed her down. They were hugging her, bringing her napkins, half-eaten Fig Newtons, handfuls of grass. "It's OK," they murmured, the way it had been said to them. Shelley felt her group surrounding her, their arms wide as though they did not know how large was the thing that they were trying to hold.

She felt someone bend down on the grass with them. "Hey," said Phil. Shelley turned around and saw him looking at her. He put his hand on her arm. She felt it resting on her, very gently. She waited for herself to move away from him.

Patrice ran over to Dana, who was standing in a crowd of campers, crying, saying, "She's dead, she's dead, she's dead."

Patrice grabbed Dana's arm. She pulled her out of the group and ran to the end of the lunch area.

"That girl's dead?" Patrice asked.

"Yeah," said Dana.

"Yuck," said Patrice.

Dana wiped the tears from her face. "No one noticed," she said.

"What?"

Dana pointed to her head. "My hair," she said.

"Oh, right," said Patrice.

"Don't you see?"

Patrice shook her head.

"Oh my God," said Dana. She turned and ran from Patrice to the parking lot.

Wendy, the Funny Bunny, began to cry. "I want to go home," she said to Diane. Even though their mothers were not due for three more hours, they ran, holding hands, to the parking lot. They went right to the wire fence, put their feet into the wire diamonds, and shook the fence so it curved under their weight. Wendy and Diane looked out at the empty parking lot, black and glittering. "Mommy," cried Wendy.

"Mommy."

"MomMEEE."

"MOMmeee."

The lot remained empty.

"Drive in when I say 'now,' " said Wendy. "Now."

"Now," said Diane. She shook the fence.

Cars rushed by.

"I hate you," said Diane to the empty parking lot.

She picked up a rock and threw it. The rock skidded across the parking lot, hit nothing.

Wendy stared at Diane as though she had just invented this movement. Diane picked up a bent milk carton and hurled it. "I hate you!" she yelled again. Wendy shook the fence. Diane threw rocks with two hands at once. Wendy jumped off the fence and picked up a tennis ball. She threw it, two-handed, from her chest; it dropped and rolled, slowly, on the ground. The two of them stood, yelling, throwing anything they could find into the air.

Roy ran for the parking lot. He leaped past the baseball diamond, holding his spray paint can tightly under his arm. He circled a clean bungalow and stood in front of it, jiggling the spray paint can in his hands.

Roy sprayed TALK TO ME JENNY on one side of the bungalow.

Gary saw Roy with the spray paint and he took off, rushing down to the bungalow, breathing hard. "Hey," he said, smiling when he saw a new message on the wall. "Genius." He smiled at Roy. Roy did not look at him.

Gary limply kicked a rock.

"Einstein," he tried.

Roy pulled the picture of Jenny Foley out of his wallet. Gary looked at the wall and mouthed the words there.

"And say what?" asked Gary.

Diane and Wendy saw Roy spray painting and rushed over, clutching crumpled soda cans. They saw what he had written and stepped back. "No!" said Diane, throwing her soda can at Jenny's name.

Dana ran down from the lunch area, holding her hand over her haircut. She saw the group gathered by the bungalow and came over and read what Roy had written.

"No way," she said. "No way, no way." She grabbed the spray paint can out of Roy's hand and rushed up to the bungalow wall. She started to spray a black line through the word TALK. "Shut up!" she said to the bungalow.

Gary leaped toward her, excitedly, and tried to grab the can. Dana turned around and sprayed black paint over Gary's shirt. "Bitch!" Gary grabbed the can from her so violently Dana fell to the ground.

Shelley was running. She came, hair flying, down from the lunch area, running toward the words on the bungalow. "You guys!" she called. Gary quickly slipped the spray paint can under his T-shirt and crossed his arms over it.

"What?" he asked.

Shelley looked at his wet, blackened T-shirt. Then she looked at the words on the bungalow.

"And say what?" she asked.

Jenny was gone. Wendy and Dana and Roy and Gary and Patrice looked at her, waiting, and all she felt was grief, an intense clutching, a new hand inside her, grabbing at anything desperately, over and over. She was fourteen years old. The campers stood, quietly, in front of her. Shelley did not know what to tell them. She was afraid of the young, thirsty way they were looking at her; all she knew was the enormous emptiness inside her that did not know how to stop Jenny from disappearing, that did not know how to protect anyone at all. She did not want to tell them this. She did not know herself how to manage it. All she could see was the terrible, gentle way the water fountain had cracked, the way a basketball was rolling slowly toward the busy intersection, the uneven way sand was blowing up around their feet.

"Time to head back," she said.

The campers stepped away from her, disappointed. They moved together like clouds, slow and blind and lonely. "You guys," said Shelley, a little desperate, "Come on, let's go. Popsicle time. It's grape today." She wanted to bring all of them back with her, walk back to lunch with all their young, sweaty weight. They stood, sneakers dirty, arms burning. Shelley began to walk up to the lunch area. The campers didn't follow her. They stood, looking at the words on the bungalow, waiting.

JULIE BLACKWOMON

The Long Way Home

It is three days after my twelfth birthday and my mother is sitting beside me on the edge of my bed. She is holding a box of sanitary napkins and a little booklet that reads *What Every Young Girl Should Know* and telling me for the third straight year that I am to read the booklet and keep the pads hidden from the sight of Daddy and Leroy. I am hardly listening. I am sneaking furtive glances out the window and patiently waiting for her to finish so I can meet the boys out on the lot for our softball game.

My mother is saying, "Look, you've thrown your pretty dress on the floor." She is bending down to pick it up. It is a white flared dress with large yellow flowers. Daddy bought it for my birthday. I am remembering the party, the coconut cake with twelve ballerinas holding twelve pink candles. Momma has straightened my hair but refused to wave it tight to my head so it will look like a process. Instead she has fluffed up the curls like she does my sister Dee Dee's hair. Momma is serving punch in a starched white apron or just standing around with her hands folded in front of her. When she catches my eye she motions with her head for me to go over and talk with the other girls who are standing in a cluster around the record player. I smile nervously back at her, but remain where I am.

My friends are all acting strange. Leroy, my brother and best friend, has been stuck up under Diedra Young all evening and Raymond and Zip-Zip are out on the back steps giggling with Peggy and Sharon. Jeffrey teases me about my knobby black knees under my new dress until I threaten to punch him in the mouth. I wander out to the kitchen to play with Fluffy, our cat, until Momma misses me and comes to drag me back to the party.

Now sitting on my bed with Momma, she is saying she will have to get me a training bra. I self-consciously reach up and touch my breasts then jerk my hands down again. I hate them. I'm always hurting them when I bump into things and now when I fight I have to worry about getting hit in the breasts too.

"Momma, can I go now? I gotta pitch today," I say. Momma puts her arm around my shoulder and pulls me close to her.

"Sugar, you've got to stop playing with those boys all the time; why don't you go play with Sheila, that nice young girl who's staying with the Jenkins?"

"But I don't know her."

"Well, you can get to know her. She's a nice enough girl and she doesn't know anybody. You can introduce her to the rest of the girls."

"But Dee knows them better than I do."

"Yeah, sugar, but Sheila doesn't have any girlfriends and you don't either, so you can be friends with each other."

I pull away from her. "I got friends," I say. I'm getting annoyed at the conversation, I want to go out and play. I get up and walk over to the window and stand there with my back to her.

"Okay," Momma says finally, "but I've invited the Jenkins over for lunch after church on Sunday and if you want to be friends with Sheila, fine, if not. . . ." She shrugs her shoulders.

"You gonna make Dee be there too?"

"Yup."

"Can we invite Zip-Zip and Jeffrey?"

She hesitates a moment. "Maybe next time."

"Okay, can I go now?" I am inching towards the door.

"Alright, scoot." She pats me on the butt as I pass her. I am running down the steps, jumping over the last two. Dee Dee, who had been listening at the door, says "Can I go with you, Cat?"

"No."

"Why not?"

"'Cause you can't."

With Dee Dee at my heels I reach the vacant lot where we play ball. There is no game today. The boys are busy gathering ammunition—dirt clods, rocks, bottles—for the fight with the white boys from across the tracks. Dee Dee whines to Leroy:

"Leroy, I wanna go."

"You can't," Leroy says.

"How come?"

"'Cause you're too young."

"I'm just as old as Jeffrey!"

"You can't go," Leroy says, "besides you're a girl."

"Cat's a girl," she says indignantly.

We ignore her. We are gathering sticks and rocks and throwing them into an empty milk crate.

"How come I can't go? Huh? How come?" Nobody answers her. We are all walking across the lot. Raymond and Leroy are carrying the ammunition; Dee Dee is standing where we left her, yelling, "I'm gonna tell Momma what you're up to too! I'm gonna tell you're going cross the tracks to fight with those white boys." Then, after a moment or two: ". . . And Cat's got Kotex in her dresser drawer!" My neck burns but I keep walking.

I am sixteen years old and sitting in Sheila's dining room. We are playing checkers and I am losing badly and not minding at all. Her cousin Bob comes in. He is stationed in Georgia and on leave from the army. He says hi to Sheila, ignores me completely and walks through to the back with his green duffel bag in his hand. His voice drifts in from the kitchen, "Where'd the little bulldagger come from?"

Sheila springs back from the table so fast her chair overturns. She yells in the kitchen doorway, "You shut your nasty mouth Bob Jenkins!" The next day we are supposed to make cookies for her aunt's birthday but she calls to suggest we do it over my house instead. I do not go back over Sheila's again unless Dee Dee is with me or there is no one home.

We are in Fairmount Park within some semi-enclosed shrubbery. Sheila and I are lying on our backs on an old army blanket. We look like Siamese twins joined together at the head. The sky is blue and I am chewing on the red and white straw that came with my Coke.

"Cat, tell me again how you used to almost be late for school all the time because you used to be waiting for me to come out of my house so we could walk to school together," Sheila says.

"I've told you a thousand times, already."

"Well, tell me again, I like to hear it."

"If you hadn't been peeping from behind the curtain yourself and waiting for *me* we both might have gotten to school on time."

She laughs softly then turns over on her stomach.

"Kiss me," she says.

I lean up on my elbow, check around to make sure nobody's peeping through the bushes then turn and press my lips to hers. After a few seconds she pulls away. "Man, Cat, I never thought I could like a girl as much as I like you."

"Me neither," I reach out and touch her hand. We kiss again, briefly, our lips barely touching. Then we turn and lie as we were before but continue holding hands.

"Cat?"

"Yeah?"

"I think I'm in love."

"Me too."

She squeezes my hand. I squeeze hers back.

"What would you do if Bob came by and saw us now?" Sheila asks.

"What would you do?"

"I don't know, I'd say 'Hi' I guess."

"Then I would too," I say.

The sun has moved and is now shining directly over us. I cover my eyes with my forearm.

"Bob would say we're both bulldaggers," Sheila says after a while.

"Yeah, I guess he would," I say.

"We aren't bulldaggers, are we Cat?"

"No, bulldaggers want to be men. We don't want to be men, right?"

"Right, we just love each other and there's nothing wrong with loving someone."

"Yeah and nobody can choose who you fall in love with."

Sheila and I are in her bedroom; her uncle is standing over the bed shouting, "What the hell's going on here?" He is home from work early. Sheila and I scramble for the sheet and clutch it across our naked bodies. I am waiting for her uncle to leave so I can get up and get dressed, but he just stands there staring, thunder in his face. Finally I release my end of the sheet and scramble to the foot of the bed. Sheila's stockings are entwined in my blouse. I cram panties into my pocket and pull blue jeans over naked, ashen legs. I am trembling. Her uncle's eyes follow me around the room like harsh spotlights.

Later at my house Daddy and I are in the dining room. Leroy and Dee Dee are in their rooms, the doors are shut tight. They've been ordered not to open them. My mother sits on the couch wringing her hands. I sit stiffly forward on the edge of a straight-backed chair, my head down, my teeth clenched.

My father stomps back and forth across the floor, his hands are first behind him, holding each other at the butt, then gesturing frantically out in front. He is asking, "What's this I hear about you being in bed with the Jenkins girl?" I sit still on the edge of my chair, looking straight ahead.

"I'm talking to you, Catherine!" His voice is booming to the rafters. I'm sure the neighbors hear. It is dark outside and a slight breeze puffs out the window curtains. I am holding a spool of thread that had been on the table. I am squeezing it in my hands, the round edges intrude into my palms. I continue to squeeze.

"You hear me talking to you, girl?" He is standing directly over me now, his voice reverberates in my ear. I squeeze the spool of thread and stare at a spider-shaped crack in the wall above the light switch. There is an itch on my left thigh but I do not scratch. Dogs bark in the backyards and one of the Williams kids is getting a spanking. I hear the strap fall, a child wailing and an angry woman's voice.

My father is saying, "Look, you'd better say something, you brazen heifer." He jerks my head around to face him. I yank it back to stare at the crack in the wall.

"You're lucky Tom Jenkins didn't have you arrested—forcing yourself on that girl like that . . ."

"What? What force? Sheila didn't say I forced her to do anything!"

"If you didn't force her then what happened?"

"Sheila didn't say that! She didn't say that! Mr. Jenkins must have said it!" I am on my feet and trembling, and screaming at the top of my young lungs.

"Then what did happen?" my father screams back at me.

I sit back down in the chair and again stare at the crack in the wall above the light switch. Trying to concentrate on it, blot out my father's voice. I cannot. I get up and run to the chair where my mother sits. I am pulling on her arm. "Momma, Sheila didn't say that did she? She didn't say I forced her?"

Momma sits there biting on her bottom lip and wringing her hands in her lap. She lays her hand on my head and doesn't speak. My father grabs my arm and yanks me away. I am enveloped in his sour breath. "Look, I am a man of God and don't you dare doubt my word!" I yank my arm away from his grip and run toward the safety of my bedroom.

"I haven't dismissed you!" I hear my father's footsteps behind me. He grabs me by my T-shirt and swings me around. I lose my footing and fall at the bottom on the steps.

"Arthur, Arthur!" My mother is running behind us. My father's knee is in my chest and he is yelling in a hoarse angry voice. "There will be no bulldaggers in my house, do you understand me, girl? THERE WILL BE NO BULLDAGGERS IN MY HOUSE."

I am sitting, beside Sheila on a bench in Fairmount Park; we are within walking distance of the spot where we used to meet with our lunches on Daddy's old army blanket. The grass is completely green except for one long crooked brown streak where the boys trampled a short cut to the basketball court. The leaves are green save for one or two brown or yellow ones beneath the bench at our feet. Sheila's head is bent.

"I am sorry," she is saying. She is picking tiny pieces of lint from a black skirt. "I'm really sorry but you don't know how my uncle is when he gets mad." I am silent. I am watching three boys I don't know play basketball on a court about twenty yards away. A tall white kid leaps up and dunks the ball.

"I just didn't know what else to do," Sheila continues, "I was scared and Uncle Jim kept saying 'She made you do it, didn't she?' and before I knew it I'd said 'yes'." A short Black kid knocks the ball out of bounds and a fat boy in a green sweatshirt darts out to retrieve it.

"Cat?" Her hand is on my forearm and I turn to look her full in the face. "I'm sorry Cat, I just didn't know what else to do." I turn again towards the basketball court, watch the tall white boy holding the ball under his arm. The fat boy in the green sweatshirt is pulling a Navy blue poncho on over his head.

"Cat, please?" Sheila is saying.

I turn to look her full in the face. "It's alright Sheila, it's alright."

It is getting windy. The basketball court empties and Sheila asks if I'll meet her at our spot next Saturday. I lie and say yes. She checks to make sure no one's looking, pecks me on the cheek, then gets up to leave. I sit watching the empty basketball court for a long time. Then I get up and take the long way home.

AMY BLOOM

When the Year
Grows Old

On a Wednesday afternoon, Kay Feldman came home from Italian
Club, which was run by Signora Maselli and filled with other misfits, girls
bright enough but too shy for the school paper, too prim or clumsy for
Modern Dance, and one boy, obviously crazy, who announced that he
planned to read all of Dante before the end of ninth grade. Kay called out for
her mother and heard nothing. There was no note on the kitchen table, only
half a cup of thickening coffee and an ashtray with stubbed-out cigarettes.

Kay's mother only drank tea, usually herbal tea, and she had never, as far
as Kay knew, ever smoked a cigarette. Kay had never even seen an ashtray in
their house. When her aunt Ruth came to visit, Kay's father made her go
outside to smoke, even in the winter. Kay could feel cold lines of sweat sliding down her sides.

Kay called out again and walked through every room, telling herself that
her mother had gone for a walk, which she sometimes did, and had just forgotten to leave a note, which was unimaginable. Kay looked through the
rooms of their house, excited beneath her anxiety, wondering whether she
would see something terrible. A body, not her mother's, of course, but
maybe some anonymous body flung across the bed, murdered by an anonymous someone else. Even better, murdered by her father, who will rot in jail
and Kay will change her name and never, ever visit him. There was no body.
The beds were unmade, which was unusual, and her mother's typewriter,
which sat on a small pine table in what they called the guest room, was
missing. Kay heard a faint mewing sound and jumped. Her father claimed
he was allergic to cats, and despite her pleas and her mother's wistful looks,

there were no pets. Kay didn't think he was allergic at all; she thought, correctly, that he hated cats and didn't want to argue.

The mewing came from the basement. Kay walked down, thinking about herself in the fictional third person, as she sometimes did: "Bravely, Portia Ives descended the creaky stairs into the dank basement . . ." The Feldman basement was not particularly dank, as basements go. Her parents would never do anything as suburban or hospitable as finishing off the basement, but it was usually dry, and the only smell was of cool concrete and minerals. At the bottom of the steps Kay sniffed repeatedly, in disbelief: those confusing, disorienting smells were the sharp reek of cat pee and the ropy, sexy scent of cigarettes.

"Oh, hi, honey, I didn't hear you come in."

Kay's mother was wearing clothes Kay didn't recognize. Her straight blond hair was pushed back by a wide black headband, and she had on a baggy black v-neck sweater, the sleeves pushed up to her elbows. Her pants were black too, and she was barefoot.

"Is there a cat in here?" Kay wanted to grab her mother, shouting, What kind of joke, what kind of demented game is this, cigarettes and cats and the beds not made?

Kay's mother giggled. The giggle was more frightening than the cigarettes. Kay's mother did not giggle; she smiled pleasantly at her husband's elaborate puns, and she pretended not to hear Kay's rude remarks.

"Yes, there is. He's not quite potty-trained, but we're getting there. Did you know that even very small kittens will begin using the kitty litter within twenty-four hours? And they've got this new kind of kitty litter, it's green and it's incredibly absorbent and soaks up most of the smell. He's in the corner there."

"Whose cat is he?" And why are you sitting on a folding chair, in the middle of the afternoon, in the goddamn basement?

"Mine, ours. How about calling him Blake—you know, 'Tyger! Tyger! burning bright / In the forests of the night, / What immortal hand or eye / Could frame thy fearful symmetry?' Do they still teach that at school? I think Blake is still my all-time favorite. I love 'Songs of Experience.'"

Kay stared at her mother. Her mother, the mother she knew, taught English as a Second Language in Adult Education and was always in the kitchen at five o'clock getting dinner started so the kitchen would be clean by the time she went to teach. Kay's mother wore khaki slacks with a narrow brown belt, brown flats, and pink or white turtlenecks. Sometimes she wore navy or mint green. When she went to teach, she put on a skirt and a cardigan with one of the turtlenecks. Kay's father said, trying to be nice, that Laura dressed like a lady. More often, he said she dressed like a nun.

"Where did you get those clothes, Mom?"

Laura looked at Kay in surprise and looked down at her black pants. She shrugged. "I found them in the trunk. I can't believe they still fit. Isn't that nice?"

At least her mother's verbal habits hadn't changed: cheerful evasion, calling everything "nice." Kay decided to act as though nothing else had changed.

"Are you coming upstairs? It's after five."

"I don't think so, honey. I'm in the middle of something, and it's going to take a little longer to get Blake acclimated. Look at him, cowering over there. Do you want to pick him up?"

Kay looked at her mother, who always warned her that animals carry germs, and looked at the kitten, a tiny bundle of strawberry blond spikes. Yesterday, if they had somehow acquired a kitten, her mother would have suggested calling him Sunshine or Buttercup, and Kay would have rolled her eyes in contempt. Kay picked up the kitten and could feel him squirming, brushing the back of her hand with a tongue like a tiny thistle.

"So what am I supposed to do? Do I have to make dinner?"

"Well, no, I wouldn't think so. Didn't you stop at Swenson's? You're not hungry yet, are you?"

Kay was having trouble with the idea that this weird beatnik knew everything her mother knew and seemed to be able to make use of it, in ways her mother was never able to manage.

"No, I guess not. He's going to be really mad, Mom, you know, when dinner's not ready."

Laura looked at her mildly. "Well, it won't be the end of the world if dinner's a little late. How anyone can eat at six, I don't know; it always seemed to me that one had hardly finished lunch. I'll finish what I'm doing and then I'll come up. We can eat around seven. I'm not teaching tonight."

Kay said nothing. In her head, she repeated the airy sound of "one had hardly finished lunch" and felt a burst of joy blanketing her worries. Perhaps this would be something good, something better than anything had ever been.

Kay heard her father, Martin, come home promptly at six o'clock, as he usually did, and she heard him call out, hiding his surprise, and his immediate anger at being surprised, with a jolly impatience. "Where the hell is everybody?"

Kay lay on her bed, stomach down, and waited for him to find her. He would only hover in her doorway; he rarely came into her bedroom.

"Hi. Where's your mother?"

"She's in the basement."

"Come on, Kay, don't be stupid. I don't have time for it."

Copying her mother's mild tone, Kay said, "She's in the basement."

"For Christ's sake." Her father stalked off.

Kay walked quietly to the top of the basement stairs. She heard her father mumbling angrily, and she heard her mother's voice cut him off so softly no words floated up the stairs. A few minutes later, Martin came up the stairs, uneasy and looking for a fight.

"Did you do your homework?"

"Yes." Kay knew better than to tell him that she had just gotten home.

"All right. Why don't you set the table or something? Your mother said dinner will be a little late."

"No problem."

"You sound like a gas station attendant when you say that. Just say, 'That will be fine,' like a normal, educated person."

In her coldest voice, Kay said, "That will be fine." She thought, And I hate you, you fat, fat, evil pig, and I hope you die.

Kay's mother came up and made hamburgers, mashed potatoes, and a green salad. She didn't speak during dinner, and the three of them ate in silence, Kay watching them both. Laura put her own dishes in the dishwasher, and as Kay and Martin sat there, she turned to leave.

"Where are you going, Laura?" Martin couldn't move fast enough to block her way, but he wasn't going to sit by while his wife acted like some second-rate Sylvia Plath.

"Downstairs. I'm working on something, and I find that the basement is the most comfortable place. Like your office at the college is for you. Fold-out couch and all."

Martin said nothing, and Kay watched his face turn a slow, swelling red. Her mother didn't stay to watch.

Martin went to read in their bedroom, hoping that tomorrow would find his wife in her usual clothes and her usual mildly depressed state, smelling like baby powder and not cigarettes.

At ten, Kay called downstairs, "I'm going to bed, Mom. I did the dishes. Good night."

"Good night, honey. That was very sweet of you, doing the dishes. I'll be up in a little bit."

"Well, I'm going to bed now." Kay had been ducking her mother's evening attentions for the last four years. Tonight, she wanted to be tucked in, but her mother stayed in the basement, resolute, in black.

In the morning, there was a note on the basement door.

Give me, O indulgent fate!
Give me yet, before I die,
A sweet, but absolute retreat
'Mongst paths so lost, and trees so high,

That the world may ne'er invade
Through such windings and such shade
My unshaken liberty.

by Anne Finch
Countess of Winchilsea

As Kay was reading it for the third time, her father scanned it over her shoulder and then crumpled it and threw it in with the coffee grounds and melon rinds.

That night her mother did not come up to make dinner. Martin went down and made more angry noises and came back up heavily, looking defeated and a little afraid. If Kay hadn't hated his guts, she would have felt sorry for him. Stupid, scared pig.

"Why don't you ask your mother to come upstairs? If she doesn't want to make dinner, we could . . . we could bring in pizza."

Kay didn't want to do anything that could be construed as helping her father, but she did want her mother to come upstairs; wanted her, even more, to witness her father's utter capitulation, to hear "bring in pizza" spoken by the man who had forbidden them to eat at fast-food joints all their lives and had taken all the fun out of family vacations by insisting that Laura cook regular meals every night in whatever cabin kitchen she found herself in.

Kay wanted to shout out, with trumpets and banners, "You can stop now, you've won. He'll bring in pizza, and he hasn't even mentioned the cat. You've won! Come back!"

Kay went downstairs and smelled the smoke and the mothballs but only a little bit of cat. The typewriter was going steadily.

"Mom?"

"I'm here."

"Dad said why don't we bring in pizza if you don't want to cook. We could get double cheese and peppers." Kay loved double cheese and peppers, and every time Martin went to a conference, Laura would hesitate and then yield, ordering a large for just the two of them, frowning as Kay ate three, then four slices.

When Laura failed to smile triumphantly, Kay's heart sank. It was not a contest, after all.

"If you want to," Laura said, balancing a Dunhill cigarette in the bowl of an unfamiliar crystal ashtray. "This ashtray belonged to my father, you never met him. He was a minor poet and a sweet man. My mother considered him a failure. I always thought so too, but now I think he was just a sweet, soft person, without ambition. Your grandmother admired ambitious men. Do you know what she said to me after she met your father for the first time? She said, 'Get pregnant.'" Laura pulled on her cigarette, looking younger and angrier than Kay had ever seen her.

"Yeah, Grandma was weird. So Mom, the pizza? Should we order it? Just one large? We could get some of the cheese breadsticks too."

"Whatever you want. I'm not hungry."

"Mom, did you eat today?"

"I'm fine, honey. See, Blake's having his dinner." They both looked at the kitten, lapping milk out of a small Wedgwood saucer, which Kay recognized as having come from the set her mother kept on display in their china cabinet.

"Okay, we'll order pizza. Mom, are you sleeping down here?"

"Well, yes, I am. This project is taking up so much time that it seems easier just to get everything set down here. It looks a lot like my room at college."

Kay looked around, unhappy but curious. It looked like the room Kay herself might have when she got to college: Klimt posters taped to the cement walls, a card table covered with two purple batik scarves, a pile of notebooks and a stack of poetry books on the cement floor, curling in the almost unnoticeable damp. Laura had unrolled an old Girl Scout sleeping bag onto the cot and added a few African-looking pillows. She had stacked two boxes of Martin's only book, discounted and autographed, to make an end table, and put a small lamp on top.

"It's nice, Mom."

Her mother beamed at her. "Thank you. 'Let the ambitious rule the earth, / let the giddy fool have mirth, / let me still in my retreat / from all roving thoughts be freed.' That's more of Anne Finch." Her mother looked at her typewriter. "I have to get back to work."

"What are you working on?"

Laura's face closed abruptly. "I'm writing some things. I wrote a lot. I have to get back to work."

"Okay, I'm going. I'll call you when the pizza comes. Okay?"

"Fine." Her mother, who always had ten words for every one of Kay's, pushed up her sleeves and started typing.

Kay and Martin ate pizza together silently. Laura said she was too busy to come up for dinner, and Kay's father ate six slices and threw the box in the garbage. He got his car keys and told Kay to clean up.

"Why should I clean up?"

"Just do it, Kay. I don't know what lunacy your mother is up to, but I can't correct papers, write a book, *and* clean the house."

Kay thought of her mother, luminous in the basement, quoting that woman poet. "I didn't say you should clean the house, did I? I just asked, why I should clean up after the two of us eat."

Martin balled his fists and set them on the table, the picture of a man trying to keep his temper. But he wasn't, Kay knew, he was only trying to scare her.

"Kay, please, clean up the kitchen. Don't make this worse than it is. Don't make me lose my temper. Why don't you go downstairs and get your mother to stop this nonsense? And tell her she has *got* to stop smoking cigarettes."

"I'll clean the kitchen if you're going to threaten me. You tell Mom to stop smoking. She's your wife."

Her father walked out of the kitchen, and Kay could hear that he didn't go out to the car; he went right to the bedroom.

Every day, not knowing what she hoped for, Kay went downstairs to visit her mother. Sometimes Laura was charming and recited poetry, but the next day she might turn weird and slow-moving, hardly able to answer Kay. Martin bought milk and fruit and dinner on his way home every night, and Kay cleaned up the kitchen after they ate the pizza or the fried chicken or the corned beef sandwiches. On the tenth day, Kay went downstairs, not thinking at all about her mother; she was crying because she was fourteen and four inches taller than the only boy who was even a little bit nice to her.

"What's the matter, honey?"

"It was just a shitty day." Since her mother's personality transplant, swearing was now no big deal. Kay was trying to figure out when she could ask for a cigarette.

"They happen." Her mother lit up and leaned back in her typing chair, turning to look at Kay. "My God, you got so beautiful this year, every time I look at you now I think, 'The brightness of her cheek would shame those stars, / As daylight doth a lamp; her eyes in heaven / Would through the airy region stream so bright / That birds would sing and think it were not night.' You are really just the Juliet. Romeos are a little hard to find in ninth grade, though."

Kay smiled, thrilled to hear her mother, who used to tell her she really could be cute if she smiled more, talk in this quirky, husky voice, a voice of lovers remembered, of disappointments survived.

"No one likes me," Kay said, realizing that at that moment, petting tiny Blake, she didn't care.

"Then they are nearsighted fools and babies. It'll happen, honey. Give everybody two or three more years and you'll be beating them off with a stick, maybe two sticks." Her mother ground out her cigarette for emphasis. "I have to get back to work. Come lie on the cot. You can take a nap while I type."

Kay lay down on the green dampish sleeping bag and put her head on one of the odd oblong pillows. Her mother pulled the folding chair closer to the cot and put one thin, colorless hand on Kay's shoulder. She sang,

"Oh, the summertime is coming
and the leaves are sweetly blooming
and the wild mountain thyme
grows around the purple heather . . .
Will you go, laddie, go?"

Kay didn't remember that her mother had sung to her nightly in that same breathy, bittersweet voice, rocking her in a small blue bedroom. Her mother sang until Kay fell asleep.

When she woke up, her mother was holding the kitten and staring at the air above the typewriter.

"Mom? Mom?"

The kitten jumped out of Laura's arms and tumbled over to his milk dish.

Kay put a hand on her mother's shoulder, and then both hands; she could feel thin skin shifting over ridges of bone beneath the dirty black sweater. Her mother didn't move, and Kay waited. After a while she could feel a slight heaving.

"What's going on?" Martin stood halfway down the stairs, peering at them, at their two sloping shapes rimmed by the harsh white light. When Kay was born, she could barely stop crying long enough to eat, and Martin would walk her all night, up and down the apartment stairs, while Laura put her head beneath two pillows and cried until dawn. For six months, they all slept on wet sheets. The only picture he had ever carried was of Kay, four months old.

"Nothing," Kay said.

Every day had frightened her more as she waited for her father's move. Obviously, something was wrong with her mother; he could send her away, and she might never come back. He could get rid of Blake, too.

"All right, Kay. Go on upstairs." He sounded the way he always did when he talked to her, as though they were strangers forced to share a seat on a terrible train ride.

Kay stood by her mother.

"Upstairs."

"What are you going to do?" Kay asked, feelings of power, of supernatural strength, surging through her chest. She will rescue her mother the way policemen shimmy through traffic to rescue toddlers, the way acrobats catch each other at the last, impossible half-second. She will swing past her father, leaving him fat and clumsy on the ground, and she and her mother will whirl through light-filled air, landing softly, not even breathing hard, on their own tiny platform.

"I just want to talk to your mother privately."

Kay stood still, squeezing her mother's shoulders, waiting for her cue.

"Martin?" Her mother's voice was softer than the kitten's.

Kay's father came down the stairs, loosening his tie. "It's me, I'm here," he said, and he leaned over the typewriter and took Laura's slack hands.

"Martin?"

Kay waited for her father's explosion, for him to yell at her mother for being stupid and repeating herself. She moved back, just a little, only her fingertips resting on her mother's dusty shoulders.

"Right here, Laura, I'm right here."

"I'm very tired. I'm not sleeping at night."

Her mother's thin whine distracted and annoyed Kay, who was trying hard to turn her into Anne Finch, into a blond, sequined acrobat effortlessly flipping from one shining trapeze to the next.

"I know, I know you can't sleep."

How could he know? Kay thought. Thick and still under his gray, conventional blankets, how could he know what her mother was doing in the night, in the basement?

"Let's go upstairs, Laura, all right? Let's go talk to Sid Schwerner, all right? He can help you sleep."

Laura pulled her hands back angrily, and Kay thought, Now! Leap into my arms, now!

"Martin, I have to get back to work."

Kay's father was smarter than she thought; he didn't yell or even try to take hold of Laura's hands again.

"Of course, I didn't mean to interrupt. Let's go meet with Sid, just for a little while, and then you can get back to work. You can't work without rest, right? Even Shakespeare, even Blake, your all-time favorite, they all rested. All right?"

Laura sighed and put her head down on the typewriter keys, and Kay felt the sigh tunnel through her spine and felt the cool metal keys of the typewriter thrown hot and hard behind her eyes. She went upstairs, not wanting to see her mother's slow ascent, wrapped in her father's brown tweed arms.

Kay could hear him through her bedroom door, talking urgently on the phone, muffling his voice like a Nazi spy; rummaging in the bedroom, dragging the zipper on her mother's ancient overnight bag. She couldn't hear her mother at all.

"All right, we're going. Kay? I'll—we'll be back later. Kay? Please come out of your room and say good-bye."

Kay pulled herself off her bed and stood in her doorway. "'Bye. Have a good time. Have fun."

Laura looked in her direction and right past her. Martin waved his hand widely, as though from a departing plane.

"All right, Kay. Take it easy. I'll call you if I need to. Don't wait up, tomorrow's a school day."

"Yes, I know. Thank you for telling me."

Martin rolled his eyes and opened the door, pulling Laura through it, still gentle even when she just stood there as if she didn't know what doors were for.

He came back the next day, without Laura. He told Kay that her mother needed a complete rest and would be home in a few weeks. He was brisk and oddly cheerful, displaying her mother's upbeat stoicism as though he had stolen it.

For the next two weeks, they lived together as they had when Laura was in the basement. Martin brought home dinner, and Kay cleaned the kitchen. She ran all her father's dark and light clothes together and washed his sweaters in hot water until he stopped making her do the laundry. She met a new girl, Rachel Gevins, and on weekends she slept over at her house and they drank rum and Cokes while the Gevinses were out at the movies. Rachel told Kay that her mother got electrolysis on her stomach. Kay told Rachel that her mother had freaked out and her father had carted her off to a funny farm. Rachel laughed and looked sad and didn't say anything, and Kay knew what it was to trust someone.

When Kay came home from her second weekend at Rachel's, she went down to the basement. "Gripping the wrought-iron banister, Dominique Beauvoir prepared to enter her past . . ." Blake, whom Kay had been surreptitiously feeding tuna fish and boned fried chicken, was gone. The litter box was gone, and so was the ten-pound bag of kitty litter. The table, the chair, the poetry books, the journals, and the cot and pillows were gone. The typewriter was gone. The air carried only faint scents of camphor and cigarettes and cat.

Kay stood in the basement, pushing out deep, uneven breaths. She will never forgive him. Beginning right now, she will never speak to him again. When Kay was little, she would walk from school to her father's office and he would lift her right onto his desk and clear a place for her among the papers so she could swing her legs over the side while she drank cocoa from the mug with the sailboats on it. He introduced her to all the pretty girls who came in and out, and they all smiled at her in a nice way and played with her hair and stood very close to her father. When she was ten, he started locking the office door, and then he said she was old enough to walk straight home by herself. Kay thought he was ashamed of her, and she was ashamed too. She wrote terrible things about him on the wall behind her dresser, but it didn't help.

If her mother does not come back now, when Kay grows up she will hire someone to murder him. Like that girl in New Jersey, she will hire some stupid guy to shoot her father in the head one night while he's reading Thomas Hardy, and she will say she doesn't know anything about it. She cries until she can barely see and locks herself in her bedroom.

When he got home, Martin rattled the doorknob a couple of times, insisting that Kay let him in. He didn't really want her to, and when she didn't, he shrugged and ate most of the fried chicken he had brought home for the two of them. He went to bed, nauseated, hating his life, still surprised by it.

Kay wouldn't leave her room the next morning, and after a few minutes Martin stopped pounding on the door. He had a breakfast meeting, and he said, feeling generous, "It won't kill you to miss a day of school, I guess. Your mother'll be home a little later anyway." He left, relieved that he had spared himself another splenetic fight.

When Kay hears the car grinding out of the driveway, she opens her door and goes back to the basement. She is waiting for a sign, and she wants to believe that she can sit there forever, that she is stonewalling God, not the other way around. The basement is not quite empty, and from her lookout on the stairs Kay can see the scraps that have been left behind. She examines the stubby pencil; nothing special, not even a tooth mark or a broken point. Kay puts it in her pocket and goes over to the corner where the cot had been. On the floor is an empty Dunhills packet, gold foil flowering out of the red box. Kay goes to her room and puts the box in her underwear drawer, tiny tobacco flakes drifting onto her white panties. She puts on her black jeans and an old black sweatshirt, turning it inside out to hide the bright lettering. She would wear a headband if she had one. Kay hears the car again and stands in the living room, waiting to see just who her father brings home.

She can hear them coming through the kitchen, hears her father grunting as he lugs in the suitcase, hears her mother murmuring thanks. Kay is barely breathing.

Her mother comes into the living room, unsmiling. Someone has dressed her in her khaki skirt and white turtleneck, but the brown belt is missing and her shirttail waves in and out of the waistband.

Kay wants to speak softly, to use her father's basement voice to win her mother back; they will read poetry and eat pizza, and in the end he will shrivel up and blow away, leaving nothing behind but his dorky black shoes. They will be fine then.

"Where's Blake?" is what she says, and her mother's mouth bunches in familiar, ugly ruffles.

"Here we go," says her father, looking at his wife.

"Well? That's not an unreasonable question, is it? I mean, the cat's just gone, you know? You know that, right, Mom? Blake's gone. He had him put to sleep or something."

Kay's mother puts her hand to her forehead, also a familiar gesture, and goes to the bedroom without looking Kay's way. Martin follows her, carrying her suitcase carefully.

In the rich late-morning light, Kay locks her bedroom door and throws the black clothes under her bed. She takes out the smooth red box and unfolds the gold foil, sniffing. Kay lies down and closes her eyes. She falls asleep, the red box clasped beneath her pillow.

MARUSYA BOCIURKIW

Here Nor There

BRITTA WAS BALD. She had small breasts and large hands. When she touched Katya, it was with her whole palm, firmly, along the side of Katya's face, or the inside of her thighs. Katya would go to Britta's tiny Berlin apartment in Kreuzberg for short intervals and at odd times: three in the morning or two in the afternoon, between Britta's bartending shifts at Oranienbar, where she passed as a man, and her waitressing shifts at the women's café, where she passed as a vegetarian.

Britta was into genderfuck and drama.

"I like it when these guys flirt with me," she told Katya. "I let them do it and then, at the crucial moment, I turn it around and say, 'Hey, look you've got the wrong idea.'"

Just hearing about it made Katya wet.

Britta kept all her clothes on when she and Katya fucked. Katya could touch, but not see, Britta's pear-shaped breasts. Only her bald head, exposed and tender. Britta would let Katya climb on top of her and then would flip her over. Katya's breath was taken away.

Man's face on a woman's body. What was it exactly that Katya was attracted to?

And *that* was the question.

Manon has hips that sway when she walks and long dark hair that smells like sandalwood and falls onto Katya's face when they sleep. Manon is always at the airport when Katya returns from her trips away, standing on the platform high above Customs, sandwiched between large European families and lone waving wives. Every time, a different token or gesture so she'll be recognized: lavender balloons, a bouquet of latex gloves, or pink confetti (this got her taken in for questioning). Manon wears her black wide-brimmed hat and her Italian leather jacket, with her red come-fuck-me lipstick and her shiny brown cowboy boots. Katya feels a sharp stab of desire. The memory of Britta drifts into another part of her body.

Once, after the long drive back to Montreal, Manon cried as Katya touched her face firmly, with her whole hand.

"You've never touched me that way before," she said, *"qu'est-ce qui se passe?"*

Katya was frustrated, to say the least.

I dreamed you had a cock, it reached across the bed, then it was a snake, circling me, holding me so tight I could hardly breathe.

At night, Katya dreamed about Britta; in the daytime, she wrote letters to Manon.

Your touch wanders along the inside of my skin. Your voice haunts my throat. I want my eyes to be your eyes. I imagine my head between your breasts, I smell your hair, even when I'm thousands of miles away.

Her letters were all honesty and all lies.

Buoyed by an academic grant, Katya travelled to Germany frequently to do research for her Ph.D. thesis on lesbian culture in pre-war Berlin. She was conducting interviews with older German women, asking them about women's cabarets and journals, lesbian movie stars and love stories. But when she played her tapes back, she found that all anybody really wanted to talk about was the changes since the Wall went down.

"It was something to fight against, something to organize around," said Birgit, the lesbian poet from the East. "Now, it's gone, almost without a trace, and it is the same with our movements, our lesbian groups, many of our feminist organizations—*kaput*, since the Wall went down. We have less funding now, that's one thing. And also we're tired, from overwork, since everything costs so much more.

"But it's something else, too. It is as though energy comes from being contained within boundaries, even if it's a boundary you don't really choose."

Katya didn't really understand any of this at the time. After she met Britta, she lost track of her project and also of herself.

Britta consumed Katya, demanded all her attention, held Katya's head tightly between her hands and looked forcefully into her eyes. When they weren't having sex and Britta wasn't working, they'd get together with Britta's crazy friends, Utta and Marion, deejays at one of the fly-by-night women's bars, getting women to dance to something besides techno music: Salt 'n Pepa or Nina Hagen. Huddled together in the music booth, they'd take Ecstasy and then set off on marathon bar and café tours, hurtling between the East and the West on the U-bahn and in cabs.

One night, it was just Katya and Britta. They went to the Globus Bar in East Berlin and danced to techno until 9 A.M. After breakfast at the anarchist café, they wandered over to the Turkish baths to freshen up. Britta was too tired to act tough. She poured warm water over Katya and tenderly washed Katya's breasts, her arms, her stomach. She was motherly, in a way Katya had never seen a butch be motherly before.

At these times, it was impossible for Katya to write letters to Manon. So she invented a system: she would write ten postcards all at once, at the beginning of her trip, and then mail one each day.

It's beautiful here. The roses along the canal are in full bloom and there are huge oak trees bent over the café where I write. This week, I will meet with a video artist from the East, to find out about her latest project: an exposé of lesbian culture in East Germany, covering the past 60 years.

Britta took Katya on long walks to her favourite spots. Not shady places by the canal, not the sweet café courtyards, but industrial wastelands: bare spaces where the Wall once stood, abandoned factory buildings overgrown with wildflowers. Places that were once on the other side of the Wall and had been inaccessible to Britta, even though they were a kilometre or less from her apartment. For Britta, it was like having a whole new country to explore.

"Listen," she said. "Listen to the sounds."

Katya listened. Nothing out of the ordinary: a few kids playing soccer and screaming at the top of their lungs. Two young mothers chatting quietly as they bumpily pushed their baby strollers along a gravel path. Some crickets. A dog barking.

"It was completely quiet here before," said Britta.

Britta and Katya fucked on the grass of an empty field, while trains bound for Moscow whistled past.

Long walks up Mount Royal, conversation moving in and out of French and English, Katya and Manon find each other again, first through language and only then through their bodies. Discreet, sensual, sitting outside Bar Sortie, their knees touching slightly, Manon hating public displays of affection.

Long periods of no talking, an assumed peaceableness that is really the reverse of the war zone in Manon's mind, the harried border crossings in Katya's heart.

I dreamed about your tight hard body last night and you saying: "Meine liebe, give it to me, give it all to me," and in my sleep, my body ached and I came till I cried.

Manon and Katya have been together for two years, but Manon never tells Katya about her jealousy. These days, she imagines shards of glass, they slice into her sleep, they hover over her stomach while Katya is in Europe. She lies in bed and imagines Katya's arms around her, then the image changes, goes out of control: she imagines Katya and Britta together, with all the details of their fucking, a self-generated film she can spend hours unreeling. Then the feel of the glass in her stomach, up through her heart and finally, resting menacingly in her throat.

Katya checks in with her: How are you feeling, do we need to talk. Manon, always sweet, kisses Katya tenderly on the cheek and says: "*Ne t'inquiète pas,* I love you still."

Manon has only lived in Montreal, has never travelled anywhere, except to the Laurentians where her mother now lives. Once, she and Katya planned a trip to San Francisco. Manon borrowed a pile of books from the library, boned up on the history, planned some visits to museums and a walking tour. The trip was cancelled; Katya's lecture fell through. And Manon was left holding onto all this knowledge of a place she'd never been. Katya had been there lots and went again the following year. Manon was working then and couldn't go.

Telling Katya about the pieces of glass is a final intimacy Manon refuses to give away. It is a place Manon knows well, where Katya has never been.

In Berlin, Britta never told Katya what it was like for her when Katya returned to Canada. Britta would walk her to the U-bahn station, surrounded by Turkish kebab houses, coffee shops and vegetable vendors, and would allow the public situation to inhibit her affection.

"See ya later, *meine liebe,*" she would say, her hands in her pockets. A kiss on Katya's neck and she was gone.

Later, Britta would cry herself to sleep with long, heaving sobs, staying in bed for days. Utta and Marion would show up faithfully and solemnly at Britta's door every morning with chunks of hash and take-out cups of coffee, finally convincing Britta to emerge and sit outdoors at the anarchist café, her bald head unprotected and innocent in the bright morning light.

While Manon and Britta each secretly wonder who it is Katya wants more, neither understands it is the condition of being in between—neither here nor there—that turns Katya on. Katya's identity exists in running for cover, to and from the opposing poles of Britta and Manon.

Katya longs for something more complete, but she's sure she'll never get it. A love that will surround her, a guarantee against abandonment. It is loss she's terrified of, not intimacy like everyone assumes. Having both Manon and Britta, she cuts her losses. Or so it seems.

Britta made love to Katya in a hard, controlled and expert way. Katya watched in wonderment as one of Britta's dildoes went into her for the first time, Britta speaking only in German: tough, dirty words that Katya couldn't understand. She shook with excitement when Britta fucked her in the middle of the night, waking her from sleep and restraining her hands in the network of hooks and straps above the bed. Britta rimmed Katya's anus with a dental dam; showed Katya how to fist her; brought out her whip and stroked Katya's ass; taught Katya how to go beyond the limits of her body's pain.

Katya took some of these things home to Manon and integrated them into their lovemaking in subtle and refined ways. Occasionally, she introduced little vanilla things, like butterfly kisses and tribadism, into her sex with Britta. Sometimes, she forgot what she was introducing to whom.

Once, she woke Britta up in the middle of the night and started fucking her.

"That's nice," said Britta sleepily, teasingly. "Where did you learn this?"

"Oh, I don't know," said Katya, not getting it. "I just like to fuck women in their sleep. They seem to like it."

Britta put her hand on Katya's and made her stop. Then she turned her back and went to sleep.

When Katya was still the new girl in town, Britta treated her like a tourist, taking her to all the standard sites: the Brandenburg Gate, Alexanderplatz and Checkpoint Charlie, where an odd museum stood, an American fantasy of what the Wall represented. Katya and Britta stared for a long time at the huge photographs of East Berliners who had tried to escape over the Wall. There was a series of photos of a man who spent years of evenings after work, digging a tunnel from his backyard into the Free World. His wife would watch him anxiously, bringing his dinners out to the tunnel when he was up late digging. There was another photo series of a woman who packed herself into a suitcase and then had the suitcase packed into the trunk of a car which managed to get across. The suitcase and car were all miraculously in the museum, with a diagram of the woman's folded-up body.

Katya was skeptical, wondering if anyone from the West ever tried to escape to the East. But Britta said quietly, later, as they sat eating *apfelkuchen* in a café across the way: "Those photos are for me about the profoundly human desire for freedom, no matter what the cost. Sometimes this freedom is not as important or as valuable as we had imagined, but we never know this until it's too late."

Berlin in June. There were sidewalk cafés everywhere, even if it was just two chairs and a table on a sidewalk. There were bicycle paths on every street, along the canals and beside outdoor markets exploding with texture and smell: Turkish breads, Indian scarves, bratwurst, vegetables and leather. There was beer that smelled like perfume and beer that tasted like fruit. There were linden trees arching over wide avenues, sending clouds of white into the air. There were old Marlene Dietrich films playing in tiny cinemas that seated 25 people. There were cafés adjoining the cinemas, where the fantasy of the movie continued into discussion: waving arms and important points through cigarette smoke and conversation. And there was the Oranienbar, where women overflowed into Oranienstrasse, draping themselves over parked cars, necking under streetlamps, leaning into each other's leather jackets.

Katya liked to go to the bar early, before Britta finished her shift. She would hang out in the crowd on the street, where Britta couldn't see her. She'd watch Britta through the large windows of the bar, serving beer in fast-motion, gay men leaning towards her and trying to whisper in her ear. Katya watched as Britta listened to the whispered comment and threw back her head and laughed, maybe touching the man briefly on the shoulder, then moving away. The more she holds back, the more she is pursued.

By the time Britta got off work, Katya was so turned on she could hardly stand up. They usually hung out on the street for a little while, having a cigarette and kissing. One night, Britta pushed Katya against a car and put her hand down Katya's jeans: discreetly, quickly. Then, Britta crossed the street and started talking to Dorothea, who had been cruising her for weeks.

Katya acted cool, lit another cigarette and waited. When Britta didn't come back, she walked down the road to the women's disco, and then to Kreuzberg and the squatter's bar. Britta finally tracked her down at 3 A.M.

She had passion and need in her eyes, which was exactly what Katya wanted.

Katya has forgotten to send any postcards for a week. Things between her and Britta have been good, ever since their big public fight outside the bar that night. She phones Manon from Britta's place, while Britta showers. Katya is stretched out on the bed, her hand in her crotch.

"Baby, I miss you so much," Katya says. "I think about you all the time. I'm thinking we shouldn't be apart so much."

Manon's voice is thin and ungenerous on the long-distance line.

"Well, maybe it's you who needs to change something, so we won't be apart so much. Otherwise, we'll be apart much more than you think."

Katya hears the warning, though the connection is bad, warms to it, softens her voice, moves her hand into her own wetness, comforts.

"Baby, I'm sorry. . . ." There is a slight shift in power, discernible even across a transatlantic phone line. It really turns Katya on.

"Baby, I'm gonna make it up to you. I need you to know that I want you so much."

That week, Britta was working twelve-hour days, between the vegetarian café and the bar, so Katya had time to herself. She arranged an interview with Antje, a lesbian in her 80s, who had lived in Berlin during the Weimar period. Katya had intended to arrange this meeting for the longest time, but life with Britta always got in the way.

Antje lived at the end of an U-bahn line, near a forest and a lake. Katya walked through an overgrown park to her tiny cottage. It felt calm here, in this neighbourhood of retired people, tending to rosebushes or walking their dogs. Katya realized she hadn't seen much of Berlin in daylight, she only seemed to go out at night.

Antje greeted her with a hug and Katya felt Antje's cheek against hers, like soft worn leather with the faintest smell of rosewater. Antje sat Katya down in an overstuffed chair and bustled with trays of pastries, cheese, bread and coffee. Katya fiddled with her tape recorder. Her mind wasn't really on the interview; she was wondering where Manon was, what Britta was up to.

Still, the interview went well. Antje seemed happy, delighted even, to be telling her stories, to have someone new in her home, to feed them with pumpernickel bread and beautiful exotic cheeses that Katya had never seen before. They drank coffee out of delicate porcelain cups and saucers decorated with orange blossoms and birds. Afternoon sun moved across the room. Antje talked, slowly and thoughtfully, brushing crumbs out of her lap, savouring each sweet memory, and smiling a crinkly, careful smile when her story turned sad.

"It is like anything else," Antje said. "We had so much, such an abundance of lesbian culture, such a rich night life, and the songs, the poetry, I can't begin to tell you. . . ."

She paused and swallowed, delicately, politely. "And we did not know how much we had, until it was gone, of course.

"They took everything away, but slowly, so very slowly. A bar closes down, you simply go to another, you're young, you want a good time, you don't ask why. Someone disappears, a writer whose work you've read, you're sad, but there are other writers, other books."

Antje was silent for several minutes, trying to reach the precise words for something important she wanted to say. She leaned over to Katya suddenly and held her hand tightly.

"You must fight. You must be clear about what you want and then you must fight for it. Or you will regret it for the rest of your life."

The next day, Katya spent hours gathering coloured pieces of the Wall from the gritty space along the canal, as a souvenir for Manon. She went to the field beside the train tracks, sat among the dried grass and the poppies and wrote Manon a long love letter. The letter was full of memories and full of promises. And Katya made a decision, writing: "Baby, I want to settle down with you."

She mailed the letter right away, so she wouldn't change it. She felt good, clean. She bought flowers for Britta and went to meet her at the bar at midnight, took her home and gave her a massage, held her tired, tight body the whole night through. In the morning, Britta let Katya fuck her unclothed for the first time and came, in a full and vulnerable way.

Katya's letter crossed Manon's letter, somewhere in the middle of the ocean. Perhaps they were both written the same day.

Manon's machine has been on for days, Katya can't get through. None of her friends seem to know where Manon has gone. Britta is working double shifts again and Katya can't get a cheap ticket to Montreal until next week. She's sure she can fix things, if she can only see Manon face-to-face.

Sex with Britta has been transcendent this week. They fucked out in the field and then in the washroom at the vegetarian café. Yesterday, Britta made her wear nipple clamps all evening, under her shirt, and this morning, she let Katya fist her: wide, soft expanse of cunt, surrounding her hand, beating like a heart, insistent and so open.

"*Meine liebe,* this is *good,*" sighed Britta. Afterwards, she looked into Katya's eyes for a long time.

Katya goes to Oranienbar at midnight. Britta is off at one, but Katya wants to hang out. She shares a cigarette with Utta and lets Annetta, the anti-fascist organizer, flirt with her just a little bit. There's a massive march the next day and Katya agrees to leaflet. If she's deported, maybe she'll get home faster.

She turns habitually to check out Britta through the window. Britta is deep in an embrace with the other bartender. They pull back, Katya breathes a sigh of relief, and then they move towards each other again and start to neck passionately. The men at the bar smile, as though they're used to it. One of them applauds. Katya goes back to the apartment. Britta gets home at 6 A.M.

Britta had been expecting anger and tears, maybe wanting them. But Katya has North American therapy words tumbling through her head: *State your needs, stay calm, don't get angry.* She says nothing.

The march begins at dusk, winding through the Turkish neighbourhoods where firebombing by neo-Nazis has been going on recently. Police in riot gear line the streets, a long blue column, light glinting off their clear plastic shields, surreal in the purple evening light. There are thousands of people, and all the dykes from the bars, the cafés and the neighbourhood are marching together, a band of leather jackets and spiked hair. Antje walks arm-in-arm with her partner Gerda. They wave eagerly at Katya. There are Turkish Maoists and American ex-patriots and Afro-German women and mothers with children who Katya has seen at the Hammam Baths and leftists and sad-looking older people who remember what it was like before.

The march lasts for hours, twisting through narrow streets. Some Maoists burn a German flag on the sidewalk and the flames cast an oddly beautiful glow in the store windows. At one point, Katya turns to Britta and says: "I love you. I'll stay, if you want me to."

Britta laughs, then gets serious, takes her aside into an alleyway and kisses her deep.

"Darlin', I gotta tell you. I'm gonna be seein' someone else now. It's a whole different thing I'm tryin'. It's really important to me. You can come visit when you want. But don't say this kinda thing anymore."

They return to the march. Some anti-fascist skinheads are breaking windows which splinter, white and sparkling, into the air. Katya keeps walking with Britta until she sees a phone booth, glowing yellow in the darkness. She runs to it, pulls out her Bell calling card, starts dialling. It's 4 A.M. in Montreal. Like a miracle, she gets through, she's crying, saying love words, saying she'll be home soon, sooner than expected. Manon agrees to meet her, but there is a silence, a wall of something that wasn't there before. Katya stays in the phone booth long after the line's gone dead, watching the march pass by, blurry and dreamlike through her tears.

REBECCA BROWN

The Death of Napoleon:
Its Influence on History

I THINK ABOUT HIM all the time. I make up stories about him and dream about him. In fact, that's not really accurate. The dreams aren't so much about him as they are about his death and me killing him. I don't know very much about him. All I know is that I have to kill him and that I think about him all the time and the ways that I can kill him and exactly how I will do it.

I thought of him tonight at the Daniels's and today at work on the subway to and from work and on the way to and from the Daniels's while we were talking and I didn't tell you. You didn't know what I was thinking about at all. We were talking about your sister and you didn't know I was thinking about him.

He's going to be on "Meet the Press." The studio is all lit up and the lights are blaring, silver and bright everywhere. It smells like sweat and makeup. Edwin Newman is there and someone is straightening his tie and coat as he's looking at some notes in a manilla folder. I notice that he's much better looking in person than on TV. I'm working on one of the cameras when I see him come out. He's short and he has on white pants, a dark coat with tails, and a red vest. His hair is slicked down, black, and he's got on a tricorn hat. He's standing about four feet away from me when I throw an extension cord at him that's in the shape of a lasso just as I'm snipping the end with a pair of heavy cutting shears. When it hits him, he turns into a red-orange glowing doughboy, like a Christmas ornament. He hops in the air, twisting and flopping. Everything is very sudden. It smells of burnt flesh and makeup and I've got him.

You and I are having a talk. We're talking about plans and goals and you've mentioned the probability of your going back to school for your masters if the promotion doesn't come through. You aren't, however, going to rule out the possibility of something totally unexpected like, for example, moving up to Vermont for a while with Bob and Debra if they were really serious and if we could get into living on a farm. You say that, mostly, you just want to be true to yourself and not fix yourself into anything that's not really you. Also, you want to consider me and do what's best for both of us. Then you ask me what I think is important for me and what I want to do and I tell you:

"I want to kill Napoleon."

"You what?"

"I want to kill Napoleon."

"What do you mean?"

"I mean I want to kill him."

"C'mon, what is this?"

"I want to kill Napoleon."

"OK, OK, I give. What's the punch line?"

"There isn't one. I just want to kill him."

Then you look at me and you say, "Right." Then you ask, "How come?" and I say, "I have to," and you say, "You don't have to." You say, "He's dead. He's been dead for a hundred and fifty years." You say, "What is this?" And you look at me.

You look at me and you wonder what's got into me. You wonder if you're dealing with me in the best way. You look kind and sympathetic. I look at you. Both of us are proud to look the other straight in the eye. It's something we've built up. You ask me why. I look straight at you and ask you, "Have you ever wanted to kill Napoleon?" and you say, "No," and I say, "Oh." Then I say, "Well, I do. I want to kill him. I mean, I have to kill him." You ask me why, and I tell you I don't know.

They're doing a remake of *King Kong* in Hollywood. They hire Napoleon as the woman abducted from the skyscraper and me as Kong. In the famous scene, I'm careful to remove him gingerly from the skyscraper. When I bring him to my face, I hardly recognize him. He looks like a cake decoration, only not so powdery; he's immaculate. I press my fingers to my palm, then fold my thumb over in a very tight fist. When I unclench my hand and ease my fingers open, I think of a Mamma Bellosi Delux Supreme With Everything. To go.

I spend a whole evening thinking of him. At home you ask me what I thought of the movie. I say I think some of it was really good, but I wasn't really concentrating on it. You ask my why and I tell you that I was thinking of Napoleon and you look at me. I was thinking how crippled I feel at not being able to abbreviate his name or call him by a nickname or a pet name. Any abbreviation or derivation sounds ridiculous. But then I reason that that is part of who he is; he is inextricably Napoleon. Nothing abbreviated or translatable, and I must kill him.

Tonight we're doing dishes after dinner. The Daniels have been over. We've played bridge and eaten lots. I am washing. You are drying and putting them away. You use a soft linen dishcloth and I use a plastic aqua-colored ball. My hands are getting pruny and my fingernails are white and soft. The water is greenish-grey with pieces of spaghetti noodles. Orange dots of grease are in it. We talk about the evening with the Daniels. We're just about finished. I've washed everything except the silverware. I pick up a handful of it. I lift it out of the water. It shines and feels slick in my hand. I dunk it back under and almost release my hand to let the pieces separate so I can scrub them individually, but then it's his puffy white neck in my hand. I look in the water and see his white, greenish face. His cheeks are bloated and he looks like panic. I tighten my hold and look. His hair loosens from being perfectly, tightly combed. It sways like seaweed or a mermaid's hair. His flesh is soft between my fingers and I tighten my grip, afraid he will be able to slip out because the water is greasy from the meatballs. His face is colored like a fish's stomach and I think how when fish drown they float up on their stomachs and their white stomachs surface like his puffy fleshy face. His lips pale into the color of peach melba yogurt. His hair sways like a mermaid's. I've never realized how long it was because it has always been stuck down. The water starts looking vaguely pink and I think that that must be from his red sash. I imagine his body being squeezed up through the drain and how it must curve like an "S" coming up through the pipe. When I feel him start to struggle, I hold even tighter, until there is only a little resistance, and re-lease him.

Then I turn on the disposal.

We're at a museum, looking at a show of lesser known contemporary artists. Hardly any of the work is representational. We talk about the work and you ask me what I think of a certain piece.

"What do you see in it?"

"Well, I don't know. Nothing really."

"It must evoke something, make you feel something."

"Yeah . . ."

"Well, what does it make you think of?"

"It reminds me of Napoleon."

"Napoleon? How come?"

"It just does."

"I don't see it at all."

"I guess I don't either. It just reminds me of him."

"Everything reminds you of Napoleon."

"Yeah. I guess so."

I think about him all the time.

I'm at the Coronation. I'm standing next to David, helping him squeeze oil out and mix it on the palette. We're about twenty yards away from him and I can smell excitement and bodies behind our corner of oil and turpentine. David is nice to me. He chats with me in French and I start to tell him that I've only studied two and a half years of high school French and that I can't remember any of it; but then I realize that I'm telling him this in perfect fluent French, and halt in mid-sentence. Fortunately he hasn't been listening and I am not a fool. He has long, thin, creamy-colored fingers, smooth-skinned hands with fine delicate lines. He is very neat and ordered. He sets the blops of paint where he wants them, equidistant from each other on the palette. I want to ask him how he can be so confident and just paint it like this, but then I notice a huge sheaf of pencil sketches and studies for this and wonder how he did them because this is the Coronation and it's never happened before. There's lots of music and noise. Glasses clink and it's more like a party than a coronation. Everyone mingles and chats. Then someone says, "OK, OK, everybody, places," and everyone gets in place. He's standing on a platform in the front and starts giving a speech in a French I can't understand. David turns to me, palm turned upright, and like a doctor saying "Suture," says, "Number nine, light." I go to hand him a palette knife but pick up a violin case instead. The lid falls open as I lift it up and out falls a sawn-off machine gun. I catch it before it hits the ground and rat-a-tat off three clips of shells at him and the rest of them, everyone except myself and David. Everyone looks red.

"We've really gotten close lately. I don't know, I just feel so good about things. I've been feeling really good lately."

"Yeah?"

"Uh huh. We have a lot more in common all the time. I really realize it more and more."

"Yeah . . ."

"I feel, like, there's more things you understand about me and I do about you that we don't even have to say."

"Yeah, really."

"Do you feel that way?"

"Sure."

"Like, I really know what you're thinking when you don't even say it."

"Yeah, really."

November. I am walking up a hill near Painswick in the Stroud valley, Gloucestershire, England. Everything is brown and grey and wet. I'm wearing dark brown shoes, slightly scuffed, with dark brown laces. The tips of the laces are the color of toffee. The path is dipped and holed from where the rain goes down. The ground is slippery and I walk cautiously. My hands, gloved and stuffed into my coat pockets, are cold. My face feels cold and hot and I know I will be red when I go back in. My glasses will fog over and I'll barely be able to see myself in the mirror when I take off my coat in the entrance hall.

I'm climbing up a hill. Behind me and below, the path twists down into Sheepscombe. Grey smoke goes up from the chimneys. I go up, and my thighs and calves hurt. I stand up to catch my breath. When I look up, I see him.

He is standing on a plateau, elevated about two feet above the top of the hill. I wonder if he's cold from exposure. I think that anyone else's boots would be smeared from the climb, but I know his aren't and I wish the sun was there to catch the glint off them. His strong head is pressed into his coat. His fine red sash is like Christmas candy, brilliant like eye-blood, straight across the stomach. He stands straight and doesn't look as if he feels the cold. He wears nothing on his hands.

He's looking straight ahead, past me, to my right. I turn around to see if I can see what he's looking at, but all I can see is the furry line between the woods and sky, and parts of smoke in tails, rising. I turn back toward him and stop. I breathe in deeply, press my hands into my pockets more and start to walk again. My toes are cold and my cold feet feel hard stones pressing on the soles. I go up slowly. He's about fifty feet away.

The path is steeper. I can't imagine him walking up here and I wonder how he got here. I walk up and feel cold go in my lungs. He stays still, looking at the fuzzy line of horizon behind me. I know that I can't see the things he can in the fuzzed horizon, or past it, and I know that this is why I love him. I feel good, having to work at the climb and I like the greyness of my breath, quickening and heavier as I try harder on the steeper path to approach him. I take my hands from my pockets, remove my gloves, and walk with my cold sweaty hands exposed.

I'm closer to him now, within shouting distance, and I want to say something. I think he must see me or know I am coming. I don't expect him to say anything and I want to say something.

I'm only twenty feet away from him. I keep climbing and I can see his boots clearly and there is no mud on them. I can see the thick seams on the sides of his tight white legs, the wrinkles over his kneecaps. I can see the rise of his shoulders as he breathes. Now I can see his clear heavy eyes fixed on the line behind me. I want to turn around again, but I don't. I keep looking at him. His wrist is red between his sleeve and the opening in his jacket. His other hand is red as well. His face is still and I am close enough to know he hears me stop and breathe. Five feet from him, I stop and look. I want to say hello and then he starts to turn to me. He's facing me, direct on, and then he starts to turn away. He lifts his right foot slightly and puts it behind himself to turn. His right thigh tightens, and his calf, pulling him around. His left hip, where his white tights and jacket meet, turns towards me. He puts his right foot on the ground and shifts his weight to that. Then he lifts his left foot forward. His eyes lower and he moves his left foot in front of himself.

Suddenly I feel desperate and I want to say his name out loud. I want to call him, "Napoleon! Napoleon!" He turns from me on a circle; the part that turns away from me goes into air. He's walking into air. I say, "Napoleon—" but I can't say it out loud. Now his back is to me, but only half of his back, the right half has disappeared. He's turned into the air. "Napoleon—" His left foot lifts again, forward, to its right; he turns. The left tail of his coat catches on air and his shoulder looks like a cliff. His hair is black and solid, shiny. His boot is smooth. The spur is silver. "Napoleon—" He lifts his foot. The spur goes up like a stone. I hear the crunch of rock beneath his moving foot. His foot is forward and right. The line moves over my vision like a card cutting over a lens. "Napoleon—" He puts his foot down. The instant it would touch, he's gone. I lunge forward, throwing myself at his boot. My hand slaps on a smooth large stone.

"Napoleon! Napoleon!"
Your hands.

"Napoleon—I love you. Napoleon—"

Everything is dark. Your hands are on me.

"Wake up. It's OK. You're just dreaming. I'm here. You're just dreaming."

I hear myself breathe and feel your hands trying to calm my body and I feel water going in my chest.

"It's only a nightmare. I'm here. Are you OK?"

"Yeah, yeah. I'm OK. Did you hear what I said?"

"I couldn't make it out, but you were screaming something. Do you remember?"

I hesitate, not looking at you. "No . . ."

He and I are standing in a train station. One of us is here to see the other one off, but I'm not sure which is which. It's cold and I only have on a sweater. He is bareheaded and his right arm is stuck inside his jacket. I feel very close with him and believe he feels so for me as well. We've just walked through the turnstile and are walking toward the track. We are silent.

I feel cold wind drifting through the station from where the trains will come in. It's a completely covered station and I can see yellow lines of light curving in as the trains come. There are several tracks. We are waiting by the first one. I feel very tender and know we will be parting in a minute.

He turns and looks up at me. "I have something for you." He speaks English with a French accent, low and woolly. He's wanting to be secretive. "It's only a little something, but I want you to have it." He pulls a coin out of his left side pocket, holds out his open palm to me, and I see a small bronze coin. "For you." He holds it out to me and I take it. "It belonged to my mother." He looks into the distance. "My mother, she was a saint." He holds the moment, then looks at me. "I want you to have it." I look down at the coin as he presses it into my palm. "Oh, Napoleon," I say very softly, gazing at the bronze dot in my palm. I raise my eyes to look at him tenderly. Then I step forward to embrace him.

He snaps back, hissing through his teeth. "Not here—anyone could see us!" His eyes flash. I know he's embarrassed about being two heads shorter than I am, and do not pursue my embrace. I look at him with apology in my eyes and he turns away to face the track where the train will arrive. He puts his hand behind his back as if both hands were behind his back, clasped and relaxed, but the other hand is in his jacket. I think how painful it must be to be so proud, and I know that he knows I understand this. I look at his firm straight back, the way his shiny heels touch each other, the firm lines of his thighs beneath his coattails. His shoulders are thrown back. We wait several minutes for the train, then see two yellow lines start across the opposite wall. The train is arriving and we move closer to the track to board. I can just see the circles of light and hear the train turning in a direct approach to the track. As the lines of light straighten and the train approaches, I remember which one of us has the ticket. When the train is about twenty feet away, I toss the coin in front of it. He spins around to ask me what I'm doing and I push him on to the track.

You tell me I've been sleeping badly lately and I say why, and you say I turn in my sleep and I often wake up sweating and clenching the sheets tight in my fist. I tell you I've been dreaming about Napoleon and killing him and you ask who and I say, "Napoleon," and you say, "No, I know it's Napoleon, but who is it really?" and I say, "What do you mean?" and you say you don't think it's just Napoleon.

You say, "It's not Napoleon you're trying to kill. It's a real person. You're trying to kill a real person," and I say, "I hadn't thought of it that way," and I hadn't.

I'm standing outside the Great Hall. It's a special day called the Hearing of Complaints and lots of people are here to petition him. Most of the people are men in old military uniforms. I'm one of the only civilians. The guard opens the door and I hear my name. He ushers me into this huge hall with tons of people standing along the sides. He's at the far end, dressed in a furry leopard robe over his standard dress. The guard holds a silver platter out to me and I put the index card with my complaints on it. Then he gives me the plate and I walk forward to the throne and him. When I get there, someone stops me and tells me to read my case. I give a long speech with words like "whereas," "heretofore," "party of the first part," and "breach of trust." Then I get to the "acquired debts requesting payment." I look up at him before I start reading. He looks uninterested. I know the other people have been petitioning for lands in Alsace-Lorraine, or the freedom of their Prussian village, or the repayment of their country estates.

I look down at my blue-lined index card on the silver tray and read:

You owe me thirty-one dollars.

You still haven't returned my favorite aqua flannel nightshirt or my blue bandanna.

You owe me two Italian dinners, one movie, and a ride to Nashville.

You owe me an incalculable number of breakfasts in bed.

You haven't returned my St. Francis medal or my Buffalo Springfield *Retrospective* album.

You owe me half of the *New Yorkers* we subscribed to and every other month's worth of the Book-of-the-Month-Club selection.

When I look up at him, he looks bored. He turns to one of the attendants next to him and asks him something I can't hear. The attendant looks at me and asks, "Is that all?" I want to say something else, but I don't. I just nod and play it cool. Then the attendant next to him says, "We'll keep your request on file for further consideration." Another attendant comes and takes the card off the plate and turns me around so I can leave. When he turns me, though, I move quicker than him. I spin back around and Frisbee the solid-silver platter right through his leopard robe. The edges sharpen as it spins through the air and I can hear the sing of air over the sharp edge. It spins into him like a turning sawmill and it hits him in the stomach like a knife in an uncooked biscuit, and I'm spinning and every time I spin I have another plate in my hand and I throw it at him and it hits another place: across his face, his pudgy white tights, the top of his slick black head. I keep going around and around and finding sharp silver Frisbees and keep throwing them at him and they stick out of him like crooked red Venetian blinds.

I start telling you about my dreams. At first I'm embarrassed and wonder if you don't want to hear them, but you tell me that you do want to hear them. You care about them and you find them interesting, too, and so I tell you and you say, "I think Napoleon is Jerry." You say you recognize the coin, the hill, the debts. I can't believe it, but then I do. Then you ask me about Jerry and if he was anything like Napoleon, if he was short or spoke French or anything, and I say no. Then you ask me what it was like with him and I say I don't remember.

"Did you trust him?"

"I don't know."

"What do you mean?"

"Well, sort of."

You look at me and say, "Look, either you trust someone or you don't. It's no matter of degree," and I say I don't remember.

We've spoken about Jerry before and you always ask me more than I want to tell, and it's good for me, but sometimes it goes too fast and I say, "I just don't remember what was real and what I'm making up."

And I wonder why I'm suddenly thinking of Jerry again because I haven't for a long time, and what suddenly reminded me of him? You didn't even know he was part of my history for a long time. Then I think about you saying that about trust, and the reason I couldn't tell you or didn't know is, if you do trust someone or think you do and then stop, does that mean you never really did? Also it means, how can you be sure if you thought you did, but then something happens and you think that maybe you didn't or shouldn't have.

I'm writing on a parchment with a long, old-fashioned, pointy-tipped pen. It says, "I thought this would hurt you most." It's a suicide note and I put it in my lap. I'm sitting in a boat without oars or a motor. I'm wearing a long heavy brocade dress and my fingers look skinny and white. I push off from the bank and float down the Seine to the palace. I know he's having a fête today and by the time I get to the palace, I'm dead. I'm dead but, since this is a dream, I can still see and feel everything, but from above and outside my body, like the movies. The boat catches in some bushes and people run down to see what's happened. They see a beautiful maiden with a long brocade dress, dead, in a boat. That's me. Then he struts up in his fine black boots. He walks on wet grass and mud by the river, but his boots remain immaculate. The sky is blue and everything is lovely. He has a glass of champagne in his hand. He approaches the boat. One of his attendants picks up the note and hands it to him. He gives the attendant his glass of champagne and reads the note. He rolls up his eyes, purses his lips, and shakes his head. He doesn't say anything but drops the note on the ground and turns back to the party.

This scene repeats itself over and over. Like trying to dial a phone number or start a car in a dream, you just can't do it, he won't respond at all. In the last repetition, though, there is a change. In this one, after he drops the note and turns away, I get out of the boat like a ghost and stab him in the back of the neck repeatedly with my pen. He dies slowly of blood loss and ink poisoning. His coat is all stained with red and blue. Then I get back into the boat and sit in the bushes.

I'm reading a book on Napoleon and you say that you wish I could get off this obsession, that it's not healthy for me, and I say you're probably right. You ask me about Jerry again and what happened and I say either, I don't remember, or, I don't want to think about it. You say you're glad you never met Jerry and you hope you never do because he sounds horrible and you wish I'd never met him either, and I don't know how I feel about that because I think maybe I did trust him and I wonder how he is.

We're playing bridge at the Daniels's. Mark and Sue are partners and my partner is him. He sits across from me at the shaky card table with the plastic canvas-looking top and deals the cards. He only uses one hand because his other one is stuck inside his coat. His pouchy, white stomach rubs against the side of the table. The Daniels have gone into the kitchen to get us all more beer and potato chips for the next rubber. I watch him deal and say, "It would be lots easier if you used both hands." He flashes his eyes at me. "It's only me," I say gingerly, "go ahead." I pause. "Take it out." He says, "I can do it with only one," in French. Then he smiles. I think he's teasing me and I get up to go around behind him, watching him deal. I stand over him and he starts humming the French national anthem. I'm sure he's joking with me and I reach over his shoulder to pull his arm out.

He cries out and drops the cards as the arm comes out with a pop. Instantly, there's a huge blast and his body is shot off the chair by an escaping rush of hot air. His body spins around the room backward, bumping on and off things as it deflates and shrinks. I can't tell if he's shouting something underneath the blast 'of air. I try to follow the quick crooked path of flight his shrinking body takes, but it's too fast and erratic. When all the air has escaped he falls on the ground and I can recognize his color scheme in the flattened plastic balloon.

We've been talking about Napoleon. You wonder why I'm obsessed with him and why I can't let him go. We see how he is Jerry, but I don't believe he's just Jerry. I don't think of Jerry by himself, or what he's like or was, but I know that he is part of Napoleon. You warn me against fabricating a mythology and not being able to control it. You warn me that I mustn't think I know everything, or that history repeats itself in the same way (I try to remember where I've heard that before, but I can't). You say you're worried because I seem to be less open with you. You say I seem like I'm always thinking of something else that I don't tell you. You say I sleep terribly these days and you wonder what it is. You say, "Tell me. I want to know. I care about it."

And I say, "Napoleon," and you say, "Look, don't give me that. Trust me, dammit. What is it really?" and I say, "Napoleon." And you're upset with me and you say, "Listen to me. *I'm* not Napoleon. You can trust me. Just tell me. What is it?"

And I want to say Napoleon again because that's all I know, but I know you don't want to hear it again, so I say, "I don't know," and you say, "Christ, why are you so obsessed? Why can't you just forget Napoleon? Why do you have to make up this mythology about yourself that isn't even true and torment yourself and cover up what's really there? Dammit, I wish you would kill him and get rid of him for good." And I believe that you love me and I want to say thank you and I want to kill Napoleon. I want to kill him for you.

And that night, you kill Napoleon.

There is no setting. Just white space and he's standing there with his back to me. I have a revolver and I'm aiming, but I can't pull the trigger. I realize all the messes I have made trying to kill him, then you're there and you say, "All you have to do is pull the trigger," and you take the revolver from me and plant one clean, beautiful, silent bullet in the back of his shiny, black hair. When the smoke clears, there's no sign of anything, just clean and white and everything is clean and beautiful.

I wake up instantly and everything is quiet and beautiful.

I don't dream about Napoleon for months or think about him. Everything is good except I'm thinking of something else that I don't know and then I start joking about Napoleon, and one day you tell me you're afraid that I'm letting my imagination run away with me. You're afraid of something in the way I laugh about him, that I don't dream about him, but I think about him when I'm awake still. Like I'm making a conscious effort. You tell me you wish I could be more trusting and strong and believing. You say you're afraid of my being secretive and you wish you had more feeling of being trusted. You say you think I fear you and you wish we didn't live with that, that it's not healthy or constructive.

Then you ask me if you can borrow forty dollars because you and Terry want to get to know each other better. You tell me you two want to spend more time with each other, and this weekend you want to go away together. And I say yes, and I think of something I want to tell you when you get back, but I don't know what it is. Then I have this dream.

It's raining and I've forgotten his name. I go walking through the streets of Paris and asking everyone if they've seen a short, almost pudgy little man with a red vest, white stretch pants, black waistcoat with tails, black shiny boots, and slicked-down hair. Then I add that they might not have been able to see any of those clothes because of his large, heavy, navy coat. No one has seen him and I can't remember his name. No one understands how vital it is that I find him. They don't know that I have to kill him. It's a night like in a Victor Hugo novel, black and grey and wet, and I feel like a sewer rat and I'm looking for this little man whose name I've forgotten. I can't believe his name has slipped my mind. I remember everything about him: his coin, his clothes, the snap of his boots, how he plays cards, the money he's borrowed from me. But I can't think of his name. I keep looking because I have to kill him. I have a pistol. It's large and heavy and has a hard wooden handle. I have to be careful because I have only one bullet and I'm afraid the powder and bullet might fall out. Then I run into an alley and I see someone from behind in a large, heavy, navy coat. He's talking to someone. Very intimately leaning over and whispering. I think their bodies are touching each other. I stop dead and hear myself breathe. The person in the coat knows I'm there and knows who I am because I hear his voice and it says, "I'm not Napoleon," and then I remember his name. He doesn't move though, but stays still with the other person, only moving slightly, and I don't know what to do. He said he wasn't Napoleon, but I recognize the coat and know that only Napoleon would realize that I was looking for him and say, "I'm not Napoleon." I know that if I don't kill him now, I never will, but then I wonder, what if this person isn't Napoleon, and then he says it again: "I'm not Napoleon," still not turning toward me and I can't see his face. Then I reason that, definitely, only Napoleon would know I was looking for him, so this must be him. I feel my body tense and I pull out the gun. I set the trigger back and start to pull. Then he turns around. The alley is dark and he moves quickly and his head is covered with a hood and I'm so upset about the gun that I can't see well, but I've already started to fire and the bullet's already going when I think I recognize him. And it's not Napoleon, and it's not Jerry; it's you.

I snap my eyes closed and scream and I don't know if the bullet hits or if it even goes off or if the blast is only the sound of my own screaming and the quick red of my hard-clenched eyes and if I've really done it.

SANDRA CISNEROS

My Name

In English my name means hope. In Spanish it means too many letters. It means sadness, it means waiting. It is like the number nine. A muddy
color. It is the Mexican records my father plays on Sunday mornings when
he is shaving, songs like sobbing.

It was my great-grandmother's name and now it is mine. She was a horse
woman too, born like me in the Chinese year of the horse—which is supposed to be bad luck if you're born female—but I think this is a Chinese lie
because the Chinese, like the Mexicans, don't like their women strong.

My great-grandmother. I would've liked to have known her, a wild horse
of a woman, so wild she wouldn't marry. Until my great-grandfather threw
a sack over her head and carried her off. Just like that, as if she were a fancy
chandelier. That's the way he did it.

And the story goes she never forgave him. She looked out the window her
whole life, the way so many women sit their sadness on an elbow. I wonder
if she made the best with what she got or was she sorry because she couldn't
be all the things she wanted to be. Esperanza. I have inherited her name, but
I don't want to inherit her place by the window.

At school they say my name funny as if the syllables were made out of tin
and hurt the roof of your mouth. But in Spanish my name is made out of
a softer something, like silver, not quite as thick as sister's name—
Magdalena—which is uglier than mine. Magdalena who at least can come
home and become Nenny. But I am always Esperanza.

I would like to baptize myself under a new name, a name more like the
real me, the one nobody sees. Esperanza as Lisandra or Maritza or Zeze the
X. Yes. Something like Zeze the X will do.

EDWIDGE DANTICAT

The Missing Peace

WE WERE PLAYING with leaves shaped like butterflies. Raymond limped from the ashes of the old schoolhouse and threw himself on top of a high pile of dirt. The dust rose in the clouds around him, clinging to the lapels of his khaki uniform.

"You should see the sunset from here." He grabbed my legs and pulled me down on top of him. The rusty grass brushed against my chin as I slipped out of his grasp.

I got up and tried to run to the other side of the field, but he caught both my legs and yanked me down again.

"Don't you feel like a woman when you are with me?" He tickled my neck. "Don't you feel beautiful?"

He let go of my waist as I turned over and laid flat on my back. The sun was sliding behind the hills, and the glare made the rocks shimmer like chunks of gold.

"I know I can make you feel like a woman," he said, "so why don't you let me?"

"My grandmother says I can have babies."

"Forget your grandmother."

"Would you tell me again how you got your limp?" I asked to distract him.

It was a question he liked to answer, a chance for him to show his bravery.

"If I tell you, will you let me touch your breasts?"

"It is an insult that you are even asking."

"Will you let me do it?"

"You will never know unless you tell me the story."

He closed his eyes as though the details were never any farther than a stage behind his eyelids.

I already knew the story very well.

"I was on guard one night," he said, taking a deep theatrical breath. "No one told me that there had been a coup in Port-au-Prince. I was still wearing my old régime uniform. My friend Toto from the youth corps says he didn't know if I was old régime or new régime. So he shot a warning at the uniform. Not at me, but at the uniform.

"The shots were coming fast. I was afraid. I forgot the password. Then one of Toto's bullets hit me on my leg and I remembered. I yelled out the password and he stopped shooting."

"Why didn't you take off your uniform?" I asked, laughing.

He ignored the question, letting his hand wander between the buttons of my blouse.

"Do you remember the password?" he asked.

"Yes."

"I don't tell it to just anyone. Lean closer and whisper it in my ear."

I leaned real close and whispered the word in his ear.

"Don't ever forget it if you're in trouble. It could save your life," he said.

"I will remember."

"Tell me again what it is."

I swallowed a gulp of dusty air and said, "Peace."

A round of gunshots rang through the air, signaling that curfew was about to begin.

"I should go back now," I said.

He made no effort to get up, but raised his hand to his lips and blew me a kiss.

"Look after yourself tonight," I said.

"Peace."

On the way home, I cut through a line of skeletal houses that had been torched the night of the coup. A lot of the old régime followers died that night. Others fled to the hills or took boats to Miami.

I rushed past a churchyard, where the security officers sometimes buried the bodies of old régime people. The yard was bordered with a chain link fence. But every once in a while, if you looked very closely, you could see a bushy head of hair poking through the ground.

There was a bed of red hibiscus on the footpath behind the yard. Covering my nose, I pulled up a few stems and ran all the way home with them.

My grandmother was sitting in the rocking chair in front of our house, making knots in the sisal rope around her waist. She grabbed the hibiscus from my hand and threw them on the ground.

"How many times must I tell you?" she said. "Those things grow with blood on them." Pulling a leaf from my hair, she slapped me on the shoulder and shoved me inside the house.

"Somebody rented the two rooms in the yellow house," she said, saliva flying out from between her front teeth. "I want you to bring the lady some needles and thread."

My grandmother had fixed up the yellow house very nicely so that many visitors who passed through Ville Rose came to stay in it. Sometimes our boarders were French and American journalists who wanted to take pictures of the churchyard where you could see the bodies.

I rushed out to my grandmother's garden, hoping to catch a glimpse of our new guest. Then I went over to the basin of rainwater in the yard and took off my clothes. My grandmother scrubbed a handful of mint leaves up and down my back as she ran a comb through my hair.

"It's a lady," said my grandmother. "Don't give her a headful of things to worry about. Things you say, thoughts you have, will decide how people treat you."

"Is the lady alone?"

"She is like all those foreign women. She feels she can be alone. And she smokes too." My grandmother giggled. "She smokes just like an old woman when life gets hard."

"She smokes a pipe?"

"Ladies her age don't smoke pipes."

"Cigarettes, then?"

"I don't want you to ask her to let you smoke any."

"Is she a journalist?" I asked.

"That is no concern of mine," my grandmother said.

"Is she intelligent?"

"Intelligence is not only in reading and writing."

"Is she old régime or new régime?"

"She is like us. The only régime she believes in is God's régime. She says she wants to write things down for posterity."

"What did you tell her when she said that?"

"That I already have posterity. I was once a baby and now I am an old woman. That is posterity."

"If she asks me questions, I am going to answer them," I said.

"One day you will stick your hand in a stew that will burn your fingers. I told her to watch her mouth as to how she talks to people. I told her to watch out for vagabonds like Toto and Raymond."

"Never look them in the eye."

"I told her that too," my grandmother said as she discarded the mint leaves.

My whole body felt taut and taint-free. My grandmother's face softened as she noticed the sheen of cleanliness.

"See, you can be a pretty girl," she said, handing me her precious pouch of needles, thimbles, and thread. "You can be a very pretty girl. Just like your mother used to be."

A burst of evening air chilled my face as I walked across to the yellow house. I was wearing my only Sunday outfit, a white lace dress that I had worn to my confirmation two years before.

The lady poked her head through the door after my first knock.

"Mademoiselle Gallant?"

"How do you know my name?"

"My grandmother sent me."

She was wearing a pair of *abakos,* American blue jeans.

"It looks as though your grandmother has put you to some inconvenience," she said. Then she led me into the front room, with its oversized mahogany chairs and a desk that my grandmother had bought especially for the journalists to use when they were working there.

"My name is really Emilie," she said in Creole, with a very heavy American accent. "What do people call you?"

"Lamort."

"How did your name come to be 'death'?"

"My mother died while I was being born," I explained. "My grandmother was really mad at me for that."

"They should have given you your mother's name," she said, taking the pouch of needles, thread, and thimbles from me. "That is the way it should have been done."

She walked over to the table in the corner and picked up a pitcher of lemonade that my grandmother made for all her guests when they first arrived.

"Would you like some?" she said, already pouring the lemonade.

"*Oui,* Madame. Please."

She held a small carton box of butter cookies in front of me. I took one, only one, just as my grandmother would have done.

"Are you a journalist?" I asked her.

"Why do you ask that?"

"The people who stay here in this house usually are, journalists."

She lit a cigarette. The smoke breezed in and out of her mouth, just like her own breath.

"I am not a journalist," she said. "I have come here to pay a little visit."

"Who are you visiting?"

"Just people."

"Why don't you stay with the people you are visiting?"

"I didn't want to bother them."

"Are they old régime or new régime?"

"Who?"

"Your people?"

"Why do you ask?"

"Because things you say, thoughts you have, will decide how people treat you."

"It seems to me, *you* are the journalist," she said.

"What do you believe in? Old régime or new régime?"

"Your grandmother told me to say to anyone who is interested, 'The only régime I believe in is God's régime.' I would wager that you are a very good source for the journalists. Do you have any schooling?"

"A little."

Once again, she held the box of cookies in front of me. I took another cookie, but she kept the box there, in the same place. I took yet another cookie, and another, until the whole box was empty.

"Can you read what it says there?" she asked, pointing at a line of red letters.

"I cannot read American," I said. Though many of the journalists who came to stay at the yellow house had tried to teach me, I had not learned.

"It is not American," she said. "They are French cookies. That says *Le Petit Ecolier.*"

I stuffed my mouth in shame.

"Intelligence is not only in reading and writing," I said.

"I did not mean to make you feel ashamed," she said, dropping her cigarette into the half glass of lemonade in her hand. "I want to ask you a question."

"I will answer if I can."

"My mother was old régime," she said. "*She* was a journalist. For a newspaper called *Libèté* in Port-au-Prince."

"She came to Ville Rose?"

"Maybe. Or some other town. I don't know. The people who worked with her in Port-au-Prince think she might be in this region. Do you remember any shootings the night of the coup?"

"There were many shootings," I said.

"Did you see any of the bodies?"

"My grandmother and me, we stayed inside."

"Did a woman come to your door? Did anyone ever say that a woman in a purple dress came to their door?"

"No."

"I hear there is a mass burial site," she said. "Do you know it?"

"Yes. I have taken journalists there."

"I would like to go there. Can you take me?"

"Now?"

"Yes."

She pulled some coins from her purse and placed them on the table.

"I have more," she said.

From the back pocket of her jeans, she took out an envelope full of pictures. I ran my fingers over the glossy paper that froze her mother into all kinds of smiling poses: a skinny brown woman with shiny black hair in short spiral curls.

"I have never seen her," I admitted.

"It is possible that she arrived in the evening, and then the coup took place in the middle of the night. Do you know if they found any dead women the day after the coup?"

"There were no bodies," I said. "That is to say no funerals."

I heard my grandmother's footsteps even before she reached the door to the yellow house.

"If you tell her that I'm here, I can't go with you," I said.

"Go into the next room and stay there until I come for you."

My grandmother knocked once and then a second time. I rushed to the next room and crouched in a corner.

The plain white sheets that we usually covered the bed with had been replaced by a large piece of purple cloth. On the cement floor were many small pieces of cloth lined up in squares, one next to the other.

"Thank you for sending me the needles," I heard Emilie say to my grandmother. "I thought I had packed some in my suitcase, but I must have forgotten them."

"My old eyes are not what they used to be," my grandmother said, in the shy humble voice she reserved for prayers and for total strangers. "But if you need some mending, I can do it for you."

"Thank you," said Emilie, "but I can do the mending myself."

"Very well then. Is my granddaughter here?"

"She had to run off," Emilie said.

"Do you know where she went?"

"I don't know. She was dressed for a very fancy affair."

My grandmother was silent for a minute as her knuckles tapped the wood on the front door.

"I will let you rest now," said my grandmother.

"Thank you for the needles," said Emilie.

Emilie bolted the door after my grandmother had left.

"Is there a way we can leave without her seeing you?" She came into the room with a flashlight and her American passport. "You might get a little beating when you go home."

"What are all these small pieces of cloth for?" I asked.

"I am going to sew them onto that purple blanket," she said. "All her life, my mother's wanted to sew some old things together onto that piece of purple cloth."

She raised a piece of white lace above her head. "That's from my mother's wedding dress."

Grabbing a piece of pink terry cloth, she said, "That's an old baby bib."

Tears were beginning to cloud her eyes. She fought them away fast by pushing her head back.

"Purple," she said, "was Mama's favorite color."

"I can ask my grandmother if she saw your mother," I said.

"When I first came, this afternoon," she said, "I showed her the pictures and, like you, she said no."

"We would tell you if we had seen her."

"I want to go to the churchyard," she said. "You say you have already taken other people there."

"I walk by it every day."

"Let's go then."

"Sometimes the yard's guarded at night," I warned her.

"I have an American passport. Maybe that will help."

"The soldiers don't know the difference. Most of them are like me. They would not be able to identify your cookies either."

"How old are you?" she asked.

"Fourteen."

"At your age, you already have a wide reputation. I have a journalist friend who has stayed in this house. He told me you are the only person who would take me to the yard."

I could not think which particular journalist would have given me such a high recommendation, there had been so many.

"Better to be known for good than bad," I said to her.

"I am ready to go," she announced.

"If she is there, will you take her away?"

"Who?"

"Your mother?"

"I have not thought that far."

"And if you see them carrying her, what will you do? She will belong to them and not you."

"They say a girl becomes a woman when she loses her mother," she said.

"You, child, were born a woman."

We walked through the footpath in my grandmother's garden, toward the main road.

"I have been having these awful dreams," Emilie whispered as she plucked some leaves off my grandmother's pumpkin vines. "I see my mother sinking into a river, and she keeps calling my name."

A round of gunshots echoed in the distance, signals from the night guards who had no other ways of speaking to one another.

We stopped on the side of the road and waited for a while and then continued on our way.

The night air blew the smell of rotting flesh to my nose. We circled the churchyard carefully before finding an entrance route. There was a rustle in the yard, like pieces of tin scraping the moist dirt.

"Who is there?"

I thought she stopped breathing when the voice echoed in the night air.

"I am an American journalist," Emilie said in breathless Creole.

She pulled out her passport and raised it toward a blinding flashlight beam. The guard moved the light away from our faces.

It was Raymond's friend, Toto. He was tall and skinny and looked barely sixteen. He was staring at me as though he was possessed by a spirit. In the night, he did not know me.

He took Emilie's passport and flipped through it quickly.

"What are you doing here?" he asked, handing the passport back to her.

"It is after curfew."

"The lady was not feeling well," I said. "So she asked me to take her for a walk."

"Didn't you hear the signals?" asked Toto. "The curfew has already started. You would not want to have blood on your nice communion dress."

Two other soldiers passed us on their way to the field. They were dragging the blood-soaked body of a bearded man with an old election slogan written on a T-shirt across his chest: ALONE WE ARE WEAK. TOGETHER WE ARE A FLOOD. The guards were carrying him, feet first, like a breech birth.

Emilie moved toward the body as though she wanted to see it better.

"You see nothing," Toto said, reaching up to turn Emilie's face. Her eyes twitched from Toto's touch on her cheek.

"Under God's sky, you do this to people!" she hollered in a brazen Creole.

Toto laughed loudly.

"We are doing that poor indigent a favor burying him," he said.

Emilie moved forward, trying to follow the guards taking the body into the yard.

"You see nothing," Toto said again, grabbing her face. She raised her arm as if to strike him. He seized her wrist in midair and whisked her hand behind her back.

"You see nothing," he said, his voice hissing between his teeth. "Repeat after me. You see nothing."

"I see nothing," I said in her place. "The lady does not understand."

"I see you," she said in Creole. "How can that be nothing?"

"Peace, let her go," I said.

"You are a coward," she told him.

He lowered his head so he was staring directly into her eyes. He twisted her arm like a wet rag.

"Peace, have mercy on her," I said.

"Let her ask for herself," he said.

She stamped her feet on his boots. He let go of her hand and tapped his rifle on her shoulder. Emilie looked up at him, angry and stunned. He moved back, aiming his rifle at her head, squinting as though he was going to shoot.

"Peace!" I hollered.

My eyes fell on Raymond's as he walked out of the field. I mouthed the word, pleading for help. *Peace. Peace. Peace.*

"They'll go," Raymond said to Toto.

"Then go!" Toto shouted. "Let me watch you go."

"Let's go," I said to Emilie. "My grandmother will be mad at me if I get killed."

Raymond walked behind us as we went back to the road.

"The password has changed," he said. "Stop saying 'peace.'"

By the time I turned around to look at his face, he was already gone.

Emilie and I said nothing to each other on the way back. The sound of bullets continued to ring through the night.

"You never look them in the eye," I told her when we got to the yellow house doorstep.

"Is that how you do it?"

I helped her up the steps and into the house.

"I am going to sew these old pieces of cloth onto my mother's blanket tonight," she said.

She took a needle from my grandmother's bundle and began sewing. Her fingers moved quickly as she stitched the pieces together.

"I should go," I said, eyeing the money still on the table.

"Please, stay. I will pay you more if you stay with me until the morning."

"My grandmother will worry."

"What was your mother's name?" she asked.

"Marie Magdalène," I said.

"They should have given you that name instead of the one you got. Was your mother pretty?"

"I don't know. She never took portraits like the ones you have of yours."

"Did you know those men who were in the yard tonight?"

"Yes."

"I didn't fight them because I didn't want to make trouble for you later," she said. "We should write down their names. For posterity."

"We have already had posterity," I said.

"When?"

"We were babies and we grew old."

"You're still young," she said. "You're not old."

"My grandmother is old for me."

"If she is old for you, then doesn't it matter if you get old? You can't say that. You can't just say what she wants for you to say. I didn't get in a fight with them because I did not want them to hurt you," she said.

"I will stay with you," I said, "because I know you are afraid."

I curled my body on the floor next to her and went to sleep.

She had the patches sewn together on the purple blanket when I woke up that morning. On the floor, scattered around her, were the pictures of her mother.

"I became a woman last night," she said. "I lost my mother and all my other dreams."

Her voice was weighed down with pain and fatigue. She picked up the coins from the table, added a dollar from her purse, and pressed the money into my palm.

"Will you whisper their names in my ear?" she asked. "I will write them down."

"There is Toto," I said. "He is the one that hit you."

"And the one who followed us?"

"That is Raymond who loves leaves shaped like butterflies."

She jotted their names on the back of one of her mother's pictures and gave it to me.

"My mother's name was Isabelle," she said, "keep this for posterity."

Outside, the morning sun was coming out to meet the day. Emilie sat on the porch and watched me go to my grandmother's house. Loosely sewn, the pieces on the purple blanket around her shoulders were coming apart.

My grandmother was sitting in front of the house waiting for me. She did not move when she saw me. Nor did she make a sound.

"Today, I want you to call me by another name," I said.

"Haughty girls don't get far," she said, rising from the chair.

"I want you to call me Marie Magdalène," I said.

She looked pained as she watched me moving closer to her.

"Marie Magdalène?"

"Yes, Marie Magdalène," I said. "I want you to call me Marie Magdalène." I liked the sound of that.

LISA HARRIS

Where the River Meets the Rain

IN COASTAL GEORGIA the rivers rise up to meet the rain almost daily. What of the land, all red and sore? Freshwater rivers, brackish water, and salt snake around islands and mainland, rise up against root-weary banks and trees, ebb and flow. What of the land covered with kudzu and long tired vipers—lazy from the heat? Tree roots break through the dirt; live oaks hold mistletoe and dangle Spanish moss. To get from island to mainland and mainland to island, people travel over drawbridges, waiting for shrimp boats and yachts to go through, waiting for the bridge to drop and form a road to carry them past oleander, with its lethal juice, in the direction of their need.

The rain falls twice a day most days, and it's almost guaranteed in the summer—sometime close to 2:00 P.M. and then again before sunrise. And this rain has its own smell, made of gardenias and rot and sweat. The rain falls in pieces of wavy glass that distort vision. And in offices and banks, beauty salons and garages, fields and bars, people stop what they are doing in anticipation of the short-lived cooling air that will follow. People—anxious to have the hot dust driven from their cars, their gardens, their houses, and their throats—sigh when the rain comes.

When the afternoon rain pulls open the sky, most people pour themselves a cool, sweetened tea and watch the land outside their windows be washed. Some of them imagine the rain as a medicine cooling their southern fever. Some of them imagine the rain as forgiveness for wrong things done but never known by others. Some of them imagine the rain as themselves, with the power to cleanse.

Once the shower is over, the sun turns the rain into a humid mist, and people return to their work—filing reports, crediting deposits, brushing out perms, draining oil, weeding the field, drinking boilermakers as they let go of the shift. Once the shower is over, people turn their gaze away from windows and look again upon the task at hand—the file poised over the manicure, the unsigned contract for Brazilian lumber at rest on the desk, the watchdog station at the vat where pulp juices simmer.

Before dawn when the clouds gather again, the peepers sing—croaking and squeaking from under magnolia leaves, from beneath mimosa branches, from their perches on exposed roots. Stars are driven back from the sky, and the rain comes from satiny blackness, making river water rise to meet the rain.

After the rain, Tessie went to the riverbank to look through debris for prizes. She had several collections, which she kept in jars and boxes and bags. She hid the containers in her room—under her bed, in the top of her closet, and in the bottom drawer of her dresser. Tessie gathered bird bones, feathers, squirrel skulls, snake vertebrae, and small pieces of colored glass. At night she put all the broken pieces of things on her bed and imagined them—a squirrel with wings, a snake with a fur tail, a bird made of glass. Tessie saw herself laid out in pieces—her brittle heart, her throbbing bones, and the glittering blue glass of her eyes, lying right next to her flesh, a zip-on outfit she wore each day to keep her blood inside.

Pieces of brown, pale green, and clear glass came from beer bottles, Coke bottles, and old jars. Tessie celebrated when she found cobalt blue chips. She searched under the turquoise sky for bleached animal bones and rocks with fossils. She looked for Indian arrowheads and old clay beads that the Ogeechee had used for trading. When Tessie was twelve, she included smoking as part of her searching—allowing herself one Pall Mall for each unique find worthy of burning tobacco.

Tessie tried to make whole beings from the gathered fragments. She recited, "T: Hi, my name is Tessie, and my ghost's name is Tammy, and we come from Tallahassee, trying to make whole beings." In her more formal moods, she chanted, "E: Hi, my name is Elizabeth, and my ghost's name is Ellie, and we come from Ellabelle, trying to piece it back together." When she missed her mother extremely, because she missed her some all the time, she took her mama's name and said, "L: Hi, my name is Laura, and my ghost's name is the same, and I come from Lithonia, trying to make sweet Laura sane."

Tessie watched the bones and glass, stones and feathers carefully. Sometimes she saw them move into shapes of wild birds, and other times she heard them whisper in a language part human and part ghost, telling her to be careful of her own magic, or telling her to step outside her container of skin—letting the bones and blood fall loose at the river bank, telling her to claim weight and sink beneath the 'Geechee River to the river of blood—made of herself and the Georgia clay. And when she followed the voices, her black hair turned into raven feathers, her eyes into cobalt glass, and her bones bleached to match the whites of her eyes and the enamel of her teeth. When she came back into the flesh, her bones remembered other stories that kept Tessie whole for a while.

The first time Tessie saw Ray, her father, naked was when she was eight. She was carrying her five babies down the narrow corridor of the trailer from the living room to her bedroom. She carried all five of them at once holding onto their straw-blond hair. When she reached her room, she dropped them on her bed. Next she went toward the bathroom and, without knocking, entered mint green space where her father stood, one foot resting on the toilet, clipping his toenails. The dark hair she had seen curling above his undershirt at the supper table grew all over his body. And hanging between his legs was a sack and a snake—purple and red, looking bruised. Tessie ran. Down the hallway. Out the door. Toward the creek to where it met the river. No longer thinking about dolls. No longer worrying about copperheads, cottonmouths, or canebrake rattlers.

She splashed into the creek and ran in its shallow waters, ran until she was chest deep in the river, and there she stayed until Ray came to get her. By then he was wearing his green worksuit, which covered most of him. Tessie wouldn't come out of the water, so Ray took off his shoes and socks and his long pants and waded in to get her. And Tessie didn't know what she thought—tired, wet, hungry, and scared. When Ray lifted her, he held her close, sorry he had scared her with his nakedness. He said five words softly in her ear, "Maybe next time you'll knock." But Tessie didn't answer him, wouldn't look at him either. She turned her face away from him while, at the same time, she held tight to his neck.

Tessie collected bits and pieces, and she collected whole things. She collected dolls—soft rubber ones that she bought at Newberry's; hard rubber dolls that she sent for through the mail; handmade corncob dolls crafted by the black men who worked her father's shrimp boat; cloth dolls her grandmother made from rags; whole dolls that she kept on her bed. And she liked the dolls, but she loved her bits and pieces of glass and bone and fallen colored feathers. Dolls were dolls, but the bits and pieces could be transformed.

She often sat at the dock waiting for her father's boat, "The Laura Jean," to come in. While she sat, she listened to the poor white and the black women as they headed shrimp and picked crabmeat from the crimson cream shells. Tessie's favorite storyteller's name was Ol'Dolly, a mixed woman—'Geechee, French, and West African.

Ol'Dolly wrapped her head in a red and green scarf, all shiny and new. And the other women who wrapped their heads were jealous because they wrapped theirs in faded rags. Ol'Dolly's headwrap made a satin crown, made Dolly proud, made her feel like crowing.

Dolly said, "I got me a ches' full of velvet and sateen—all colors."

"Uh-huh."

"Sure ya do, Dolly."

"Keep talkin' it up, Dolly. Go on."

Dolly ignored the hecklers and kept talking. "Ever night when I get home, firs' thing I does is scrub myself with lemon and lye to kill this fish smell. Then I goes into my cabin and I opens up my trunk. Piece by piece I takes out the cloth and lays it on my cheek. Velvet and sateen—fabrics for a queen, I think. And I think myself into magic. I takes out the needle and thread and I sew—dresses and capes, headwraps, and pinafores, but I'm thrifty, like my mama taught me. So I makes the clothes to fit little people."

Ol'Dolly wipes her hand on the cleanest cloth, and then she reaches inside her big blouse. She pulls out five wooden dolls dressed in clothes from a fairy tale, clothes made of greens and red and purples. The dolls' faces are painted black with round white eyes and full red lips. Tessie sits on her hands so she won't grab the dolls from Ol'Dolly. That's how bad she wants one.

Ol'Dolly calls her, "Come here, Tessiedoll, and hold these lady queens for me. If I holds onto them, they soon be smelling of the sea. Ain't no lady wanna smell like fish. Humf—sure you know I don't wanna be smellin' that way."

Tessie rushed to Ol'Dolly's side and gathered up the five black-faced queens in their regal clothes.

"Fact is, Tessiedoll, you might should take those ladies home and put them on a shelf. What Ol'Dolly gonna do with five fancy ladies in her cabin? 'Sides, I can always make me some mo'. You take 'em. Go on, girl."

Tessie's heart flew, swirled, and spun. "Ol'Dolly, thank you, thank you! Such beautiful ladies. I'll take very good care of them, m'am, I promise you that. And when I play with them, I'll think of you and your trunk of fancy cloth."

Tessie didn't wait for the shrimp boat. She put the dollies in her pockets and walked down the sand road, made her way through the trailer park. She tiptoed into the trailer, past where her mother slept on the scratchy couch, into her bedroom. She lined the new dolls up on her windowsill and she named them Dolly's Dolls. She made a little sign that she hung with tape, "Five Lady Queens" by Old Dolly.

The first night the dolls slept in Tessie's room, she kept waking to the smell of burnt wood, but there was no fire. The second night, she woke to rustling fabric, and when she opened her eyes, she saw the dolls grown large as pine trees dancing around the room, but she wasn't afraid. The third night, Tessie awoke to singing and rustling and the smell of burnt wood. And before her the five dolls danced, singing strange words with smoke coming from their wooden mouths. From then on, dolls became as important to her as chips of glass, as red river water, as herself.

Creek beds ran red with the Georgia clay. The water swirled and spit, cascaded and frothed, chastised and beckoned Tessie, who sat inside her trailer looking out at rising water—the red water of a wet Georgia spring. She bit at her hangnails and the callus on her third finger where she rested her pencils and pens, pressing intensely while she did her work at school, pressing so hard that her middle finger appeared deformed. During the summer she hardly wrote at all, avoiding pens and pencils and paper, but still reading books, reading anything she could get ahold of, walking two miles to the olive green bookmobile, where Mr. Hanks stayed seated behind the wheel even when he checked out the books.

Reading didn't give her calluses. It gave her ideas that let her ignore her surroundings, that let her erase the arguments between her mother and father, that let her forget about rising red water and copperheads hanging from riverbank trees. Reading let her imagine the dry plains of the midwest, the snow-peaked mountains of the north, and the wild trails of the untamed west. And Tessie knew she was becoming all these landscapes—her throat the dry plains, her emotions the cold of the northeast when her father touched her, and the wild, untamed west when she touched herself.

Tessie touched herself in many different ways, all the time, night and day, rain or shine, soft and hard. Each morning after she cooked her father's eggs and grits, she washed the dishes and scrubbed down the counters. Then she washed her hair and body, scrubbing her face, making the bright light of herself shine through her skin. She knew it was a brave thing to let people see her light, because it dared people who thought less of her to say anything mean. And people did think less of her—since her mother was in and out of the state mental hospital at Milledgeville and her father was a brute who ran dope on his shrimp boat. With her face all clean, she was more than the girl who lived in the turquoise and white trailer parked on Lot 71 in Little Bit of Paradise Park.

And Tessie touched herself gently at night under the faded cotton blanket, tickling her own skin the way she read mothers often did to put their babies to sleep. And the dolls chanted Tessie into ecstasy, hovering over her bed, loving her. She rubbed her shoulders hard, the way a woman rubs a man after he's been working in a factory all day, and then she rubbed herself in patterns, leading into a darkness reserved for lovers, a darkness that came with sleep, the unknown darkness of death.

So Tessie learned some things: she learned she could be wrong, she learned that bits and pieces were not the only things that could be transformed, she learned that the river and the rain met and kissed. She wanted to search Ol'Dolly out and tell her about the dolls at night, but she reasoned two ways: that Dolly already knew or that Dolly would never believe her. So when she went down to the dock to wait for her daddy or to fetch some shrimp, she skirted Ol'Dolly and the women who smelled of the sea. After supper with her mama and daddy, Tessie either sneaked to the river or shut herself into the bedroom, where the dolls talked to her. She loved to see them move, and the burnt wood smell was incense to her, the only smell that covered the paper mill and the docks.

Tessie smelled turnip greens and bacon, wisteria and rain. She ate hot cornbread topped with butter and sipped her sweetened iced tea. Laura Jean made dinner, but declared, "It's too hot to eat. Thank you very much." So she sat at her end of the table smoking Pall Malls and sipping a Royal Crown. A silent supper meant the food was good, otherwise Ray yelled and fussed, and no one ate except him—because he complained.

Laura Jean ignored Ray; she knew he ate no matter what, as long as she gave him a couple of beers to wash it down, and as long as at least one thing was batter fried. But Tessie, well, she was more particular.

When Laura Jean was pregnant, when Ray still tried to please her, he went into Savannah to a pet store and bought her a Siamese cat. Then he went by the Piggly Wiggly and picked up some tuna-flavored cat food. He could have fed it fish from the boat, but he thought canned food would make Laura Jean love him more.

Laura Jean loved that kitty, named it Baby. Loving as a woman when she's treated right. But the canned food was wrong. Baby wouldn't eat it, wanted shrimp and fish instead, wanted fresh meat. And Laura Jean didn't blame her cat—the smell knocked her over, brought back the morning sickness that in the last trimester had made her lose five pounds a month when she was first pregnant. Laura Jean walked half a mile to the butcher's place and bought sliced filet mignon for Baby.

When Ray found out that Laura Jean had been dipping into his beer money for Baby's food, the only thing that saved her from being beaten was her pregnancy. He promised he'd let her have it later, but Ray forgot his bad promises with the same regularity that he forgot the good ones—a diamond, a house, and that he'd quit drinking.

Laura Jean bore her first child, a daughter, October 25th, when the best expression of a Georgia autumn appeared—golden leaves, and green leaves spotted with gold, a red leaf or an orange one every so often, a few big brown magnolia leaves, and still-blooming black-eyed Susans along the roadside, in the fields, along the banks of the Ogeechee. Laura Jean bore her daughter at high noon and gave her Opal for a middle name—Elizabeth Opal. The fiery golds from the trees outside the hospital in the full sun of a Savannah autumn and her daughter's sapphire blue eyes made Laura Jean dream of fire opals with all their sparkling colors.

Whatever drug they gave Laura Jean to knock her out worked. And when she awoke in the recovery room, she shouted a prayer at the nurse who told her she had a beautiful baby girl, 21 inches long, 8 pounds and 10 ounces. "That baby's full of fire, Mrs. Sipes. You've got yourself a handful."

Laura Jean responded by saying, "Rejoice, oh ye flocks, for unto you a child is born, unto you a daughter is given, and her name shall be unspoken and her flights unmapped and unrecorded. Her pink-skinned wings will carry her. All glory shines around, and the wise follow stars in her eyes."

The recovery room nurse called for a sedative and gave Laura Jean the shot herself. She'd never heard someone yell quite so loud and certainly never heard something quite so strange. What the woman said sounded as if it were the New Testament, but the nurse didn't think it was. While Mrs. Sipes slept, the nurse pulled her records to see if she was married to a minister or had any previous record of mental illness. Neither. She was married to a man who worked at the paper mill. Nothing about mental instability. So she checked Mrs. Sipes's chart to see what drug had been administered during delivery. When she saw it was morphine, she wasn't quite as taken aback—nothing that a little sleep wouldn't cure.

Ray wouldn't let Laura Jean call their daughter Opal. "That's a stone. You wouldn't want to call this girl Diamond or Ruby. Anyways, opals bring bad luck, they crack easy."

"But, Ray, my grandmother's name was Pearl and I had a great-aunt Ruby, I don't see what you are getting so het up—"

"No, by God. She's my child, too, and we ain't having part of her name sound like she belongs in a jewelry store."

Tessie told long intricate stories at the supper table. She ate the few things she liked, while she ate she talked. And while she talked, she controlled the table. High on her list of things to avoid were her mama's potato salad and turnip greens. The potato salad—made out of mashed potatoes, sweet pickles, hard boiled eggs, and salad dressing—stuck in her mouth. The turnip greens smelled the same as the bathroom at June's Country Corner, where her daddy dragged her. There was something about the iron in the dark green leaves that reacted with the metal fillings in her teeth. When she chewed, she received little shocks up her jaw and into her temple.

Tessie walked home with her best friend, Janie, every day. Laura Jean knew that, so she didn't worry about her. But one day when Tessie was forty-five minutes late, Laura Jean went out looking for her in the Ford Galaxy station wagon.

She found the girls walking home, but Tessie was leaning on Janie's shoulder for support. Tessie wanted to talk right away, but Laura Jean told her to hush and save it for supper. She drove Janie back to her house. Then Laura Jean took Tessie home, hurried her inside, and sat her down at the table with Ray.

Tessie had crystal marbles: ruby, sapphire, and emerald.

"John Henry dared me to a game of marbles, Mama. I met him outside on the red clay. You know how it always has a layer of dust on it? Well, I let John Henry draw the circle. Everybody stood round staring. No one cheered for either of us.

"I shot with my ruby crystal and won John Henry's ball bearing. He snorted and hocked an oyster inside the circle. Then I went in for lunch. I laid the crystals and ball bearing on a napkin in front of me at the lunch table.

"On my way home, John Henry picked me up and held my arms so I couldn't scratch him. Then he threw me on the sidewalk. My knees hit first, split open like a watermelon. John Henry pulled out a knife and cut the straps on my bookbag. He dumped everything on the sidewalk. He stole his ball bearing that I had won fair and square, and he took my crystals."

Her father belched and looked at her with his watered blue eyes. "Quit tellin' tales, Tess, and eat your turnips."

Laura Jean reached across the table to touch Tessie's hand. "It's all right, Baby," she said when she made contact.

Ray's fist hit the table. "And you. Quit callin' her Baby, makes me think of that damn chink cat."

Janie lived in a real house made out of wood that sat on a piece of land big enough for a vegetable garden. She grew okra and lady peas, limas and watermelon, collards and beefsteak tomatoes. She had to share her bedroom, and there wasn't any indoor plumbing. "At least at Little Bit, you got a toilet and running water, Tessie," Janie spoke in a soft drawl, her voice warm and sticky as mimosa flowers. "And you got a roof that doesn't leak and neighbors all around, and in a heartbeat you can play a game of Tin Can Annie or shoot some marbles. All I got here is chores and Daddy and Mommy." But that wasn't how Tessie saw it. She envied the white frame house with its red tin roof, and she envied the space all around and the garden. Lot 71 was crowded right between Lots 70 and 72. She heard Jeb Fisher pee and flush, she heard him swear when he cut himself shaving, and she heard him cry at night when his wife, Linda, told him, "Keep you hands to yourself. I just took my bath." Through the screen door on the other side, she saw fat Mrs. Bowser in her unfastened robe, the layers of flesh rolling down her front, her breasts downcast, her nipples disappearing into the mound of her stomach.

For Tessie, space was a dream and silence was its color. And in that place, she had music and running water, a daddy like Janie's, and her mother had returned, stayed by her side—sane and funny, lighting one Pall Mall after another while she told stories about growing up on the 'Geechee River as she tickled Tessie's back with her long red nails.

Laura Jean expected people to use both of her names, and if they didn't, she wouldn't answer. When she was crazy, she did what people in the trailer park called "went off." "Oh, Tessie's mama has went off again." Like that. She didn't wander or explode. Her blue eyes were fixed ahead of her while she sat on her couch describing other worlds. When she went off, she stopped in the middle of what she was doing, sat down, and stared.

Laura Jean went in and out of Milledgeville. Paranoid schizophrenic. When she went off, she spent her days talking with God over Pall Malls and coffee. She saw women arrive while Ray was trying to make love to her, and she told him to stop because her substitutes had arrived. She quit doing the housework because she could see elves doing it for her. Besides, if she did it, she couldn't talk to God as much.

Electric shock treatments made her quieter—not saner. She drew into herself; the stays at Milledgeville grew longer.

Rain fell day after day, filling the creek beds and turning the hard red clay into slick, eroding danger zones. Nothing but dark purple clouds and rain so thick it fell in sheets, blanketing vision. Creeks ran into freshwater rivers, which ran into brackish water, which ran into the tidal waters and then into the ocean. From Little Bit of Paradise Trailer Park's Lot 71, Tessie saw the rain fall day after day in sheets, saw it wash down the red creek bed, turning clay into silt.

When the rain stopped, mosquitoes spilled from the air, rose from the swamps, swarmed outside her trailer door. Mosquito Control drove through the Park spraying the white poison in the air, and no one minded. Each person yearned for the silent spring air, the silent summer air, hating the hissing, buzzing sound of mosquitoes, which were measured by the number of them that landed on an exposed arm in a minute's time.

Tessie hated the mosquitoes, but she hated the confinement of the trailer more, starved as she was for space. Mosquitoes bit her hungrily, bites on top of bites until quarter-sized welts appeared. The Avon Lady sold Skin-So-Soft as a repellant, and it did work, so Tessie layered it on and watched as the mosquitoes dove into it and suffocated; their long, delicate wings quivering out of sync. Her entire body smelling bittersweet.

Many snakes lived in the Park. One had lived there for five years, as long as Tessie had, and it was big. The others heard the thud of human feet coming down the path and disappeared, but the big one moved more slowly, and even with the people swimming and on the bank talking, it didn't run away. It hung out in the willow tree, head up and watchful.

Janie didn't like the snake, didn't like its size or its attitude. She kept her daddy's shotgun in the bedroom closet, loaded. She started getting up a half hour earlier and walking down to the creek the long way around, staying away from the side where the trees were and where the snakes lived. She stood steady for thirty minutes waiting for the big snake. Tessie told her, "It's the wrong time of day, Janie. Those snakes are still sleeping. They aren't going to come out unless there's sun for them to lay in. You might as well stay in bed and sleep. Besides, it's bad luck to kill snakes." Janie didn't listen to Tessie, but she didn't see the snake either.

One morning several weeks into her hunt, when Tessie was scrambling her egg and waiting for the toast to pop out, she heard the shot. She felt as if she had been hit. She took the pan off the burner and forgot about the toast. She put her pale pink flip-flops on and moved swiftly down the path to the creek.

Janie had waded in, ignoring the stones that offended her tender feet, and shot the big snake where it lay sleeping on the willow branch. She held the wounded snake by its neck. Then she threw it on the ground and pounded its head with the butt of her gun. "I don't want it to suffer," she said.

Each time the butt hit, Tessie felt a twinge in her vertebrae, a hispid pain. Her earrings rattled when she shook her head. She hugged herself and tiny flecks of skin fell. In her mouth, her tongue split.

Rub a hand against cottonwood bark to keep a cottonmouth away. Rub a back against a standing rock to gain strength. Rub a forehead slowly across pine bark to ward off sadness. Lie down on the side of your body. Rub a cheek against the night-cooled red clay. Rest there. When the snakes begin to night hunt, they will consider the body a log; they will not rattle, hiss, or bite—still as the body is, the same temperature as the clay. They will coil close when the hunt is done. They will coil close to sleep. Tessie memorized the rules for sleeping in the swamp with snakes.

Like a snake, Tessie's body became the temperature of those things closest to her. In the swamp, Tessie was not afraid. She didn't know many Jesus stories, but she did know about him wandering in the wilderness with the devil, and the story made her laugh. She thought Jesus should have been much more afraid of the city of Jerusalem than of anything in the wilderness. She preferred swamp to Savannah, snakes to people.

Cottonwood and cottonmouth. Canebrakes and canebrake rattlers. Copper bracelets and copperheads. Tessie thought of things in pairs. Milk and honey, black and white, glory and power, bourbon and water, sun and rain, now and never, life and death, sound and silence, him and her, mother and father, crazy and sane. Usually the pairs were also opposites, but not always. And whether the pairs were the same or opposite, the words made Tessie think of stories.

Cottonwoods and cottonmouths, canebrakes and canebrake rattlers were natural and sane, gave Tessie's world order, because what each did was predictable, followed a pattern. She knew that the trees provided shade, were good for climbing. She loved to break the cane and suck the sugar from the end. And snakes, which everyone around her feared, detested, killed, were her friends. While other little girls slept with stuffed animals from Newberry's, Tessie slept on the riverbank with snakes curled around her, at first mistaking her for a log, but eventually they knew her for what she was—human. And they let her pick them up, they let her pet their bellies until they slept, her hand urging the ingested frog or rodent farther down their digestive tract.

SUSAN HAWTHORNE

Such a Tomboy

DON'T BE SUCH A TOMBOY. Don't bite your nails. Where did you get so dirty so quickly? Act like a lady. Don't chew with your mouth open—it's rude. Go and wash your hands before you come and sit up at the table. Have you cleaned your shoes? Sit still for five minutes. Have you collected the eggs and fed the chooks? Your hem's hanging. Go and get a needle and thread. *But I don't like sewing, and anyway, I can't do it.* You're such a tomboy. Hold your knife and fork properly, or you'll never be invited to dinner at Buck House. Sit up straight. Don't slouch. Try not to sit with your legs wide open. It's not ladylike. Don't accept lifts from strange men. Be friendly. Act like a lady, not like a tomboy. Enjoy yourself at the party. Always be polite. Be interested in what others say to you. There's a ladder in your stockings. If ever your underpants fall down when you're walking down the street, step out of them, pick them up and put them in your bag. Don't leave them lying in the street. Your petticoat is hanging. Don't look cheap. Where have you been? Why can't you keep your clothes clean? If you don't ask, you don't want. Did you remember to brush the horse down? Don't be such a tomboy. Have you set the table? Where are the salt and pepper shakers? Have you cleaned your teeth? Go and put on some deodorant. Tidy your room. Go and get the cow up from the paddock so I can milk her. Why don't you put on that nice dress I bought for you? You look so soft and feminine in it. *But I don't like it, it's prissy.* Now that you've got your period you'll have to try and act like a lady. Be yourself. Don't go swimming when you've got your period. Always wash yourself properly. Don't wear nylon underpants. Use cold water to wash out bloodstains. Don't listen to what the other girls say. It's probably not true. Always ask a boy what his father does. You can tell a lot about a person from their table manners. Don't do anything silly. Make the gravy for the roast—always use flour. Did you put salt in the porridge? If you add baking powder to the beans they'll keep their color. Learn to be a lady. When you stay with someone, be polite—offer to dry the dishes, help out, don't just sit there. Always smile. Smile and the whole world smiles with you, cry and you cry alone. Wednesday's child is full of woe. I think you'll have to bring the sheep in by yourself from Walleroobie tomorrow. Don't do things just because others do them. People respect a girl who says no. When you're travelling, wash out your panties at night. Take one of those stretch clotheslines with you. Don't borrow money from others. If you do, pay it back straightaway. Keep your independence. A girl needs her own income. You shouldn't work for money if you don't have to. You should stop working when you get married. Maybe you'll marry a doctor. Keep up your maths. Learn to follow the share market. Always finish what you start. If a job's worth doing, it's worth doing well. Have you fed the dogs, watered the garden, swept the back path, cleaned the aviary? Virgins shouldn't use tampons.

Why did you turn out to be a lesbian?

Upon reading Jamaica Kincaid's "Girl"

PAM HOUSTON

Selway

It was June the seventh and we'd driven eighteen hours of pavement and sixty miles of dirt to find out the river was at highwater, the highest of the year, of several years, and rising. The ranger, Ramona, wrote on our permit, "We do not recommend boating at this level," and then she looked at Jack.

"We're just gonna go down and take a look at it," he said, "see if the river gives us a sign." He tried to slide the permit away from Ramona, but her short dark fingers held it against the counter. I looked from one to the other. I knew Jack didn't believe in signs.

"Once you get to Moose Creek you're committed," she said. "There's no time to change your mind after that. You've got Double Drop and Little Niagara and Ladle, and they just keep coming like that, one after another with no slow water in between."

She was talking about rapids. This was my first northern trip, and after a lazy spring making slow love between rapids on the wide desert rivers, I couldn't imagine what all the fuss was about.

"If you make it through the Moose Creek series there's only a few more real bad ones; Wolf Creek is the worst. After that the only thing to worry about is the takeout point. The beach will be under water, and if you miss it, you're over Selway Falls."

"Do you have a river guide?" Jack said, and when she bent under the counter to get one he tried again to slide the permit away. She pushed a small, multifolded map in his direction.

"Don't rely on it," she said. "The rapids aren't even marked in the right place."

"Thanks for your help," Jack said. He gave the permit a sharp tug and put it in his pocket.

"There was an accident today," Ramona said. "In Ladle."

"Anybody hurt?" Jack asked.

"It's not official."

"Killed?"

"The water's rising," Ramona said, and turned back to her desk.

At the put-in, the water crashed right over the top of the depth gauge. The grass grew tall and straight through the slats of the boat ramp.

"Looks like we're the first ones this year," Jack said.

The Selway has the shortest season of any river in North America. They don't plow the snow till the first week in June, and by the last week in July there's not enough water to carry a boat. They only allow one party a day on the river that they select from a nationwide lottery with thousands of applicants each year. You can try your whole life and never get a permit.

"Somebody's been here," I said. "The people who flipped today."

Jack didn't answer. He was looking at the gauge. "It's up even from this morning," he said. "They said this morning it was six feet."

Jack and I have known each other almost a year. I'm the fourth in a series of long-term girlfriends he's never gotten around to proposing to. He likes me because I'm young enough not to sweat being single and I don't put pressure on him the way the others did. They wanted him to quit running rivers, to get a job that wasn't seasonal, to raise a family like any man his age. They wouldn't go on trips with him, not even once to see what it was like, and I couldn't imagine that they knew him in any way that was complete if they hadn't known him on the river, if they hadn't seen him row.

I watched him put his hand in the water. "Feel that, baby," he said. "That water was snow about fifteen minutes ago."

I stuck my foot in the water and it went numb in about ten seconds. I've been to four years of college and I should know better, but I love it when he calls me baby.

Jack has taken a different highwater trip each year for the last fifteen, on progressively more difficult rivers. When a river is at high water it's not just deeper and faster and colder than usual. It's got a different look and feel from the rest of the year. It's dark and impatient and turbulent, like a volcano or a teenage boy. It strains against its banks and it churns around and under itself. Looking at its fullness made me want to grab Jack and throw him down on the boat ramp and make love right next to where the river roared by, but I could tell by his face he was trying to make a decision, so I sat and stared at the river and wondered if it was this wild at the put-in what it would look like in the rapids.

"If anything happened to you . . ." he said, and threw a stick out to the middle of the channel. "It must be moving nine miles an hour." He walked up and down the boat ramp. "What do you think?" he said.

"I think this is a chance of a lifetime," I said. "I think you're the best boatman you know." I wanted to feel the turbulence underneath me. I wanted to run a rapid that could flip a boat. I hadn't taken anything like a risk in months. I wanted to think about dying.

It was already early evening, and once we made the decision to launch, there were two hours of rigging before we could get on the water. On the southern rivers we'd boat sometimes for an hour after dark just to watch what the moon did to the water. On the Selway there was a rapid that could flip your boat around every corner. It wasn't getting pitch dark till ten-thirty that far north, where the June dusk went on forever, but it wasn't really light either and we wouldn't be able to see very far ahead. We told ourselves we'd go a tenth of a mile and make camp, but you can't camp on a sheer granite wall, and the river has to give you a place to get stopped and get tied.

I worked fast and silent, wondering if we were doing the right thing and knowing if we died it would really be my fault, because as much as I knew Jack wanted to go, he wouldn't have pushed me if I'd said I was scared. Jack was untamable, but he had some sense and a lot of respect for the river. He relied on me to speak with the voice of reason, to be life-protecting because I'm a woman and that's how he thinks women are, but I've never been protective enough of anything, least of all myself.

At nine-fifteen we untied the rope and let the river take us.

"The first place that looks campable," Jack said.

Nine miles an hour is fast in a rubber raft on a river you've never boated when there's not quite enough light to see what's in front of you. We were taking on water over the bow almost immediately, even though the map didn't show any rapids for the first two miles. It was hard for me to take my eyes off Jack, the way his muscles strained with every stroke, first his upper arms, then his upper thighs. He was silent, thinking it'd been a mistake to come, but I was laughing and bailing water and combing the banks for a flat spot and jumping back and forth over my seat to kiss him, and watching while his muscles flexed.

My mother says I thrive on chaos, and I guess that's true, because as hard a year as I've had with Jack I stayed with it, and I won't even admit by how much the bad days outnumbered the good. We fought like bears when we weren't on the river, because he was so used to fighting and I was so used to getting my own way. I said I wanted selfless devotion and he took a stand on everything from infidelity to salad dressing, and it was always opposite to mine. The one thing we had going for us, though, was the sex, and if we could stop screaming at each other long enough to make love it would be a day or sometimes two before something would happen and we'd go at it again. I've always been afraid to stop and think too hard about what great sex in bad times might mean, but it must have something to do with timing, that moment making love when you're at once absolutely powerful and absolutely helpless, a balance we could never find when we were out of bed.

It was the old southern woman next door, the hunter's widow, who convinced me I should stay with him each time I'd get mad enough to leave. She said if I didn't have to fight for him I'd never know if he was mine. She said the wild ones were the only ones worth having and that I had to let him do whatever it took to keep him wild. She said I wouldn't love him if he ever gave in, and the harder I looked at my life, the more I saw a series of men— wild in their own way—who thought because I said I wanted security and commitment, I did. Sometimes it seems this simple: I tamed them and made them dull as fence posts and left each one for someone wilder than the last. Jack is the wildest so far, and the hardest, and even though I've been proposed to sixteen times, five times by men I've never made love to, I want him all to myself and at home more than I've ever wanted anything.

"Are you bailing? I'm standing in water back here," he said, so I bailed faster but the waves kept on crashing over the bow.

"I can't move this boat," he said, which I knew wasn't entirely true, but it was holding several hundred gallons of water times eight pounds a gallon, and that's more weight than I'd care to push around.

"There," he said. "Camp. Let's try to get to shore."

He pointed to a narrow beach a hundred yards downstream. The sand looked black in the twilight; it was long and flat enough for a tent.

"Get the rope ready," he said. "You're gonna have to jump for it and find something to wrap around fast."

He yelled *jump* but it was too early and I landed chest-deep in the water and the cold took my breath but I scrambled across the rocks to the beach and wrapped around a fallen trunk just as the rope went tight. The boat dragged the trunk and me ten yards down the beach before Jack could get out and pull the nose of it up on shore.

"This may have been real fuckin' stupid," he said.

I wanted to tell him how the water made me feel, how horny and crazy and happy I felt riding on top of water that couldn't hold itself in, but he was scared, for the first time since I'd known him, so I kept my mouth shut and went to set up the tent.

In the morning the tent was covered all around with a thin layer of ice and we made love like crazy people, the way you do when you think it might be the last time ever, till the sun changed the ice back to dew and got the tent so hot we were sweating. Then Jack got up and made coffee, and we heard the boaters coming just in time to get our clothes on.

They threw us their rope and we caught it. There were three of them, three big men in a boat considerably bigger than ours. Jack poured them coffee. We all sat down on the fallen log.

"You launched late last night?" the tallest, darkest one said. He had curly black hair and a wide open face.

Jack nodded. "Too late," he said. "Twilight boating."

"It's up another half a foot this morning," the man said. "It's supposed to peak today at seven."

The official forest service document declares the Selway unsafe for boating above six feet. Seven feet is off their charts.

"Have you boated this creek at seven?" Jack asked. The man frowned and took a long drink from his cup.

.   "My name's Harvey," he said, and stuck out his hand. "This is Charlie and Charlie. We're on a training trip." He laughed. "Yahoo."

Charlie and Charlie nodded.

"You know the river," Jack said.

"I've boated the Selway seventy times," he said. "Never at seven feet. It was all the late snow and last week's heat wave. It's a bad combination, but it's boatable. This river's always boatable if you know exactly where to be."

Charlie and Charlie smiled.

"There'll be a lot of holes that there's no way to miss. You got to punch through them."

Jack nodded. I knew Harvey was talking about boat flippers. Big waves that form in holes the river makes behind rocks and ledges and that will suck boats in and hold them there, fill them with water till they flip, hold bodies, too, indefinitely, until they go under and catch the current, or until the hole decides to spit them out. If you hit a hole with a back wave bigger than your boat perfectly straight, there's a half a chance you'll shoot through. A few degrees off in either direction, and the hole will get you every time.

"We'll be all right in this tank," Harvey said, nodding to his boat, "but I'm not sure I'd run it in a boat that small. I'm not sure I'd run it in a boat I had to bail."

Unlike ours, Harvey's boat was a self-bailer, inflatable tubes around an open metal frame that let the water run right through. They're built for high water, and extremely hard to flip.

"Just the two of you?" Harvey said.

Jack nodded.

"A honeymoon trip. Nice."

"We're not married," Jack said.

"Yeah," Harvey said. He picked up a handful of sand. "The black sand of the Selway," he said. "I carried a bottle of this sand downriver the year I got married. I wanted to throw it at my wife's feet during the ceremony. The minister thought it was pretty strange, but he got over it."

One of the Charlies looked confused.

"Black sand," Harvey said. "You know, black sand, love, marriage, Selway, rivers, life; the whole thing."

I smiled at Jack, but he wouldn't meet my eyes.

"You'll be all right till Moose Creek," Harvey said. "That's when it gets wild. We're gonna camp there tonight, run the bad stretch first thing in the morning in case we wrap or flip or tear something. I hope you won't think I'm insulting you if I ask you to run with us. It'll be safer for us both. The people who flipped yesterday were all experienced. They all knew the Selway."

"They lost one?" Jack said.

"Nobody will say for sure," Harvey said. "But I'd bet on it."

"We'll think about it," Jack said. "It's nice of you to offer."

"I know what you're thinking," Harvey said. "But I've got a kid now. It makes a difference." He pulled a picture out of his wallet. A baby girl, eight or nine months old, crawled across a linoleum floor.

"She's beautiful," I said.

"She knocks me out," Harvey said. "She follows everything with her finger; bugs, flowers, the TV, you know what I mean?"

Jack and I nodded.

"It's your decision," he said. "Maybe we'll see you at Moose Creek."

He stood up, and Charlie and Charlie rose behind him. One coiled the rope while the other pushed off.

Jack poured his third cup of coffee. "Think he's full of shit?" he said.

"I think he knows more than you or I ever will," I said.

"About this river, at least," he said.

"At least," I said.

In midday sunshine, the river looked more fun than terrifying. We launched just before noon, and though there was no time for sightseeing I bailed fast enough to let Jack move the boat through the rapids, which came quicker and bigger around every bend. The map showed ten rapids between the put-in and Moose Creek, and it was anybody's guess which of the fifty or sixty rapids we boated that day were the ones the forest service had in mind. Some had bigger waves than others, some narrower passages, but the river was continuous moving white water, and we finally put the map away. On the southern rivers we'd mix rum and fruit juice and eat smoked oysters and pepper cheese. Here, twenty fast miles went by without time to take a picture, to get a drink of water. The Moose Creek pack bridge came into sight, and we pulled in and tied up next to Harvey's boat.

"White fuckin' water," Harvey said. "Did you have a good run?"

"No trouble," Jack said.

"Good," Harvey said. "Here's where she starts to kick ass." He motioned with his head downriver. "We'll get up at dawn and scout everything."

"It's early yet," Jack said. "I think we're going on." I looked at Jack's face, and then Harvey's.

"You do what you want," Harvey said. "But you ought to take a look at the next five miles. The runs are obvious once you see them from the bank, but they change at every level."

"We haven't scouted all day," Jack said. I knew he wanted us to run alone, that he thought following Harvey would be cheating somehow, but I believed a man who'd throw sand at his new wife's feet, and I liked a little danger but I didn't want to die.

"There's only one way through Ladle," Harvey said. "Ladle's where they lost the girl."

"The girl?" Jack said.

"The rest of her party was here when we got here. Their boats were below Ladle. They just took off, all but her husband. He wouldn't leave, and you can't blame him. He was rowing when she got tossed. He let the boat get sideways. He's been wandering around here for two days, I guess, but he wouldn't get back in the boat."

"Jesus Christ," Jack said. He sat down on the bank facing the water.

I looked back into the woods for the woman's husband and tried to imagine a posture for him, tried to imagine an expression for his face. I thought about my Uncle Tim, who spent ten years and a lifetime of savings building his dream home. On the day it was completed he backed his pickup over his four-year-old daughter while she played in the driveway. He sold the house in three days and went completely gray in a week.

"A helicopter landed about an hour ago," Harvey said. "Downstream, where the body must be. It hasn't taken off."

"The water's still rising," Jack said, and we all looked to where we'd pulled the boats up on shore and saw that they were floating. And then we heard the beating of the propeller and saw the helicopter rising out over the river.

We saw the hundred feet of cable hanging underneath it and then we saw the woman, arched like a dancer over the thick black belt they must use for transplanting wild animals, her long hair dangling, her arms slung back. The pilot flew up the river till he'd gained enough altitude, turned back, and headed over the mountain wall behind our camp.

"They said she smashed her pelvis against a rock and bled to death internally," Harvey said. "They got her out in less than three minutes, and it was too late."

Jack put his arm around my knees. "We'll scout at dawn," he said. "We'll all run this together."

Harvey was up rattling coffeepots before we had time to make love and I said it would bring us bad luck if we didn't but Jack said it would be worse than bad luck if we didn't scout the rapids. The scouting trail was well worn. Harvey went first, then Jack, then me and the two Charlies. Double Drop was first, two sets of falls made by water pouring over clusters of house-sized boulders that extended all the way across the river.

"You can sneak the first drop on the extreme right," Harvey said. "There's no sneak for the second. Just keep her straight and punch her through. Don't let her get you sideways."

Little Niagara was a big drop, six feet or more, but the run was pretty smooth and the back wave low enough to break through.

"Piece of cake," Harvey said.

The sun was almost over the canyon wall, and we could hear Ladle long before we rounded the bend. I wasn't prepared for what I saw. One hundred yards of white water stretched from shore to shore and thundered over rocks and logjams and ledges. There were ten holes the size of the one in Double Drop, and there was no space for a boat in between. The currents were so chaotic for such a long stretch there was no way to read which way they'd push a boat. We found some small logs and climbed a rock ledge that hung over the rapid.

"See if you can read this current," Harvey said, and tossed the smallest log into the top of the rapid. The log hit the first hole and went under. It didn't come back up. One of the Charlies giggled.

"Again," Harvey said. This time the log came out of the first hole and survived two more before getting swallowed by the biggest hole, about midway through the rapid.

"I'd avoid that one for sure," Harvey said. "Try to get left of that hole." He threw the rest of the logs in. None of them made it through. "This is bigtime," he said.

We all sat on the rock for what must have been an hour. "Seen enough?" Harvey said. "We've still got No Slouch and Miranda Jane."

The men climbed down off the rock, but I wasn't quite ready to leave. I went to the edge of the ledge, lay flat on my stomach, and hung over until my head was so full of the roar of the river I got dizzy and pulled myself back up. The old southern woman said men can't really live unless they face death now and then, and I know by men she didn't mean mankind. And I wondered which rock shattered the dead woman's pelvis, and I wondered what she and I were doing out here on this river when Harvey's wife was home with that beautiful baby and happy. And I knew it was crazy to take a boat through that rapid and I knew I'd do it anyway but I didn't any longer know why. Jack said I had to do it for myself to make it worth anything, and at first I thought I was there because I loved danger, but sitting on the rock I knew I was there because I loved Jack. And maybe I went because his old girlfriends wouldn't, and maybe I went because I wanted him for mine, and maybe it didn't matter at all why I went because doing it for me and doing it for him amounted, finally, to exactly the same thing. And even though I knew in my head there's nothing a man can do that a woman can't, I also knew in my heart we can't help doing it for different reasons. And just like a man will never understand exactly how a woman feels when she has a baby, or an orgasm, or the reasons why she'll fight so hard to be loved, a woman can't know in what way a man satisfies himself, what question he answers for himself, when he looks right at death.

My head was so full of the sound and the light of the river that when I climbed down off the bank side of the ledge I didn't see the elk carcass until I stepped on one of its curled hooves. It was a young elk, probably not dead a year, and still mostly covered with matted brown fur. The skull was picked clean by scavengers, polished white by the sun and grinning. The sound that came out of my mouth scared me as much as the elk had, and I felt silly a few minutes later when Harvey came barreling around the corner followed by Jack.

Harvey saw the elk and smiled.

"It startled me is all," I said.

"Jesus," Jack said. "Stay with us, all right?"

"I never scream," I said. "Hardly ever."

No Slouch and Miranda Jane were impressive rapids, but they were nothing like Ladle and both runnable to the left. On the way back to camp we found wild strawberries, and Jack and I hung back and fed them to each other and

I knew he wasn't mad about me screaming. The boats were loaded by ten-thirty and the sun was warm. We wore life jackets and helmets and wet suits. Everybody had diver's boots but me, so I wore my loafers.

"You have three minutes in water this cold," Harvey said. "Even with a wet suit. Three minutes before hypothermia starts, and then you can't swim, and then you just give in to the river."

Harvey gave us the thumbs-up sign as the Charlies pushed off. I pushed off right behind them. Except for the bail bucket and the spare oar, everything on the boat was tied down twice and inaccessible. My job was to take water out of the boat as fast as I could eight pounds at a time, and to help Jack remember which rapid was coming next and where we had decided to run it.

I saw the first of the holes in Double Drop and yelled, "Right," and we made the sneak with a dry boat. We got turned around somehow after that, though, and had to hit the big wave backwards. Jack yelled, "Hang on, baby," and we hit it straight on and it filled the boat, but then we were through it and in sight of Little Niagara before I could even start bailing.

"We're going twelve miles an hour at least," Jack yelled. "Which one is this?"

"Niagara," I yelled. "Right center." The noise of the river swallowed my words and I only threw out two bucketfuls before we were over the lip of Niagara and I had to hold on. I could hear Ladle around the bend and I was throwing water so fast I lost my balance and that's when I heard Jack say, "Bail faster!" and that's when I threw the bail bucket into the river and watched, unbelieving, as it went under, and I saw Jack see it too but we were at Ladle and I had to sit down and hold on. I watched Harvey's big boat getting bounced around like a cork, and I think I closed my eyes when the first wave crashed over my face because the next thing I knew we were out of the heaviest water and Harvey was standing and smiling at us with his fist in the air.

I could see No Slouch around the bend and I don't remember it or Miranda Jane because I was kneeling in the front of the boat scooping armfuls of water the whole time.

We all pulled up on the first beach we found and drank a beer and hugged each other uncertainly, like tenants in an apartment building where the fires have been put out.

"You're on your own," Harvey said. "We're camping here. Take a look at Wolf Creek, and be sure and get to shore before Selway Falls." He picked up a handful of black sand and let it run through his fingers. He turned to me. "He's a good boatman, and you're very brave."

I smiled.

"Take care of each other," he said. "Stay topside."

We set off alone and it clouded up and started to rain and I couldn't make the topography match the river map.

"I can't tell where we are," I told Jack. "But Wolf Creek can't be far."

"We'll see it coming," he said, "or hear it."

But it wasn't five minutes after he spoke that we rounded a bend and were in it, waves crashing on all sides and Jack trying to find a way between the rocks and the holes. I was looking too, and I think I saw the run, fifty feet to our right, right before I heard Jack say, "Hang on, baby," and we hit the hole sideways and everything went white and cold. I was in the waves and underwater and I couldn't see Jack or the boat, I couldn't move my arms or legs apart from how the river tossed them. Jack had said swim down to the current, but I couldn't tell which way was down and I couldn't have moved there in that washing machine, my lungs full and taking on water. Then the wave spit me up, once, under the boat, and then again, clear of it, and I got a breath and pulled down away from the air and felt the current grab me, and I waited to get smashed against a rock, but the rock didn't come and I was at the surface riding the crests of some eight-foot rollers and seeing Jack's helmet bobbing in the water in front of me.

"Swim, baby!" he yelled, and it was like it hadn't occurred to me, like I was frozen there in the water. And I tried to swim but I couldn't get a breath and my limbs wouldn't move and I thought about the three minutes and hypothermia and I must have been swimming then because the shore started to get closer. I grabbed the corner of a big ledge and wouldn't let go, not even when Jack yelled at me to get out of the water, and even when he showed me an easy place to get out if I just floated a few yards downstream it took all I had and more to let go of the rock and get back in the river.

I got out on a tiny triangular rock ledge, surrounded on all sides by walls of granite. Jack stood sixty feet above me on another ledge.

"Sit tight," he said. "I'm going to go see if I can get the boat."

Then he was gone and I sat in that small space and started to shake. It was raining harder, sleeting even, and I started to think about freezing to death in that space that wasn't even big enough for me to move around in and get warm. I started to think about the river rising and filling that space and what would happen when Jack got back and made me float downstream to an easier place, or what would happen if he didn't come back, if he died trying to get the boat back, if he chased it fifteen miles to Selway Falls. When I saw the boat float by, right side up and empty, I decided to climb out of the space.

I'd lost one loafer in the river, so I wedged myself between the granite walls and used my fingers, mostly, to climb. I've always been a little afraid of heights, so I didn't look down. I thought it would be stupid to live through the boating accident and smash my skull free-climbing on granite, but as I inched up the wall I got warmer and kept going. When I got to the top there were trees growing across, and another vertical bank I hadn't seen from below. I bashed through the branches with my helmet and grabbed them one at a time till they broke or pulled out and then I grabbed the next one higher. I dug into the thin layer of soil that covered the rock with my knees and my elbows, and I'd slip down an inch for every two I gained. When I came close to panic I thought of Rambo, as if he were a real person, as if what I was doing was possible, and proven before, by him.

And then I was on the ledge and I could see the river, and I could see Jack on the other side, and I must have been in shock, a little, because I couldn't at that time imagine how he could have gotten to the other side of the river, I couldn't imagine what would make him go back in the water, but he had, and there he was on the other side.

"I lost the boat," he yelled. "Walk downstream till you see it."

I was happy for instructions and I set off down the scouting trail, shoe on one foot, happy for the pain in the other, happy to be walking, happy because the sun was trying to come out again and I was there to see it. It was a few miles before I even realized that the boat would be going over the falls, that Jack would have had to swim one more time across the river to get to the trail, that I should go back and see if he'd made it, but I kept walking downstream and looking for the boat. After five miles my bare foot started to bleed, so I put my left loafer on my right foot and walked on. After eight miles I saw Jack running up the trail behind me, and he caught up and kissed me and ran on by.

I walked and I walked, and I thought about being twenty-one and hiking in mountains not too far from these with a boy who almost drowned and then proposed to me. His boots had filled with the water of a river even farther to the north, and I was wearing sneakers and have a good kick, so I made it across just fine. I thought about how he sat on the far bank after he'd pulled himself out and shivered and stared at the water. And how I ran up and down the shore looking for the shallowest crossing, and then, thinking I'd found it, met him halfway. I remembered when our hands touched across the water and how I'd pulled him to safety and built him a fire and dried his clothes. Later that night he asked me to marry him and it made me happy and I said yes even though I knew it would never happen because I was too young and free and full of my freedom. I switched my loafer to the other foot and wondered if this danger would make Jack propose to me. Maybe he was the kind of man who needed to see death first, maybe we would build a fire to dry ourselves and then he would ask me and I would say yes because by the time you get to be thirty, freedom has circled back on itself to mean something totally different from what it did at twenty-one.

I knew I had to be close to the falls and I felt bad about what the wrecked boat would look like, but all of a sudden it was there in front of me, stuck on a gravel bar in the middle of the river with a rapid on either side, and I saw Jack coming back up the trail toward me.

"I've got it all figured out," he said. "I need to walk upstream about a mile and jump in there. That'll give me enough time to swim most of the way across to the other side of the river, and if I've read the current right, it'll take me right into that gravel bar."

"And if you read the current wrong?" I said.

He grinned. "Then it's over Selway Falls. I almost lost it already the second time I crossed the river. It was just like Harvey said. I almost gave up. I've been running twelve miles and I know my legs'll cramp. It's a long shot but I've got to take it."

"Are you sure you want to do this?" I said. "Maybe you shouldn't do this."

"I thought the boat was gone," he said, "and I didn't care because you were safe and I was safe and we were on the same side of the river. But there it is asking me to come for it, and the water's gonna rise tonight and take it over the falls. You stay right here where you can see what happens to me. If I make it I'll pick you up on that beach just below. We've got a half a mile to the takeout and the falls." He kissed me again and ran back upriver.

The raft was in full sunshine, everything tied down, oars in place. Even the map I couldn't read was there, where I stuck it, under a strap.

I could see Jack making his way through the trees toward the edge of the river, and I realized then that more than any other reason for being on that trip, I was there because I thought I could take care of him, and maybe there's something women want to protect after all. And maybe Jack's old girlfriends were trying to protect him by making him stay home, and maybe I thought I could if I was there, but as he dropped out of sight and into the water I knew there'd always be places he'd go that I couldn't, and that I'd have to let him go, just like the widow said. Then I saw his tiny head in the water and I held my breath and watched his position, which was perfect, as he approached the raft. But he got off center right at the end, and a wave knocked him past the raft and farther down the gravel bar. He got to his feet and went down again. He grabbed for a boulder on the bottom and got washed even farther away. He was using all his energy to stay in one place and he was fifty yards downriver from the raft. I started to pray then, to whomever I pray to when I get in real trouble, and it may have been a coincidence but he started moving forward. It took him fifteen minutes and strength I'll never know to get to the boat, but he was in it, and rowing, and heading for the beach.

Later, when we were safe and on the two-lane heading home, Jack told me we were never in any real danger, and I let him get away with it because I knew that's what he had to tell himself to get past almost losing me.

"The river gave us both a lesson in respect," he said, and it occurred to me then that he thought he had a chance to tame that wild river, but I knew I was at its mercy from the very beginning, and I thought all along that that was the point.

Jack started telling stories to keep himself awake: the day his kayak held him under for almost four minutes, the time he crashed his hang glider twice in one day. He said he thought fifteen years of highwater was probably enough, and that he'd take desert rivers from now on.

The road stretched out in front of us, dry and even and smooth. We found a long dirt road, turned, and pulled down to where it ended at a chimney that stood tall amid the rubble of an old stone house. We didn't build a fire and Jack didn't propose; we rolled out our sleeping bags and lay down next to the truck. I could see the light behind the mountains in the place where the moon would soon rise, and I thought about all the years I'd spent saying love and freedom were mutually exclusive and living my life as though they were exactly the same thing.

The wind carried the smell of the mountains, high and sweet. It was so still I could imagine a peace without boredom.

GISH JEN

What Means Switch

THERE WE ARE, nice Chinese family—father, mother, two born-here girls. Where should we live next? My parents slide the question back and forth like a cup of ginseng neither one wants to drink. Until finally it comes to them, what they really want is a milkshake (chocolate) and to go with it a house in Scarsdale. What else? The broker tries to hint: the neighborhood, she says. Moneyed. Many delis. Meaning rich and Jewish. But someone has sent my parents a list of the top ten schools nation-wide (based on the opinion of selected educators and others) and so *many-deli* or not we nestle into a Dutch colonial on the Bronx River Parkway. The road's windy where we are, very charming; drivers miss their turns, plough up our flower beds, then want to use our telephone. "Of course," my mom tells them, like it's no big deal, we can replant. We're the type to adjust. You know—the lady drivers weep, my mom gets out the Kleenex for them. We're a bit down the hill from the private plane set, in other words. Only in our dreams do our jacket zippers jam, what with all the lift tickets we have stapled to them, Killington on top of Sugarbush on top of Stowe, and we don't even know where the Virgin Islands are—although certain of us do know that virgins are like priests and nuns, which there were a lot more of in Yonkers, where we just moved from, than there are here.

This is my first understanding of class. In our old neighborhood everybody knew everything about virgins and non-virgins, not to say the technicalities of staying in-between. Or almost everybody, I should say; in Yonkers I was the laugh-along type. Here I'm an expert.

"You mean the man . . .?" Pig-tailed Barbara Gugelstein spits a mouthful of coke back into her can. "That is *so* gross!"

Pretty soon I'm getting popular for a new girl, the only problem is Danielle Meyers, who wears blue mascara and has gone steady with two boys. "How do *you* know," she starts to ask, proceeding to edify us all with how she French-kissed one boyfriend and just regular kissed another. ("Because, you know, he had braces.") We hear about his rubber bands, how once one popped right into her mouth. I begin to realize I need to find somebody to kiss too. But how?

Luckily, I just about then happen to tell Barbara Gugelstein I know karate. I don't know why I tell her this. My sister Callie's the liar in the family; ask anybody. I'm the one who doesn't see why we should have to hold our heads up. But for some reason I tell Barbara Gugelstein I can make my hands like steel by thinking hard. "I'm not supposed to tell anyone," I say.

The way she backs away, blinking, I could be the burning bush.

"I can't do bricks," I say—a bit of expectation management. "But I can do your arm if you want." I set my hand in chop position.

"Uhh, it's okay," she says. "I know you can, I saw it on TV last night."

That's when I recall that I too saw it on TV last night—in fact, at her house. I rush on to tell her I know how to get pregnant with tea.

"With tea?"

"That's how they do it in China."

She agrees that China is an ancient and great civilization that ought to be known for more than spaghetti and gunpowder. I tell her I know Chinese. "*Be-yeh fa-foon,*" I say. "*Shee-veh. Ji nu.*" Meaning, "Stop acting crazy. Rice gruel. Soy sauce." She's impressed. At lunch the next day, Danielle Meyers and Amy Weinstein and Barbara's crush, Andy Kaplan, are all impressed too. Scarsdale is a liberal town, not like Yonkers, where the Whitman Road Gang used to throw crabapple mash at my sister Callie and me and tell us it would make our eyes stick shut. Here we're like permanent exchange students. In another ten years, there'll be so many Orientals we'll turn into Asians; a Japanese grocery will buy out that one deli too many. But for now, the mid-sixties, what with civil rights on TV, we're not so much accepted as embraced. Especially by the Jewish part of town—which, it turns out, is not all of town at all. That's just an idea people have, Callie says, and lots of them could take us or leave us same as the Christians, who are nice too; I shouldn't generalize. So let me not generalize except to say that pretty soon I've been to so many bar and bas mitzvahs, I can almost say myself whether the kid chants like an angel or like a train conductor, maybe they could use him on the commuter line. At seder I know to forget the bricks, get a good pile of that mortar. Also I know what is schmaltz. I know that I am a goy. This is not why people like me, though. People like me because I do not need to use deodorant, as I demonstrate in the locker room before and after gym. Also, I can explain to them, for example, what is tofu (*der-voo,* we say at home). Their mothers invite me to taste-test their Chinese cooking.

"Very authentic." I try to be reassuring. After all, they're nice people, I like them. "De-lish." I have seconds. On the question of what we eat, though, I have to admit, "Well, no, it's different than that." I have thirds. "What my mom makes is home style, it's not in the cookbooks."

Not in the cookbooks! Everyone's jealous. Meanwhile, the big deal at home is when we have turkey pot pie. My sister Callie's the one introduced them—Mrs. Wilder's, they come in this green-and-brown box—and when we have them, we both get suddenly interested in helping out in the kitchen. You know, we stand in front of the oven and help them bake. Twenty-five minutes. She and I have a deal, though, to keep it secret from school, as everybody else thinks they're gross. We think they're a big improvement over authentic Chinese home cooking. Ox-tail soup—now that's gross. Stir-fried beef with tomatoes. One day I say, "You know Ma, I have never seen a stir-fried tomato in any Chinese restaurant we have ever been in, ever."

"In China," she says, real lofty, "we consider tomatoes are a delicacy."

"Ma," I say. "Tomatoes are *Italian*."

"No respect for elders." She wags her finger at me, but I can tell it's just to try and shame me into believing her. "I'm tell you, tomatoes *invented* in China."

"*Ma*."

"Is true. Like noodles. Invented in China."

"That's not what they said in *school*."

"In *China*," my mother counters, "we also eat tomatoes uncooked, like apple. And in summertime we slice them, and put some sugar on top."

"Are you sure?"

My mom says of course she's sure, and in the end I give in, even though she once told me that China was such a long time ago, a lot of things she can hardly remember. She said sometimes she has trouble remembering her characters, that sometimes she'll be writing a letter, just writing along, and all of sudden she won't be sure if she should put four dots or three.

"So what do you do then?"

"Oh, I just make a little sloppy."

"You mean you *fudge?*"

She laughed then, but another time, when she was showing me how to write my name, and I said, just kidding, "Are you sure that's the right number of dots now?" she was hurt.

"I mean, of course you know," I said. "I mean, *oy*."

Meanwhile, what I know is that in the eighth grade, what people want to hear does not include how Chinese people eat sliced tomatoes with sugar on top. For a gross fact, it just isn't gross enough. On the other hand, the fact that somewhere in China somebody eats or has eaten or once ate living monkey brains—now that's conversation.

"They have these special tables," I say, "kind of like a giant collar. With a hole in the middle, for the monkey's neck. They put the monkey in the collar, and then they cut off the top of its head."

"Whadda they use for cutting?"

I think. "Scalpels."

"*Scalpels?*" says Andy Kaplan.

"Kaplan, don't be dense," Barbara Gugelstein says. "The Chinese *invented* scalpels."

Once a friend said to me, You know, everybody is valued for something. She explained how some people resented being valued for their looks; others resented being valued for their money. Wasn't it still better to be beautiful and rich than ugly and poor, though? You should be just glad, she said, that you have something people value. It's like having a special talent, like being good at ice-skating, or opera-singing. She said, You could probably make a career out of it.

Here's the irony: I am.

Anyway. I am ad-libbing my way through eighth grade, as I've described. Until one bloomy spring day, I come in late to homeroom, and to my chagrin discover there's a new kid in class.

Chinese.

So what should I do, pretend to have to go to the girls' room, like Barbara Gugelstein the day Andy Kaplan took his ID back? I sit down; I am so cool I remind myself of Paul Newman. First thing I realize, though, is that no one looking at me is thinking of Paul Newman. The notes fly:

"I think he's cute."

"Who?" I write back. (I am still at an age, understand, when I believe a person can be saved by aplomb.)

"I don't think he talks English too good. Writes it either."

"Who?"

"They might have to put him behind a grade, so don't worry."

"He has a crush on you already, you could tell as soon as you walked in, he turned kind of orangish."

I hope I'm not turning orangish as I deal with my mail, I could use a secretary. The second round starts:

"What do you mean who? Don't be weird. Didn't you *see* him??? Straight back over your right shoulder!!!!"

I have to look; what else can I do? I think of certain tips I learned in Girl Scouts about poise. I cross my ankles. I hold a pen in my hand. I sit up as though I have a crown on my head. I swivel my head slowly, repeating to myself, *I could be Miss America.*

"Miss Mona Chang."

Horror raises its hoary head.

"Notes, please."

Mrs. Mandeville's policy is to read all notes aloud.

I try to consider what Miss America would do, and see myself, back straight, knees together, crying. Some inspiration. Cool Hand Luke, on the other hand, would, quick, eat the evidence. And why not? I should yawn as I stand up, and boom, the notes are gone. All that's left is to explain that it's an old Chinese reflex.

I shuffle up to the front of the room.

"One minute please," Mrs. Mandeville says.

I wait, noticing how large and plastic her mouth is.

She unfolds a piece of paper.

And I, Miss Mona Chang, who got almost straight A's her whole life except in math and conduct, am about to start crying in front of everyone.

I am delivered out of hot Egypt by the bell. General pandemonium. Mrs. Mandeville still has her hand clamped on my shoulder, though. And the next thing I know, I'm holding the new boy's schedule. He's standing next to me like a big blank piece of paper. "This is Sherman," Mrs. Mandeville says.

"Hello," I say.

"*Non how a,*" I say.

I'm glad Barbara Gugelstein isn't there to see my Chinese in action.

"*Ji nu,*" I say. "*Shee veh.*"

Later I find out that his mother asked if there were any other Orientals in our grade. She had him put in my class on purpose. For now, though, he looks at me as though I'm much stranger than anything else he's seen so far. Is this because he understands I'm saying "soy sauce rice gruel" to him or because he doesn't?

"Sher-man," he says finally.

I look at his schedule card. Sherman Matsumoto. What kind of name is that for a nice Chinese boy?

(Later on, people ask me how I can tell Chinese from Japanese. I shrug. You just kind of know, I say. *Oy!*)

Sherman's got the sort of looks I think of as pretty-boy. Monsignor-black hair (not monk-brown like mine), bouncy. Crayola eyebrows, one with a round bald spot in the middle of it, like a golf hole. I don't know how anybody can think of him as orangish; his skin looks white to me, with pink triangles hanging down the front of his cheeks like flags. Kind of delicate-looking, but the only truly uncool thing about him is that his spiral notebook has a picture of a kitty cat on it. A big white fluffy one, with a blue ribbon above each perky little ear. I get much opportunity to view this, as all the poor kid understands about life in junior high school is that he should follow me everywhere. It's embarrassing. On the other hand, he's obviously even more miserable than I am, so I try not to say anything. Give him a chance to adjust. We communicate by sign language, and by drawing pictures, which he's better at than I am; he puts in every last detail, even if it takes forever. I try to be patient.

A week of this. Finally I enlighten him. "You should get a new notebook."

His cheeks turn a shade of pink you mostly only see in hyacinths.

"Notebook." I point to his. I show him mine, which is psychedelic, with big purple and yellow stick-on flowers. I try to explain he should have one like this, only without the flowers. He nods enigmatically, and the next day brings me a notebook just like his, except that this cat sports pink bows instead of blue.

"Pret-ty," he says. "You."

He speaks English! I'm dumbfounded. Has he spoken it all this time? I consider: Pretty. You. What does that mean? Plus actually, he's said *plit-ty*, much as my parents would; I'm assuming he means pretty, but maybe he means pity. Pity. You. Pity. You.

"Jeez," I say finally.

"You are wel-come," he says.

I decorate the back of the notebook with stick-on flowers, and hold it so that these show when I walk through the halls. In class I mostly keep my book open. After all, the kid's so new; I think I really ought to have a heart. And for a livelong day nobody notices.

Then Barbara Gugelstein sidles up. "Matching notebooks, huh?"

I'm speechless.

"First comes love, then comes marriage, and then come chappies in a baby carriage."

"Barbara!"

"Get it?" she says. "Chinese Japs."

"Bar-*bra*," I say to get even.

"Just make sure he doesn't give you any *tea*," she says.

Are Sherman and I in love? Three days later, I hazard that we are. My thinking proceeds this way: I think he's cute, and I think he thinks I'm cute. On the other hand, we don't kiss and we don't exactly have fantastic conversations. Our talks *are* getting better, though. We started out, "This is a book." "Book." "This is a chair." "Chair." Advancing to, "What is this?" "This is a book." Now, for fun, he tests me.

"What is this?" he says.

"This is a book," I say, as if I'm the one who has to learn how to talk.

He claps. "Good!"

Meanwhile, people ask me all about him, I could be his press agent.

"No, he doesn't eat raw fish."

"No, his father wasn't a kamikaze pilot."

"No, he can't do karate."

"Are you sure?" somebody asks.

Indeed he doesn't know karate, but judo he does. I am hurt I'm not the one to find this out; the guys know from gym class. They line up to be flipped, he flips them all onto the floor, and after that he doesn't eat lunch at the girls' table with me anymore. I'm more or less glad. Meaning, when he was there, I never knew what to say. Now that he's gone, though, I seem to be stuck at the "This is a chair" level of conversation. Ancient Chinese eating habits have lost their cachet; all I get are more and more questions about me and Sherman. "I dunno," I'm saying all the time. *Are* we going out? We do stuff, it's true. For example, I take him to the department stores, explain to him who shops in Alexander's, who shops in Saks. I tell him my family's the type that shops in Alexander's. He says he's sorry. In Saks he gets lost; either that, or else I'm the lost one. (It's true I find him calmly waiting at the front door, hands behind his back, like a guard.) I take him to the candy store. I take him to the bagel store. Sherman is crazy about bagels. I explain to him that Lender's is gross, he should get his bagels from the bagel store. He says thank you.

"Are you going steady?" people want to know.

How can we go steady when he doesn't have an ID bracelet? On the other hand, he brings me more presents than I think any girl's every gotten before. Oranges. Flowers. A little bag of bagels. But what do they mean? Do they mean thank you, I enjoyed our trip; do they mean I like you; do they mean I decided I liked the Lender's better even if they are gross, you can have these? Sometimes I think he's acting on his mother's instructions. Also I know at least a couple of the presents were supposed to go to our teachers.

He told me that once and turned red. I figured it still might mean something that he didn't throw them out.

More and more now, we joke. Like, instead of "I'm thinking," he always says, "I'm sinking," which we both think is so funny, that all either one of us has to do is pretend to be drowning and the other one cracks up. And he tells me things—for example, that there are electric lights everywhere in Tokyo now.

"You mean you didn't have them before?"

"Everywhere now!" He's amazed too. "Since Olympics!"

"Olympics?"

"1960," he says proudly, and as proof, hums for me the Olympic theme song. "You know?"

"Sure," I say, and hum with him happily. We could be a picture on a UNICEF poster. The only problem is that I don't really understand what the Olympics have to do with the modernization of Japan, any more than I get this other story he tells me, about that hole in his left eyebrow, which is from some time his father accidentally hit him with a lit cigarette. When Sherman was a baby. His father was drunk, having been out carousing; his mother was very mad but didn't say anything, just cleaned the whole house. Then his father was so ashamed he bowed to ask her forgiveness.

"Your mother cleaned the house?"

Sherman nods solemnly.

"And your father *bowed?*" I find this more astounding than anything I ever thought to make up. "That is so weird," I tell him.

"Weird," he agrees. "This I no forget, forever. *Father* bow to *mother!*"

We shake our heads.

As for the things he asks me, they're not topics I ever discussed before. Do I like it here? Of course I like it here, I was born here, I say. Am I Jewish? Jewish! I laugh. *Oy!* Am I American? "Sure I'm American," I say. "Everybody who's born here is American, and also some people who convert from what they were before. You could become American." But he says no, he could never. "Sure you could," I say. "You only have to learn some rules and speeches."

"But I Japanese," he says.

"You could become American anyway," I say. "Like I *could* become Jewish, if I wanted to. I'd just have to switch, that's all."

"But you Catholic," he says.

I think maybe he doesn't get what means switch.

I introduce him to Mrs. Wilder's turkey pot pies. "Gross?" he asks. I say they are, but we like them anyway. "Don't tell anybody." He promises. We bake them, eat them. While we're eating, he's drawing me pictures.

"This American," he says, and he draws something that looks like John Wayne. "This Jewish," he says, and draws something that looks like the Wicked Witch of the West, only male.

"I don't think so," I say.

He's undeterred. "This Japanese," he says, and draws a fair rendition of himself. "This Chinese," he says, and draws what looks to be another fair rendition of himself.

"How can you tell them apart?"

"This way," he says, and he puts the picture of the Chinese so that it is looking at the pictures of the American and the Jew. The Japanese faces the wall. Then he draws another picture, of a Japanese flag, so that the Japanese has that to contemplate. "Chinese lost in department store," he says. "Japanese know how go." For fun, he then takes the Japanese flag and fastens it to the refrigerator door with magnets. "In school, in ceremony, we this way," he explains, and bows to the picture.

When my mother comes in, her face is so red that with the white wall behind her she looks a bit like the Japanese flag herself. Yet I get the feeling I better not say so. First she doesn't move. Then she snatches the flag off the refrigerator, so fast the magnets go flying. Two of them land on the stove. She crumples up the paper. She hisses at Sherman, *"This is the U.S. of A., do you hear me?"*

Sherman hears her.

"You call your mother right now, tell her come pick you up."

He understands perfectly. I, on the other hand, am stymied. How can two people who don't really speak English understand each other better than I can understand them? "But Ma," I say.

"Don't *Ma* me," she says.

Later on she explains that World War II was in China, too. "Hitler," I say. "Nazis. Volkswagens." I know the Japanese were on the wrong side, because they bombed Pearl Harbor. My mother explains about before that. The Napkin Massacre. *"Nan-king,"* she corrects me.

"Are you sure?" I say. "In school, they said the war was about putting the Jews in ovens."

"Also about ovens."

"About both?"

"Both."

"That's not what they said in school."

"Just forget about school."

Forget about school? "I thought we moved here for the schools."

"We moved here," she says, "for your education."

Sometimes I have no idea what she's talking about.

"I like Sherman," I say after a while.

"He's nice boy," she agrees.

Meaning what? I would ask, except that my dad's just come home, which means it's time to start talking about whether we should build a brick wall across the front of the lawn. Recently a car made it almost into our living room, which was so scary, the driver fainted and an ambulance had to come. "We should have discussion," my dad said after that. And so for about a week, every night we do.

"Are you just friends, or more than just friends?" Barbara Gugelstein is giving me the cross-ex.

"Maybe," I say.

"Come on," she says, "I told you *everything* about me and Andy."

I actually *am* trying to tell Barbara everything about Sherman, but everything turns out to be nothing. Meaning, I can't locate the conversation in what I have to say. Sherman and I go places, we talk, one time my mother threw him out of the house because of World War II.

"I think we're just friends," I say.

"You think or you're sure?"

Now that I do less of the talking at lunch, I notice more what other people talk about—cheerleading, who likes who, this place in White Plains to get earrings. On none of these topics am I an expert. Of course, I'm still friends with Barbara Gugelstein, but I notice Danielle Meyers has spun away to other groups.

Barbara's analysis goes this way: To be popular, you have to have big boobs, a note from your mother that lets you use her Lord and Taylor credit card, and a boyfriend. On the other hand, what's so wrong with being unpopular? "We'll get them in the end," she says. It's what her dad tells her. "Like they'll turn out too dumb to do their own investing, and then they'll get killed in fees and then they'll have to move to towns where the schools stink. And my dad should know," she winds up. "He's a broker."

"I guess," I say.

But the next thing I know, I have a true crush on Sherman Matsumoto. *Mis*ter Judo, the guys call him now, with real respect; and the more they call him that, the more I don't care that he carries a notebook with a cat on it.

I sigh. "Sherman."

"I thought you were just friends," says Barbara Gugelstein.

"We were," I say mysteriously. This, I've noticed, is how Danielle Meyers talks; everything's secret, she only lets out so much, it's like she didn't grow up with everybody telling her she had to share.

And here's the funny thing: The more I intimate that Sherman and I are more than just friends, the more it seems we actually are. It's the old imagination giving reality a nudge. When I start to blush, he starts to blush; we reach a point where we can hardly talk at all.

"Well, there's first base with tongue, and first base without," I tell Barbara Gugelstein.

In fact, Sherman and I have brushed shoulders, which was equivalent to first base I was sure, maybe even second. I felt as though I'd turned into one huge shoulder, that's all I was, one huge shoulder. We not only didn't talk, we didn't breathe. But how can I tell Barbara Gugelstein that? So instead I say, "Well there's second base and second base."

Danielle Meyers is my friend again. She says, "I know exactly what you mean," just to make Barbara Gugelstein feel bad.

"Like *what* do I mean?" I say.

Danielle Meyers can't answer.

"You know what I think?" I tell Barbara the next day. "I think Danielle's giving us a line."

Barbara pulls thoughtfully on one of her pigtails.

If Sherman Matsumoto is never going to give me an ID to wear, he should at least get up the nerve to hold my hand. I don't think he sees this. I think of the story he told me about his parents, and in a synaptic firestorm realize we don't see the same things at all.

So one day, when we happen to brush shoulders again, I don't move away. He doesn't move away either. There we are. Like a pair of bleachers, pushed together but not quite matched up. After a while, I have to breathe, I can't help it. I breathe in such a way that our elbows start to touch too. We are in a crowd, waiting for a bus. I crane my neck to look at the sign that says where the bus is going; now our wrists are touching. Then it happens: He links his pinky around mine.

Is that holding hands? Later, in bed, I wonder all night. One finger, and not even the biggest one.

Sherman is leaving in a month. Already! I think, well, I suppose he will leave and we'll never even kiss. I guess that's all right. Just when I've resigned myself to it, though, we hold hands all five fingers. Once when we are at the bagel shop, then again in my parents' kitchen. Then, when we are at the playground, he kisses the back of my hand.

He does it again not too long after that, in White Plains.

I invest in a bottle of mouthwash.

Instead of moving on, though, he kisses the back of my hand again. And again. I try raising my hand, hoping he'll make the jump from my hand to my cheek. It's like trying to wheedle an inchworm out the window. You know, *This way, this way.*

All over the world, people have their own cultures. That's what we learned in social studies.

If we never kiss, I'm not going to take it personally.

It is the end of the school year. We've had parties. We've turned in our textbooks. Hooray! Outside the asphalt already steams if you spit on it. Sherman isn't leaving for another couple of days, though, and he comes to visit every morning, staying until the afternoon, when Callie comes home from her big-deal job as a bank teller. We drink Kool-Aid in the backyard and hold hands until they are sweaty and make smacking noises coming apart. He tells me how busy his parents are, getting ready for the move. His mother, particularly, is very tired. Mostly we are mournful.

The very last day we hold hands and do not let go. Our palms fill up with water like a blister. We do not care. We talk more than usual. How much airmail is to Japan, that kind of thing. Then suddenly he asks, will I marry him?

I'm only thirteen.

But when old? Sixteen?

If you come back to get me.

I come. Or you can come to Japan, be Japanese.

How can I be Japanese?

Like you become American. Switch.

He kisses me on the cheek, again and again and again.

His mother calls to say she's coming to get him. I cry. I tell him how I've saved every present he's ever given me—the ruler, the pencils, the bags from the bagels, all the flower petals. I even have the orange peels from the oranges.

All?

I put them in a jar.

I'd show him, except that we're not allowed to go upstairs to my room. Anyway, something about the orange peels seems to choke him up too. *Mister* Judo, but I've gotten him in a soft spot. We are going together to the bathroom to get some toilet paper to wipe our eyes when poor tired Mrs. Matsumoto, driving a shiny new station wagon, skids up onto our lawn.

"Very sorry!"

We race outside.

"Very sorry!"

Mrs. Matsumoto is so short that about all we can see of her is a green cotton sun hat, with a big brim. It's tied on. The brim is trembling.

I hope my mom's not going to start yelling about World War II.

"Is all right, no trouble," she says, materializing on the steps behind me and Sherman. She's propped the screen door wide open; when I turn I see she's waving. "No trouble, no trouble!"

"No trouble, no trouble!" I echo, twirling a few times with relief.

Mrs. Matsumoto keeps apologizing; my mom keeps insisting she shouldn't feel bad, it was only some grass and a small tree. Crossing the lawn, she insists Mrs. Matsumoto get out of the car, even though it means trampling some lilies-of-the-valley. She insists that Mrs. Matsumoto come in for a cup of tea. Then she will not talk about anything unless Mrs. Matsumoto sits down, and unless she lets my mom prepare her a small snack. The coming in and the tea and the sitting down are settled pretty quickly, but they negotiate ferociously over the small snack, which Mrs. Matsumoto will not eat unless she can call Mr. Matsumoto. She makes the mistake of linking Mr. Matsumoto with a reparation of some sort, which my mom will not hear of.

"Please!"

"No no no no."

Back and forth it goes: "No no no no." "No no no no." "No no no no." What kind of conversation is that? I look at Sherman, who shrugs. Finally Mr. Matsumoto calls on his own, wondering where his wife is. He comes over in a taxi. He's a heavy-browed businessman, friendly but brisk—not at all a type you could imagine bowing to a lady with a taste for tie-on sunhats. My mom invites him in as if it's an idea she just this moment thought of. And would he maybe have some tea and a small snack?

Sherman and I sneak back outside for another farewell, by the side of the house, behind the forsythia bushes. We hold hands. He kisses me on the cheek again, and then—just when I think he's finally going to kiss me on the lips—he kisses me on the neck.

Is this first base?

He does it more. Up and down, up and down. First it tickles, and then it doesn't. He has his eyes closed. I close my eyes too. He's hugging me. Up and down. Then down.

He's at my collarbone.

Still at my collarbone. Now his hand's on my ribs. So much for first base. More ribs. The idea of second base would probably make me nervous if he weren't on his way back to Japan and if I really thought we were going to get there. As it is, though, I'm not in much danger of wrecking my life on the shoals of passion; his unmoving hand feels more like a growth than a boyfriend. He has his whole face pressed to my neck skin so I can't tell his mouth from his nose. I think he may be licking me.

From indoors, a burst of adult laughter. My eyelids flutter. I start to try and wiggle such that his hand will maybe budge upward.

Do I mean for my top blouse button to come accidentally undone?

He clenches his jaw, and when he opens his eyes, they're fixed on that button like it's a gnat that's been bothering him for far too long. He mutters in Japanese. If later in life he were to describe this as a pivotal moment in his youth, I would not be surprised. Holding the material as far from my body as possible, he buttons the button. Somehow we've landed up too close to the bushes.

What to tell Barbara Gugelstein? She says, "Tell me what were his last words. He must have said something last."

"I don't want to talk about it."

"Maybe he said, Good-bye?" she suggests. "Sayonara?" She means well.

"I don't want to talk about it."

"Aw, come on, I told you everything about . . ."

I say, "Because it's private, excuse me."

She stops, squints at me as though at a far-off face she's trying to make out. Then she nods and very lightly places her hand on my forearm.

The forsythia seemed to be stabbing us in the eyes. Sherman said, more or less, *You will need to study how to switch.*

And I said, *I think you should switch. The way you do everything is weird.*

And he said, *You just want to tell everything to your friends. You just want to have boyfriend to become popular.*

Then he flipped me. Two swift moves, and I went sprawling through the air, a flailing confusion of soft human parts such as had no idea where the ground was.

It is the fall, and I am in high school, and still he hasn't written, so finally I write him.

I still have all your gifts, I write. *I don't talk so much as I used to. Although I am not exactly a mouse either. I don't care about being popular anymore. I swear. Are you happy to be back in Japan? I know I ruined everything. I was just trying to be entertaining. I miss you with all my heart, and hope I didn't ruin everything.*

He writes back, *You will never be Japanese.*

I throw all the orange peels out that day. Some of them, it turns out, were moldy anyway. I tell my mother I want to move to Chinatown.

"Chinatown!" she says.

I don't know why I suggested it.

"What's the matter?" she says. "Still boy-crazy? That Sherman?"

"No."

"Too much homework?"

I don't answer.

"Forget about school."

Later she tells me if I don't like school, I don't have to go every day. Some days I can stay home.

"Stay home?" In Yonkers, Callie and I used to stay home all the time, but that was because the schools there were *waste of time.*

"No good for a girl be too smart anyway."

For a long time I think about Sherman. But after a while I don't think about him so much as I just keep seeing myself flipped onto the ground, lying there shocked as the Matsumotos get ready to leave. My head has hit a rock; my brain aches as though it's been shoved to some new place in my skull. Otherwise I am okay. I see the forsythia, all those whippy branches, and can't believe how many leaves there are on a bush—every one green and perky and durably itself. And past them, real sky. I try to remember about why the sky's blue, even though this one's gone the kind of indescribable grey you associate with the insides of old shoes. I smell grass. Probably I have grass stains all over my back. I hear my mother calling through the back door, "Mon-a! Everyone leaving now," and "Not coming to say good-bye?" I hear Mr. and Mrs. Matsumoto bowing as they leave—or at least I hear the embarrassment in my mother's voice as they bow. I hear their car start. I hear Mrs. Matsumoto directing Mr. Matsumoto how to back off the lawn so as not to rip any more of it up. I feel the back of my head for blood—just a little. I hear their chug-chug grow fainter and fainter, until it has faded into the whuzz-whuzz of all the other cars. I hear my mom singing, "*Mon-*a! *Mon-*a!" until my dad comes home. Doors open and shut. I see myself standing up, brushing myself off so I'll have less explaining to do if she comes out to look for me. Grass stains—just like I thought. I see myself walking around the house, going over to have a look at our churned-up yard. It looks pretty sad, two big brown tracks, right through the irises and the lilies of the valley, and that was a new dogwood we'd just planted. Lying there like that. I hear myself thinking about my father, having to go dig it up all over again. Adjusting. I think how we probably ought to put up that brick wall. And sure enough, when I go inside, no one's thinking about me, or that little bit of blood at the back of my head, or the grass stains. That's what they're talking about—that wall. Again. My mom doesn't think it'll do any good, but my dad thinks we should give it a try. Should we or shouldn't we? How high? How thick? What will the neighbors say? I plop myself down on a hard chair. And all I can think is, we are the complete only family that has to worry about this. If I could, I'd switch everything to be different. But since I can't, I might as well sit here at the table for a while, discussing what I know how to discuss. I nod and listen to the rest.

PAGAN KENNEDY

Shrinks

A FEW MONTHS AGO, Sara's mother started taking Prozac. Every Sunday now, she called with more proof of her indebtedness to the drug. "I've quit my job, honey. I'm starting a catering company," she said breathlessly one day, as if she had that minute run in from giving notice. Then, a few weeks later, "I've thrown out my entire wardrobe. I'm only going to wear happy clothes."

Once in a while Sara couldn't help saying something snide like, "What's next, Mom, a tummy tuck?" After all, this happiness of her mother's was a betrayal of sorts.

"Oh, Sara," her mother would say, "give it a rest." Or more likely, she'd advise Sara to stop seeing her feminist therapist and go to someone with an MD: Her mother had no use for shrinks who couldn't dispense pills.

Riding the train downtown to meet her mother, Sara tried not to catch glimpses of herself in the window, which had been turned by the darkness outside into a black mirror. She thought, "At least I've had more than her," meaning shrinks. Back before the Prozac, she and her mother had spent an afternoon on the phone counting them. Her mother had an amazing memory for shrinks. "You started at seven with that Dr. Prescott. I didn't start until I was sixteen," she'd said, as if excusing herself for her low score. At the end of tallying Sara's shrinks, they'd realized she'd had almost thirty, if you included the counselors at school, the doctors she'd decided against after seeing them once and the ones she'd gone to just to get this or that medicine.

"Very impressive, Sara," her mother had said, in the same stiff way she used to congratulate her after a piano recital.

"Anyone could do it, Mom."

"No, hon, it shows how serious you are about solving your problems. I'm proud of you."

Sara understood what she was really referring to. Her mother had always believed that when she found the right man, the right job, the right pill, her life would begin again. Her mother hadn't considered herself properly alive since Sara's father left her seventeen years ago.

Back before that happened, Sara had only dabbled in psychiatry: the summer she was seven, her mother made matching daisy-print dresses for Sara and herself, and a few days later announced, "You're going to see a psychiatrist just like Mommy." Sara always associated her first session with the terry-cloth pinafore that matched her mom's, with feeling like a little lady as she waited by herself in the reception room, reading *Highlights* the way her mother read the *New Yorker*. All she could remember about her first psychiatrist was the way he asked her about dreams she couldn't remember, and his toys, her favorite of which was the pretend doctor's kit. Inside was a vial of candy pills. "Go ahead," he'd say, "eat one." No matter how many candy pills she ate, the vial was always full again by the next session.

Her mother gave her real pills, too: purple ones for going to sleep; a yellow one to ease her through the first day of third grade; a white one when she got too excited about riding the bumper cars at Playland.

After her father left, when Sara was ten, she switched shrinks and began going twice a week. The new psychiatrist didn't have any toys, only a desk, a reclining couch and a box of Kleenex.

"What's the bed for?" she asked him in the first session.

"In case you feel like lying down," he said.

"But why would I feel like lying down?"

"You might; try it," he said.

She tried to lie stiff on her back, but she couldn't keep still; she rolled to her stomach, to her side.

"You don't have to," he said. "It's not necessary."

"Yes it is," she said. Finally, she settled on her back with her hands on her stomach. She knew that her mother must lie in the same position when she had therapy, carefully resting her perfect bonnet of hair on the pillow.

"Tell me about your father," the shrink's voice had said. She couldn't see him from where she lay; instead she spoke to his framed diplomas, which hung on the opposite wall.

"Daddy's moved to California," she said.

"How do you feel about that?"

"I don't know."

But after several more years of therapy, she knew exactly what she felt, or what she was supposed to feel. Even when she'd graduated to other worries, the shrinks kept dredging up the divorce, and she dutifully went over it with them, giving them what she later realized was her mother's version of the story: without warning or provocation, her father said he couldn't live with them anymore and announced he'd taken a job on the West Coast. Sara, the shrinks said, felt rejected.

Sara sometimes suspected that she was no more unhappy than any of her high school friends. But her mother said, "Sara, normal people jump out of bed in the morning with a smile. We have to fix whatever's making you so depressed." Her mother, in fact, had been through vials of pills searching for the ingredient she thought made other people so happy; she hadn't found it, but she had hopes for Sara, and would drop her off at the shrink's office saying, "Now, honey, if he prescribes you Premerin, make sure you get some Desaril with it so you can sleep," or "Sara, don't let him give you Ellivil. We don't want you to bloat up, do we?"

During college, Sara began going to a feminist social worker instead of a psychiatrist. With her new shrink, she revised the family story: perhaps her mother, brainwashed by the patriarchy, sought to mold Sara into a perfect, plastic girl with no problems. Since that breakthrough, she'd gone to a string of feminists.

Nowadays, Sara was seeing Tillie, a short, squat grandmother who wore serapes she'd woven herself. On her wall, bigger than any of her university degrees, was a blown-up newspaper photo of herself twenty years ago, sprawled in the street, with police officers leaning over her. That she had once laid her body down in front of trucks carrying boys off to Vietnam—or rather, off to an army base in New Jersey—was somehow one of Tillie's credentials for therapy. She valued Life.

"Honey," she'd say, "you've been telling me over and over again that you want to quit your job. Now let's discuss how you're going to do that."

But even discussing it made Sara queasy. For four years, she'd worked in a library filing the bound periodicals. She couldn't imagine anything else but days filled with the particular squeak of the floor in the stacks, of watching the dust swirl like fruit flies when she opened an old almanac.

She'd never had a real job in an office, but she'd seen it on TV—people rushing around in suits, phones ringing, the glare of fluorescent lights. Going to work in such a place would be like having to wake up from her dreaming days of shuffling between the iron shelves, trailing one hand along their lines of book spines.

"I'm just too neurotic right now to even think about it," Sara would say.

"What about your boyfriend?" Tillie would remind her. "You say the relationship's going nowhere."

If Sara's job could have been turned into a man—as frogs are turned into princes—it would have been her boyfriend, Andy. He had the musty, outmoded air of the library about him, the way he kept his blinds drawn all day, reading under a sickly circle of light. Sara had dropped out of grad school after a year, but he was the type who would be in it forever. He even looked like a sloth, with his furry sweaters and one lock of hair that hung over his eyes.

"But what if I never get a boyfriend again?" Sara would say. "What if I die alone?"

Tillie would lean forward and wave a hand emphatically, as if trying to erase a chalk board. "You just need a Cause in your life. Something outside of yourself."

All the feminist shrinks said she needed something like that. It was the one point on which they seemed to agree with her mother: Sara was missing some crucial ingredient in her life. When she found it, she would begin a new, happy existence full of meaning, love and light.

After that day when she and her mother had counted them up on the phone, Sara couldn't stop thinking about her thirty shrinks; she was not yet thirty years old, so it averaged out to more than one a year, which seemed like some kind of accomplishment. The next time her mother called, Sara said, "How long's a football field? I bet if you put them all end to end, all the shrinks I've had, there'd almost be enough for a line across a football field— thirty times five-and-a-half feet, right?" And she went on and did the math.

"You've always loved numbers," her mother said. "If only you could put that to use."

But Sara hadn't been listening. She'd been imagining the shrinks lying end-to-end across the field. She kept on thinking about them for a long time after. When she was supposed to be working, for instance, a random word on a book spine would remind her of the shrinks, and with a little glow of pride she'd remember them. At first she pictured them in a typical football stadium with lime markings and raspy Astroturf, the vast arena lit up by spotlights as if for a nighttime game. But later she refined the image to make it more comforting: she got rid of the football field and imagined instead an abandoned meadow she used to play in as a kid. As she made the shrinks lie head to toe across the meadow, she took stock of them—the ones still living and the dead ones; the child psychiatrists; the Freudians, Rogerians and feminists; the ones who dressed like doctors and the ones who dressed like golfers; the ones who blamed everything on her dysfunctional family and the silent ones. They reclined on their backs in the ticklish, unmown grass in the late afternoon, as swallows swooped and called in the pink sky. In particular, she treasured the quiet of the scene—no sound except the tremulous, surprising flutter of birds as they dipped into the field to catch one last insect. She didn't have to explain anything, to talk and cry and answer questions for those shrinks in the meadow. Instead, she stood on the hill above them, watching how the smoke from their pipes and cigarettes wafted up in lacy puffs to turn gold in the evening light, like the fleecy clouds of eighteenth-century paintings.

Best of all was how, in the tall grass, the line of shrinks would look like a path that led somewhere, a secret road made of rumpled tweed and crossed arms and faces puckered in meditative consideration of her own problems. She liked to think the shrinks blurred into a taut line, an umbilical cord that would pull her along into her new, perfect life.

Sara hurried out into the six-o'clock darkness. People trotted past her, their scarves waving from their necks like frantic arms. She crossed the street and saw her mother inside Ciao, reading the menu. In the brightly lit restaurant, her mother looked like a mannequin in a store window—skin pale as moonlight but hard as plastic.

It was the first time Sara had seen her since the Prozac, and her stomach tightened. When she opened the door to the restaurant, her mother turned and, with a distracted, exuberant look, came over to kiss her. A bit of the bright-colored silk around her mother's neck floated into Sara's mouth. For a moment, with her mother clutching her, she had a feeling of panic. It seemed to her that, in stepping into the restaurant, she had stepped into a strange country. With its sprays of forsythia and fragile, trembling circles of candlelight, the restaurant seemed part of the beautiful world of her mother's new life.

Her mother pulled back. "I'm exhausted," she said. "I can't wait to sit down." This made Sara feel much better; even if it was only aching feet, her mother still knew pain.

"You look nice. I think you've lost weight," Sara said.

"Don't laugh, but I do Jane Fonda."

Sara didn't know how to answer, now that sarcastic comments were ruled out. Her mother B.P., before Prozac, would say that exercise was a crock; but now she gushed on about how she loved it, and Sara was reduced to polite clichés.

As they settled at their table, her mother talked of the client she had landed that day, and of star fruit and mint leaves, which she referred to as her company's signature garnishes. Sara half-listened, marveling at how her mother had redone herself. She used to wear droopy sweater dresses; she used to be one of those gray-complected women you see everywhere in buses and grocery stores.

Her mother had always had it in her though; Sara could see it now in the way she had ordered their lives, had risen so quickly from secretary to office manager. Even depressed, her mother had grit. Sara, on the other hand, would never have grit. She wanted to tell her mother this, to say, "Look, for me maybe there is no great happiness," but she knew this would not sway her mother, or more specifically that the Prozac coursing through her mother's bloodstream made her deaf to common sense.

Her mother led the conversation expertly—as she must do with her clients now—so that just as they began sipping their decaf, she got down to business. "You know, your cousin Beanie's husband practices up here. I want you to go see him, hon. He'll fix you up. If you're not covered, I'll pay for whatever it takes to get you prescribed. I really think he's the one to help you."

Sara agreed to go. After all, her mother had always said she'd slough off her depression once she found the right pill, and she had. Perhaps Prozac would give Sara the courage to go back to grad school, to ditch Andy. Still, she had a doomed feeling about the whole thing; even if she did take Prozac, surely her lack of grit, her attitude problem, would prevent it from working, as if Prozac were some sort of impartial judge that only gave you the happiness you deserved.

Sara's mother turned over her business card and scrawled the name and number on it. And after her mother rushed off to catch a plane, Sara was left on the sidewalk in front of the restaurant, clutching this white square bearing her mother's scribbles, like a prescription written on stiff paper.

Andy opened the door and she walked in past him, dumping her bag on the sofa.

"Mom's going to get me Prozac," she said as she took off her coat and draped it over his roommate's bike.

He trailed after her as she hurried through the apartment turning on lights, the radio, the fan. She always did this, even during day. When they'd first started going out, he'd objected—he hated wasting the energy—but after a few months, he'd grown used to it.

"I thought you didn't want the Prozac," he said.

"I may as well try it. You should see what it's done for her."

"But Sara," he said. "Isn't this backsliding? I mean, letting her tell you what pills to take like when you were a kid?"

"This one works, though. I have the same genetics she does, so maybe it will help me, too." She laughed, "Though actually, I doubt it. I'm beyond hope." She headed to the kitchen, to get the pantry light.

She claimed to turn on the lights and radio to scare off burglars. That's how she'd put it, "burglars," as if she were a little kid. Later, when he'd asked her about it again, she'd said, "Okay, I'll tell you the real reason. Because I think it will keep me distracted, which is better than being neurotic," and then she'd giggled.

But lately, he'd begun to realize she had quite a different reason for turning on the lights and for all her other rigid rituals, like the way she insisted on boiling canned food to kill botulism, and her habit of constantly referring to her neuroses as if they were old friends. "What's this mole on my arm?" she'd say, and then, "God, I'm such a hypochondriac." She wasn't much more screwed up than the next person, he thought, but she'd been in psychoanalysis so long that she'd learned to magnify every fear, instead of letting it pass. She was, he'd come to realize, like a person whose wounds never get a chance to heal because she can't stop picking at the scabs.

Sara went out to the kitchen and opened the refrigerator.

"Are you hungry?" he asked.

"No, my mother stuffed me. I just want to see what you have." After a minute, she let the fridge close with a smack.

"I'm just worried about this Prozac thing," he said. "I mean, does it really help or is it like Valium?" He heard that whiny tone come into his voice, as it always did when he tried to get her to think rationally.

"I don't care what it does. I just want it," she laughed nervously.

"But I'm worried that this will make you worse in the end. I mean, what about that article in *Newsweek?*"

"Oh, Andy," she said, "that article was hype. Don't worry so much." And then she laughed, and he started laughing, too, at her telling him not to worry.

Dr. Manning's office was in a turreted and long-lawned mansion, the kind of mental hospital that looks like a prep school. She knew the type. The reception area was furnished in that tasteful way—mahogany tables and Liberty prints—that meant one thing to her: liberally prescribed drugs.

"Go right on up," the receptionist said.

But just outside the doctor's office, a rotund, rumpled man motioned to her from down the hall. "Come here," he called. "Over here."

Sara pointed to the office, but he kept waving for her to follow him. "I have an appointment," she said when she caught up.

"It's all right," he said. "That's my office." As she followed him along the hall, he added, "The Xerox machine is broken and I have to copy these forms. I'm very absent-minded, you see, so if I don't do these now, I never will." He led her into a room where a copy machine was still beeping.

"There," he said, pushing the green button for emphasis. "It says E5. E5!"

Sara, who was always fixing the machine at work, said, "That means it needs toner."

The doctor turned in a circle, confused.

"It's right here." She ripped open a cardboard box and unhooked the machine's front panel to put the bottle in, crinkling her nose at the smell. She closed the panel and wiped her hands on her jeans.

"You're Beanie's cousin, huh?" he said, feeding papers into the machine. He squinted up at her. "You know, come to think of it, you remind me of Beanie. She's the soul of practicality. But Sara, why did you choose a psychiatrist who's related to you, more or less?"

"Look, maybe I *should* go to someone else," she said. He seemed to be a real flake, and now she thought maybe he wasn't worth her mother's money.

"No," he barked, gathering up the papers that the machine had spit out. Suddenly he became another person entirely. "Our session has begun. Repairing this machine was part of it, for reasons I shall divulge later."

He trotted back to his office and Sara jogged behind, protesting. "Oh, you make everyone fix a Xerox machine, huh? Is this a new school of therapy? Jesus. You should be paying me." He ignored her, which made her feel rather relieved. She had never talked back to a shrink, and she wasn't sure what the consequences could be. But even as she ranted at him, she reminded herself that as long as she got Prozac, it would be worth dealing with this guy. Besides, the session was shaping up to be more interesting than the standard hour of chrome chairs and significant pauses you get with MDs.

He settled behind his desk and gestured for Sara to sit opposite him.

"Look," he said, "if you really are like Beanie, you hardly need my help. So tell me why you're here."

"My mom wants me to get Prozac." Sara told him about her mother, the miraculous cure. "Do you think I should go on it? Would it help me?"

He held up one pudgy hand. "Hold on. First of all, this euphoria your mother is experiencing is probably temporary—it happens with some people when they go on the drug. Give her another month or two, and then we'll decide whether it helps her."

Sara felt a little gleeful at this, at the idea of her mother calling and cursing the drug. "You mean it will stop working?"

"It's good for some compulsives. But it helps people cope—no more than that."

"Well, should I take it then?" Sara leaned forward. She was almost afraid to hear the answer. Somehow, she felt this was the moment of judgment, when he decided whether she was beyond hope or not.

"What's wrong with you?" He crossed his fat legs and his glasses slid down his tiny, ill-formed nose.

"I'm not happy."

"And what on earth does that mean?" He leaned over the desk, screwing up his shrewd eyes.

"I don't know. I'm just not."

"Well, do you make it to your job on time? Are you in danger of harming yourself or others? Are you capable of having sexual relations? Do you eat and sleep normally? In other words, do you behave like a healthy person?"

"Well, yes, but . . ." She didn't know exactly where this was leading.

"Then it sounds as if you can do quite well without Prozac, and even better without me," he said with a little slap on the table and a dismissive tilt of his head, as if he expected her to jump up and leave the office that moment.

"Wait. I don't believe this." Sara heard her voice get loud. "That's not professional. You can't just spend ten minutes with me and say I'm fine."

"You can cope. Most of my patients cannot. My colleagues seem to think it's their job to ensure their patients' happiness. But, Miss Baker," Sara was not sure when he'd switched to her last name, "happiness is something that cannot be measured, cannot be defined. It's one of the great mysteries. Certainly it's beyond the scope of psychiatry. My job is to get people up and running, so to speak, as when you fixed that Xerox machine. I see a person flashing E5 and I give him or her toner. But I don't see you flashing anything, Miss Baker."

"But," Sara said, still puzzling over this analogy, "I've been to forty shrinks and not one of them ever said I was normal." It was really thirty, of course, but forty sounded better.

"Forty shrinks, forty winks," he said, almost to himself, then louder: "Look, if we could measure happiness, if it were something real, it's quite possible that you might be the happier of the two of us. But happiness aside, I think you can survive admirably, unlike myself. Certainly you can fix a Xerox machine, which is beyond me, and you probably wouldn't lose your patients' records as I do. So the idea of your paying me a generous sum for consultation is rather ridiculous, don't you think?"

When she came out of the building, Andy was already waiting. She got in his car and slammed the door behind her.

"Well," he said, driving down the hill, "did you get it?"

"Yeah." She waved the piece of paper with the prescription on it so he was almost afraid it would fly out the window. "But it probably won't work and it costs a dollar a pill. I'm not even sure if I'm covered for it. And if I take it, I have to see that quack every month."

Andy leaned forward to look both ways, and then swung the car out onto the highway. "So he did think you needed it, huh?"

"No," she sniffed in a way that told him she was trying to recover her dignity. "He says I'm fine. I guess compared to him, I am. He's a total nut."

"So, but, he gave you the prescription anyway?"

"Yeah. He says I should decide for myself, but his professional opinion is that I should take all the money it would cost and put it in an IRA. As if I had the money in the first place."

"He said that?" Andy thought she was kidding, but when he glanced over at her, she was gazing earnestly at the piece of paper she had flattened out on her lap.

"What does it say, exactly," he nodded at her lap.

"I don't know. Latin," she said without lifting her head, as if she couldn't stop staring at it. "I wish I could read it."

They paused at a red light beside the river, and she watched how the water glared in the sun and then turned translucent brown as it passed under the shadow of the trees. Suddenly, her disappointment was tremendous, unbearable. "They never make it anything you can read," she said again, feeling her eyes get teary. "So you can't even understand what's going on inside you when you take it. The worst part is, they don't even know what it does to you themselves."

"Well, are you going to get it?" Andy said, quite reasonably, because he was used to the way she got worked up about things like this. It was nothing against him. "Should we go by a drug store?"

The light changed and he drove on.

After a few minutes, she said, almost whispered, "I don't know." When she looked over at him, he was leaning down to fiddle with the radio knob. As was his habit when they couldn't decide where to go next, he'd turned off a side street to drive in circles through the suburbs.

A strange idea occurred to Sara: Perhaps what she'd always thought of as dullness in Andy was happiness—not the kind of ecstatic happiness she and her mother had sought, the kind you could point to, that made you dye your hair blond and get a set of business cards printed. Andy's happiness wasn't in anything he did as much as the way he did it. Even now, he seemed content to drive aimlessly until she told him where to go. It was then she decided to ask his advice. It would be the first time she had ever done so.

"Andy, should I? Is it worth it?" she said, her voice sounding oddly tender. It seemed to her that she was asking him some larger question than whether she should take the pill.

He switched off the radio, as if to concentrate. "Hmm. Well, let's see," he said, and he turned onto a wide, shady street that neither of them knew.

BINNIE KIRSHENBAUM

For Widgit Stands

THAT WAS THE SAME YEAR I had my father take down my closet door and hang beads in its place. I put up a poster of Janis Joplin on one wall and a macramé ornament on another. I was reading Herman Hesse, Kahlil Gibran, and *Jonathan Livingston Seagull,* which I thought to be deep, heady stuff. I wore a peace sign button on the lapel of my navy pea jacket. Heidi Rosenthal was my best friend.

Each night during Walter Cronkite, I braided my waist-length hair into corn rows, and in the morning I undid them. The result was hair that rippled down my back. I got the idea for rippled hair from Donna Huston, although her hair rippled naturally. Donna Huston was the most hippie girl in my grade, if not in all of Hamilton Junior High. She could've been a centerfold for *Life* magazine with that hair, and the way her Sweet Orr bellbottoms slid under the heels of her Fred Braun shoes. Her blouses were gauzy and made in India, land of many cool things like incense, the Maharishi, silver ankle bracelets with bells attached.

Appearances, however, sometimes deceived. In Social Studies class, when Mr. Tisch pulled down the map of the world and called on Donna Huston to point out Vietnam, she went looking for it in South America.

More than anything then, I yearned to be older, older than twelve going on thirteen, old enough to sit in, to strike, to protest and riot. It was with envy that I watched the film footage from the University of Michigan, of radicals chanting, "Hell no! We won't go!" and burning their draft cards and the American flag. Mounted police broke through the throngs of students. Placards went flying. Hippies ran for cover as the club-wielding cops bashed skulls, then handcuffed and tossed the hippies into the paddywagon as if they were suitcases being loaded onto a conveyer belt.

Alas, by the time I was of age to hurl a bottle at a cop, it was all over.

After the report on the campus riot, Walter Cronkite had news from Vietnam. There were more casualties to report. I didn't think he should call dead people *casualties*. I thought he ought to say *dead people*. I imagined writing Walter Cronkite a letter to that effect, which he would read on the air. I went to sleep with the vision of Walter Cronkite holding up an envelope and telling America, "I have a letter here from a young girl. . . ." Desperate for a way to protest, to make my voice heard, I hungered not merely to enlist in the revolution, but to be the one with the bullhorn.

At school, during homeroom, Miss O'Connor, as she did every day, took attendance and then said, "All rise for the Pledge of Allegiance." In that instant it came to me, a flash of brilliance, the way to be the Mark Rudd, the Angela Davis, the Abbie Hoffman of the twelve-year-old set. I would boycott the Pledge. I would stand tall, but keep silent, a silence that would resonate from student to student, from homeroom to homeroom throughout the junior highs of America. What a day it would be when the teachers said, "All rise for the Pledge of Allegiance," and young people everywhere clamped their mouths shut. That would've been as cool as having a war but no one shows up to fight it.

Although I'd never have admitted it—not even to myself because I liked to think I'd have gladly done jail time for the cause—I took sly comfort knowing there'd be no serious repercussion over my boycott of the Pledge. Not that Miss O'Connor was in any way sympathetic to my politics, but there'd been some trouble in the past with Miss O'Connor requiring her homeroom to recite, along with the Pledge, the Lord's Prayer. My mother was president of the P.T.A. that year and sat in on the meeting when some Jewish boy's parents made a stink about that. Miss O'Connor argued that the Lord's Prayer was non-denominational. "It's for all the religions and races," she said.

The Jewish boy's mother, a professor at Sarah Lawrence, wasn't swayed. "God doesn't belong in the public schools," she said, and she voiced concern for atheists and Zen Buddhists.

Miss O'Connor, who was best friends with the convent of nuns over at St. Eugene's, believed that God belonged everywhere and that atheists and whatnots deserved to have hot lead poured into their intestines. But she said none of that. Instead she said, "It's no different than having them recite the Pledge of Allegiance."

"Yes," the Jewish boy's father agreed, "and they don't have to recite that either."

To avoid the possibility of a court case, the principal told Miss O'Connor the Lord's Prayer had to go and no one had to recite anything they didn't want to recite. After the boy's parents left, the principal placated Miss O'Connor. "You know how the Jews get," he said.

And because Miss O'Connor already hated my guts—she hated all the hippies—I really had nothing to lose, although that didn't stop me from acting as if I did. Defiantly, I pinned my arms to my sides—no right hand draped over my heart—and I kept my mouth closed tightly while the class droned *I pledge allegiance to the flag mumble mumble America mumble for widgit stands,* and then a finger, Lydia Langorelli's finger to be exact, poked me in the back.

Lydia Langorelli had to repeat the third and fifth grades. Consequently, she was developed. While the rest of the girls in our class had rosebud breasts, Lydia had big hooters entombed in one of those old-fashioned conical cupped bras. She wore black eyeline, Maybelline from Woolworth's, and nylon stockings with runs in them. She was not at all a hippie.

This was not the first time Lydia poked me in the back. The week before she'd poked me and asked, "You got a comb?"

Of course I had a comb. Only I wasn't real keen on loaning it to Lydia Langorelli. But, I reminded myself, sharing property was an integral part of hippiedom, and so I fished out my comb from my fringed suede bag.

"Good," Lydia snatched it from me, and like it was a bowling trophy, she held up my faux-mother-of-pearl comb and announced to the whole class, "Now I can clean out my hairbrush."

The boys laughed, and the girls cried, "Ewww, gross," as Lydia ran my comb through her filthy hairbrush, catching dandruff and grease and probably lice too.

A poke in the back from Lydia Langorelli was never going to be the highlight of my day. Glumly I turned around to see what she wanted this time.

"The Pledge," she chomped on pink chewing gum. "We're saying the Pledge."

America, right or wrong, love it or leave it; Lydia Langorelli was staunchly patriotic the way only the downtrodden could be. Lydia clung to the hope that if she pledged allegiance to the flag fervently enough, if tears sprung to her eyes during the National Anthem, then someday America would do right by her. Thus far, America had dealt Lydia Langorelli dirt.

Although no one I knew had ever actually been there, it was common knowledge that Lydia lived in a crummy apartment over Pete's Pizza and Sub Shop, where her father swept up and washed dishes for a living. When Lydia was just a little kid, her mother took off for a better life but turned up dead in a motel room in South Yonkers.

The rest of us at Hamilton Junior High lived in houses. Nice houses, and we had a plethora of luxuries to rebel against: charge accounts at Lord and

Taylor's, pink bedroom sets, country clubs that discriminated quietly. That we would eventually go off to college was a given.

I wasn't about to get into it—why I would not vow allegiance to a nation whose government was morally bereft—with Lydia Langorelli. She could never have grasped the concept of civil disobedience because to get left back twice, you had to be a real moron. I turned my back on her *and justice for all*. As if we'd been standing at attention for hours, twenty-two of us seventh-graders collapsed in our seats.

Again, Lydia's finger jabbed into my shoulder blade. "How come you didn't say the Pledge?" Obviously, she wasn't going to let the subject drop, so I gave her as succinct an answer as possible. While Lydia blew a large pink bubble, I explained, "It goes against my belief system."

Sucking the gum back into her mouth, Lydia said, "You don't believe in America? What are you? Some kind of Commie?" Then Lydia Langorelli told me, "After school. Today. I'm going to beat the shit out of you."

Beating the crap out of me was the one thing at which she was bound to excel. Those greaser girls were famous for biting, clawing, scratching, kicking, hair-pulling fights. And Lydia was the queen of the greasers. Not to mention she was twice my size. I didn't even know how to throw a punch. Violence was so uncool. I felt like I was going to throw up.

"Lydia Langorelli," Miss O'Connor's voice snapped like a whip. "Are you chewing gum? Get rid of that." Miss O'Connor quivered all over as if she were talking about something as nasty as a used condom instead of a wad of Bazooka.

Lydia spit the gum into her hand, but rather than wrapping it up in a piece of looseleaf paper like you were supposed to, Lydia slapped her palm against the top of my head. She ground the pink gum into my hair.

My hair! My long, rippled, picture-of-the-young-hippie hair! Gum in my hair was so disastrous, I momentarily forgot that wasn't going to be the worst of it.

I met up with Heidi in the hall and showed her what Lydia'd done to me. "What can I do?"

Heidi seemed to remember something about peanut butter as a solution. Or maybe it was margarine. "Either way," she said, "go to Home Ec."

I nodded and then told her the rest. "She's going to beat me up after school."

Heidi gasped and clutched her books as if two notebooks and *The Red Pony* were a bullet-proof vest. "Lydia Langorelli will kill you," Heidi said. "She'll mop the floor with you. You're dead meat." Seven years later, Heidi dropped out of college and joined the Church of Scientology.

Mrs. Rice, the orthopedic-shod dominatrix of the Home Ec rooms, reigned over six ovens, six double sinks, six refrigerators. Girls had to take Home Ec, where we made tuna casseroles and cinnamon toast. Boys took Shop. They got to build bookends and learn to use a blow torch.

"How did this happen?" Mrs. Rice wanted to know how gum wound up in my hair, but I only shrugged because, no matter what, it wasn't cool to rat.

"Young ladies do not shrug their shoulders," Mrs. Rice reprimanded me, and before I knew what she was up to, she'd whipped a pair of scissors from her apron pocket and snipped. The wad of gum, with two feet of my hair attached, looked like a scalp Lydia Langorelli could've hung from her belt.

I stopped in the girls' room to assess the damage. A circle of porcupine quills, one inch in diameter, stood straight up on the top of my head. I looked like a Hare Krishna in reverse.

Other than homeroom, Lydia was not in any of my classes because I was *accelerated* and she was *slow*. The only time I might've run into her during the day was at lunch. But I had no appetite, and instead of sliding my tray along in the cafeteria line, I hid out in Mr. Ellman's room.

I'd assumed Mr. Ellman would be eating his lunch in the faculty cafeteria, but he was at his desk munching granola and grading papers. Mr. Ellman was my English teacher. He had sort of long hair and referred to television as "the boob tube." Also, he let it be known he became a teacher because teachers got draft deferments.

"What's with your hair?" he asked. "Is that the newest in what's happening?"

"Yes," I said, and I half expected him to say groovy. But Mr. Ellman, embarrassed that he wasn't up on the newest trend, dropped the subject of hair and asked, "What can I do for you?"

I pretended I came to talk to him about the war. He told me I should write letters to my congressman demanding troop withdrawal. I didn't know who my congressman was, but I didn't mention that. Nor did I mention anything about Lydia Langorelli's plans to beat me to a bloody pulp. Not even when Mr. Ellman asked, "Are you okay? You look like something's bothering you." Mr. Ellman was the kind of teacher who liked kids to confide in him. Consequently, no one ever did.

"It's the war," I said. "Young men dying, getting maimed and beat up. And what for? America? For which it stands?" My chin jerked, and I started to cry.

Mr. Ellman was at a loss as to what to do. A man teacher could not hug me or pat me or dry my tears without courting disaster. One wrong move and he would've found himself wading through the rice paddies.

Seventh period, I had Biology. While my lab partner hacked up an earthworm, dread danced in my stomach. I pictured myself sitting on the ground in the lotus position as Lydia kicked me in the head. I tried to draw inspiration from Gandhi and Martin Luther King engaging in passive resistance. I was banking on passive resistance being a kind of invisible shield; therefore the blows inflicted wouldn't hurt much. I watched the clock on the wall, the red second hand sweeping around like it was in a hurry to get someplace. My hands went clammy.

Although I hadn't told anyone except Heidi that Lydia was going to beat me up after school, and I'd sworn her to secrecy, word had spread. When the bell rang, no one went home or to band practice or to cheerleading. Instead, two feet off of school property, they all congregated in a circle. The air was crisp and smelled of burning leaves.

Lydia took off her leather jacket and gave it to some other greaser girl to hold. I handed my books to Heidi, and the cries went up, "Girl fight! Girl fight!" Then the crowd hushed so as not to miss the sound of Lydia's knuckles making contact with my face.

I heard the crunch, and I went down. My hands splayed behind me, so I wasn't flat out but sort of sitting. Lydia moved in and, as if to see if I were dead yet, she prodded me in the ribs with the point of her scuffed black shoe. I flinched and looked up at her, at her white lipstick, at the cheap sleeveless nylon shell she wore, at the pair of dunce caps she had for breasts, at the yellow discolorations on her arms which days before had been purple and blue. And from someplace deep down where you know things you didn't think you knew, things you weren't supposed to know, much less ever talk about, *I knew* and I said, "You have sex with your father."

As if I'd decked her in a soft and tender place, her eyes bugged from the unexpected low blow and then swirled into a kaleidoscope of pain and fear. Suddenly, she was the prey, as stunned as the cobra who thought the mongoose just another rodent. She mouthed the word "No," but instead of a rush of compassion, I experienced a rush of adrenaline. Fueled by victory, crazed by power, I got up and shrieked at the top of my lungs for the whole school to hear, "Lydia Langorelli fucks her father. She gives him blow jobs and cooks him spaghetti."

The crowd was with me all the way. Everyone, including the girl holding Lydia's leather jacket, hooted and laughed and whistled because this turn of events was far more thrilling than merely watching Lydia beat the shit out of me. Besides, Lydia was just some greaser who'd been left back twice. And no one, no one in the whole *I pledge allegiance to the flag of the United States of America* gave a widgit about Lydia Langorelli.

CRIS MAZZA

Is It Sexual Harassment Yet?

Even before the Imperial Penthouse switched from a staff of exclusively male waiters and food handlers to a crew of fifteen waitresses, Terence Lovell was the floor captain. Wearing a starched ruffled shirt and black tails, he embodied continental grace and elegance as he seated guests and, with a toreador's flourish, produced menus out of thin air. He took all orders but did not serve—except in the case of a flaming meal or dessert, and this duty, for over ten years, was his alone. One of his trademarks was to never be seen striking the match—either the flaming platter was swiftly paraded from the kitchen or the dish would seemingly spontaneously ignite on its cart beside the table, a quiet explosion, then a four-foot column of flame, like a fountain with floodlights of changing colors.

There'd been many reasons for small celebrations at the Lovell home during the past several years: Terence's wife, Maggie, was able to quit her job as a keypunch operator when she finished courses and was hired as a part-time legal secretary. His son was tested into the gifted program at school. His daughter learned to swim before she could walk. The newspaper did a feature on the Imperial Penthouse with a half-page photo of Terence holding a flaming shish-kebab.

Then one day on his way to work, dressed as usual in white tie and tails, Terence Lovell found himself stopping off at a gun store. For that moment, as he approached the glass-topped counter, Terence said his biggest fear was that he might somehow, despite his professional elegant manners, appear to the rest of the world like a cowboy swaggering his way up to the bar to order a double. Terence purchased a small hand gun—the style that many cigarette lighters resemble—and tucked it into his red cummerbund.

It was six to eight months prior to Terence's purchase of the gun that the restaurant began to integrate waitresses into the personnel. Over the next year or so, the floor staff was supposed to eventually evolve into one made up of all women with the exception of the floor captain. It was still during the early weeks of the new staff, however, when Terence began finding gifts in his locker. First there was a black lace and red satin garter. Terence pinned it to the bulletin board in case it had been put into the wrong locker, so the owner could claim it. But the

I know they're going to ask about my previous sexual experiences. What counts as sexual? Holding hands? Wet kisses? A finger up my ass? Staring at a man's bulge? He wore incredibly tight pants. But before all this happened, I wasn't a virgin, and I wasn't a virgin in so many ways. I never had an abortion, I never had VD, never went into a toilet stall with a woman, never castrated a guy at the moment of climax. But I know enough to know. As soon as you feel like *someone,* you're no one. Why am I doing this? *Why?*

flowers he found in his locker were more of a problem—they were taken from the vases on the tables. Each time that he found a single red rosebud threaded through the vents in his locker door, he found a table on the floor with an empty vase, so he always put the flower back where it belonged. Terence spread the word through the busboys that the waitresses could take the roses off the tables each night after the restaurant was closed, but not before. But on the whole, he thought—admittedly on retrospect—the atmosphere with the new waitresses seemed, for the first several weeks, amiable and unstressed.

Then one of the waitresses, Michelle Rae, reported to management that Terence had made inappropriate comments to her during her shift at work. Terence said he didn't know which of the waitresses had made the complaint, but also couldn't remember if management had withheld the name of the accuser, or if, when told the name at this point, he just didn't know which waitress she was. He said naturally there was a shift in decorum behind the door to the kitchen, but he wasn't aware that anything he said or did could have possibly been so misunderstood. He explained that his admonishments were never more than half-serious, to the waitresses as well as the waiters or busboys: "Move your butt," or "One more mix-up and you'll be looking at the happy end of a skewer." While he felt a food server should appear

So, you'll ask about my sexual history but won't think to inquire about the previous encounters I *almost* had, or *never* had: it wasn't the old ships-in-the-night tragedy, but let's say I had a ship, three or four years ago, the ship of love, okay? So once when I had a lot of wind in my sails (is this a previous sexual experience yet?), the captain sank the vessel when he started saying stuff like, "You're not ever going to be the most important thing in someone else's life unless it's something like he kills you—and then only if he hasn't killed anyone else yet nor knocked people off for a living—otherwise no one's the biggest deal in anyone's life but their own." Think about that. He may've been running my ship, but it turns out *he* was navigating by remote control. When the whole thing blew up, he was unscathed. Well, now I try to live as though I wrote that rule, as though it's *mine*. But that hasn't made me like it any better.

There are so many ways to humiliate someone. Make someone so low they leave a snail-trail. Someone makes a joke, you don't laugh. Someone tells a story—a personal story, something that mattered—you don't listen, you aren't moved. Someone wears a dance leotard to work, you don't notice. But underneath it all, you're planning the real humiliation. The symbolic humiliation. The humiliation of humiliations. Like I told you, I learned this before, I already know the *type*: he'll be remote, cool, distant—*seeming* to

unruffled, even languid, on the floor, he pointed out that movement was brisk in the kitchen area, communication had to get the point across quickly, leaving no room for confusion or discussion. And while talking and joking on a personal level was not uncommon, Terence believed the waitresses had not been working there long enough for any conversations other than work-related, but these included light-hearted observations: a customer's disgusting eating habits, vacated tables that appeared more like battle-grounds than the remains of a fine dinner, untouched expensive meals, guessing games as to which couples were first dates and which were growing tired of each other, whose business was legitimate and whose probably dirty, who were wives and which were the mistresses, and, of course, the rude customers. Everyone always had rude-customer stories to trade. Terence had devised a weekly contest where each food server produced their best rude-customer story on a 3×5 card and submitted it each Friday. Terence then judged them and awarded the winner a specially made shish-kebab prepared after the restaurant had closed, with all of the other waiters and waitresses providing parodied royal table service, even to the point of spreading the napkin across the winner's lap and dabbing the corners of his or her mouth after each bite.

be gentle and tolerant but actually cruelly indifferent. It'll be great fun for him to be aloof or preoccupied when someone is in love with him, genuflecting, practically prostrating herself. If he doesn't respond, she can't say he hurt her, she never got close enough. He'll go on a weekend ski trip with his friends. She'll do calisthenics, wash her hair, shave her legs, and wait for Monday. Well, not *this* time, no sir. Terence Lovell is messing with a sadder-but-wiser chick.

The rude-customer contest was suspended after the complaint to management. However, the gifts in his locker multiplied during this time. He continued to tack the gifts to the bulletin board, whenever possible: the key chain with a tiny woman's high-heeled shoe, the 4×6 plaque with a poem printed over a misty photograph of a dense green moss-covered forest, the single black fishnet stocking. When he found a pair of women's underwear in his locker, instead of tacking them to the bulletin board, he hung them on the inside doorknob of the woman's restroom. That was the last gift he found in his locker for a while. Within a week he received in the mail the same pair of women's underwear.

Since the beginning of the new staff, the restaurant manager had been talking about having a staff party to help the new employees feel welcome and at ease with the previous staff. But in the confusion of settling in, a date had never been set. Four or five months after the waitresses began work, the party had a new purpose: to ease the tension caused by the complaint against Terence. So far, nothing official had been done or said about Ms. Rae's allegations.

During the week before the party, which was to be held in an uptown nightclub with live music on a night the Imperial Penthouse was closed,

Yes, I was one of the first five women to come in as food servers, and I expected the usual resistance—the dirty glasses and ash-strewn linen on our tables (before the customer was seated), planting long hairs in the salads, cold soup, busboys delivering tips that appeared to have been left on greasy plates or in puddles of gravy on the tablecloth. I could stand those things. It was like them saying, "We know you're here!" But no, not *him.* He didn't want to return to the days of his all-male staff. Why would he want that? Eventually he was going to be in charge of an all-woman floor.

Terence asked around to find out if Michelle Rae would be attending. All he discovered about her, however, was that she didn't seem to have any close friends on the floor staff.

Michelle did come to the party. She wore a green strapless dress which, Terence remembered, was unbecomingly tight and, as he put it, made her rump appear too ample. Her hair was in a style Terence described as finger-in-a-light-socket. Terence believed he probably would not have noticed Michelle at all that night if he were not aware of the complaint she had made. He recalled that her lipstick was the same shade of red as her hair and there were red tints in her eye shadow.

Terence planned to make it an early evening. He'd brought his wife, and, since this was the first formal staff party held by the Imperial Penthouse, had to spend most of the evening's conversation in introducing Maggie to his fellow employees. Like any ordinary party, however, he was unable to remember afterwards exactly what he did, who he talked to, or what they spoke about, but he knew that he did not introduce his wife to Michelle Rae.

Terence didn't see Maggie go into the restroom. It was down the hall, toward the kitchen. And he didn't see Michelle Rae follow her. In fact, no one did. Maggie returned to the dance area with her face flushed, breathing heavily, her eyes filled with tears, tugged at his arm and,

Sound familiar? A harem? A pimp's stable? He though it was so hilarious, he started saying it every night: "Line up, girls, and pay the pimp." Time to split tips. See what I mean? But he only flirted a little with them to cover up the obviousness of what he was doing to me. Just a few weeks after I started, I put a card on the bulletin board announcing that I'm a qualified aerobic dance instructor and if anyone was interested, I would lead an exercise group before work. My card wasn't there three hours before someone (and I don't need a detective) had crossed out "aerobic" and wrote "erotic," and he added a price per session! I had no intention of charging anything for it since I go through my routine everyday anyway, and the more the merrier is an aerobic dance motto—we like to share the pain. My phone number was clear as day on that card—if he was at all intrigued, he could've called and found out what I was offering. I've spent ten years exercising my brains out. Gyms, spas, classes, health clubs . . . no bars. He could've just once picked up the phone, I was always available, willing to talk this out, come to a settlement. He never even tried. Why should he? He was already king of Nob Hill. You know that lowlife bar he goes to? If anyone says how he was such an amiable and genial supervisor . . . you bet he was genial, he was halfway drunk. It's crap about him being a big family man. Unless his living room had a pool table, those beer mirrors on

with her voice shaking, begged Terence to take her home. It wasn't until they arrived home that Maggie told Terence how Michelle Rae had come into the restroom and threatened her. Michelle had warned Mrs. Lovell to stay away from Terence and informed her that she had a gun in her purse to help *keep* her away from Terence.

Terence repeated his wife's story to the restaurant manager. The manager thanked him. But, a week later, after Terence had heard of no further developments, he asked the manager what was going to be done about it. The manager said he'd spoken with both Ms. Rae and Mrs. Lovell, separately, but Ms. Rae denied the incident, and, as Mrs. Lovell did not actually see any gun, he couldn't fire an employee simply on the basis of what another employee's wife said about her, especially with the complaint already on file, how would that look? Terence asked, "But isn't there some law against this?" The manager gave Terence a few days off to cool down.

The Imperial Penthouse was closed on Mondays, and most Monday evenings Terence went out with a group of friends to a local sports bar. Maggie Lovell taught piano lessons at home in the evenings, so it was their mutual agreement that Terence go out to a movie or, more often, to see a football game on television. On one such evening, Maggie received a phone call from a woman who said

the wall, and the sticky brown bar itself—the wood doesn't even show through anymore, it's grime from people's hands, the kind of people who go there, the same way a car's steering wheel builds up that thick hard black layer which gets sticky when it rains and you can cut it with a knife. No, his house may not be like that, but he never spent a lot of time at his house. I know what I'm talking about. He'll say he doesn't remember, but I wasn't ten feet away while he was flashing his healthy salary (imported beer), and he looked right through me—no, *not* like I wasn't there. When a man looks at you the way he did at me, he's either ignoring you or undressing you with his eyes, but probably *both*. And that's just what he did and didn't stop there. He's not going to get away with it.

Wasn't it his idea to hire us in the first place? No, he wasn't there at the interview, but looked right at me my first day, just at me while he said, "You girls probably all want to be models or actresses. You don't give *this* profession enough respect. Well," he said, "you will." Didn't look at anyone else. He meant me. I didn't fail to notice, either, I was the only one with red hair. Not dull

she was calling from the restaurant—there'd been a small fire in one of the storage rooms and the manager was requesting that Terence come to the restaurant and help survey the damage. Mrs. Lovell told the caller where Terence was.

The Imperial Penthouse never experienced any sort of fire, and Terence could only guess afterwards whether or not that was the same Monday evening that Michelle Rae came to the sports bar. At first he had considered speaking to her, to try to straighten out what was becoming an out-of-proportion misunderstanding. But he'd already been there for several hours—the game was almost over—and he'd had three or four beers. Because he was, therefore, not absolutely certain what the outcome would be if he talked to her, he checked his impulse to confront Ms. Rae, and, in fact, did not acknowledge her presence.

When a second complaint was made, again charging Terence with inappropriate behavior and, this time, humiliation, Terence offered to produce character witnesses, but before anything came of it, a rape charge was filed with the district attorney and Terence was brought in for questioning. The restaurant suspended Terence without pay for two weeks. All the waitresses, except Ms. Rae, were interviewed, as well as several ex-waitresses—by this time the restaurant was already experiencing some turnover of the new

auburn . . . flaming red. They always assume, don't they? You know, the employees restrooms were one toilet each for men and women, all the customary holes drilled in the walls, stuffed with paper, but if one restroom was occupied, we could use the other, so the graffiti was heterosexual, a dialogue. It could've been healthy, but he never missed an opportunity. I'd just added my thoughts to an on-going discussion of the growing trend toward androgyny in male rock singers—they haven't yet added breasts and aren't quite at the point of cutting off their dicks—and an hour later, there it was, the thick black ink pen, the block letters: "Let's get one thing clear—do you women want it or *not?* Just what is the *thrust* of this conversation?" What do you *call* an attitude like that? And he gets *paid* for it! You know, after you split a tip with a busboy, bartender, and floor captain, there's not much left. *He* had an easy answer: earn bigger tips. *Earn* it, work your *ass* off for it, you know. But who's going to tip more than 15% unless. . . . Well, unless the waitress wears no underwear. He even said that the best thing about taking part of our tip money was it made us move our asses that much prettier. There was another thing he liked about how I had to earn bigger tips—reaching or bending. And then my skirt was "mysteriously," "accidentally" lifted from behind, baring my butt in front of the whole staff. Many of those interviewed reported that Michelle Rae had been asking them if they'd slept with Terence. In one case Ms. Rae was said to have told one of her colleagues that she, Michelle, knew all about her co-worker's affair with the floor captain. Some of the waitresses said that they'd received phone calls on Mondays; an unidentified female demanded to know if Terence Lovell was, at that moment, visiting them. A few of those waitresses assumed it was Michelle Rae while others said they'd thought the caller had been Mrs. Lovell.

When the district attorney dropped the rape charge for lack of evidence, Michelle Rae filed suit claiming harassment, naming the restaurant owner, manager and floor captain. Meanwhile Terence began getting a series of phone calls where the caller immediately hung up. Some days the phone seemed to ring incessantly. So once, in a rage of frustration, Terence grabbed the receiver and made a list of threats—the worst being, as he remembered it, "kicking her lying ass clear out of the state"—before realizing the caller hadn't hung up that time. Believing the caller might be legitimate—a friend or a business call— Terence quickly apologized and began to explain, but the caller, who never gave her name, said, "Then I

kitchen staff. He pretended he hadn't noticed. Then winked and smiled at me later when I gave him his share of my tips. Told me to keep up the good work. Used *ass* every chance he got in my presence for weeks afterwards. Isn't this sexual harassment yet?

Of course I was scared. He knew my work schedule, and don't think he didn't know where I live. Knew my days off, when I'd be asleep, when I do my aerobic dance routine every day. I don't mind *who*ever wants to do aerobic dance with me—but it has to be at my place where I've got the proper flooring and music. It was just an idle, general invitation—an announcement—I wasn't *begging . . . any*one, him included, could come once or keep coming, that's all I meant, just harmless, healthy exercise. Does it mean I was looking to start my dancing career in that palace of high-class entertainment *he* frequents? Two pool tables, a juke box and big-screen TV. What a lousy front—looks exactly like what it re-guess you're not ready." When Terence asked her to clarify—ready for what?—she said, "To meet somewhere and work this out. To make my lawsuit obsolete garbage. To do what you really want to do to me. To finish all this."

Terence began refusing to answer the phone himself, relying on Maggie to screen calls, then purchasing an answering machine. As the caller left a message, Terence could hear who it was over a speaker, then he could decide whether or not to pick up the phone and speak to the party directly. He couldn't disconnect the phone completely because he had to stay in touch with his lawyer. The Imperial Penthouse was claiming Terence was not covered on their lawsuit insurance because he was on suspension at the time the suit was filed.

When he returned to work there was one more gift in Terence's locker: what looked like a small stiletto switchblade, but, when clicked open, turned out to be a comb. A note was attached, unsigned, which said, "I'd advise you to get a gun."

Terence purchased the miniature single-cartridge hand gun the following day. After keeping it at work in his locker for a week, he kept it, unloaded, in a dresser drawer at home, unable to carry it to work every day, he said, because the outline of the gun was clearly recognizable in the pocket of his tux pants.

ally *is*, his lair, puts on his favorite funky music, his undulating blue and green lights, snorts his coke, dazzles his partner—his doped-up victim—with his moves and gyrations, dances her into a corner and rapes her before the song's over, up against the wall—*that* song's in the juke box too. You think I don't *know?* I was having a hassle with a customer who ordered rare, complained it was overdone, wanted it *rare,* the cook was busy, so Terence grabs another steak and throws it on the grill—tsss on one side, flips it, tsss on the other—slams it on a plate. "Here, young lady, you just dance this raw meat right out to that john." I said I don't know how to dance. "My dear," he said, "*everyone* knows how to dance, it's all a matter of moving your ass." Of course the gun was necessary! I tried to be reasonable. I tried everything!

One Monday evening as Terence was leaving the sports bar—not drunk, but admittedly not with his sharpest wits either—three men stopped him. Terence was in a group with another man and three women, but, according to the others, the culprits ignored them, singling out Terence immediately. It was difficult for Terence to recall what happened that night. He believed the men might've asked him for his wallet, but two of the others with him say the men didn't ask for anything but were just belligerent drunks looking for a fight. Only one member of Terence's party remembered anything specific that was said, addressed to Terence: "Think you're special?" If the men had been attempting a robbery, Terence decided to refuse, he said, partly because he wasn't fully sober, and partly because it appeared the attackers had no weapons. In the ensuing fight—which, Terence said, happened as he was running down the street, but was unsure whether he was chasing or being chased—Terence was kicked several times in the groin area and sustained several broken ribs. He was hospitalized for two days.

Maggie Lovell visited Terence in the hospital once, informing him that she was asking her parents to stay with the kids until he was discharged because she was moving into a motel. She wouldn't tell Terence the name of the motel, in-

Most people—you just don't know what goes on back there. You see this stylish, practically regal man in white tie and tails, like an old fashioned prince ... or Vegas magician ... but back there in the hot, steamy kitchen, what's *wrong* with him? Drunk? Drugs? He played sword fight with one of the undercooks, using the longest skewers, kept trying to jab each other in the crotch. The chef yelled at the undercook, but Terence didn't say a word, went to the freezer, got the meatballs out, thawed them halfway in the microwave, then started threading them onto the skewer. Said it was an ancient custom, like the Indians did with scalps, to keep trophies from your victims on your weapon. He added vegetables in between the meatballs—whole bell peppers, whole onions, even whole eggplant, starting dousing the whole thing with brandy. His private bottle? Maybe. He said we should put it on the menu, he wanted someone to order it, his delux kebab. He would turn off all the chandeliers and light the dining room with the burning food. Then he stopped. He and I were alone! He said, "The only thing my delux kebab needs is a fresh, ripe tomato." Isn't this incredible! He wanted to know how I would like to be the next juicy morsel to be poked onto the end of that thing. He was still pouring brandy all over it. Must've been a gallon bottle, still half full when he put it on the

sisting she didn't want anyone to know where she was, not even her parents, and besides, she informed him, there probably wouldn't even be a phone in her room. Terence, drowsy from pain killers, couldn't remember much about his wife's visit. He had vague recollections of her leaving through the window, or leaning out the window to pick flowers, or slamming the window shut, but when he woke the next day and checked, he saw that the window could not be opened. Terence never saw his wife again. Later he discovered that on the night of his accident there had been an incident at home. Although Terence had instructed his eight-year-old son not to answer the phone, the boy had forgotten, and, while his mother was giving a piano lesson, he picked up the receiver just after the machine had clicked on. The entire conversation was therefore recorded. The caller, a female, asked the boy who he was, so he replied that he was Andy Lovell. "The heir apparent," the voice said softly, to which Andy responded, "What? I mean, pardon?" There was a brief pause, then the caller said, "I'd really like to get rid of your mom so your dad could fuck me. If you're halfway like him, maybe I'll let you fuck me too." There is another pause on the tape. Investigators disagree as to whether it is the caller's breathing or the boy's that can be heard. The boy's voice, obviously trembling, then said, "What?" The female caller snapped,

counter, twirled the huge shish-kebab again, struck his sword fighting pose and cut the bottle right in half. I can hardly believe it either. When the bottle cracked open, the force of the blow made the brandy shoot out, like the bottle had opened up and split—it splattered the front of my skirt. In the next second his kebab was in flames—maybe he'd passed it over a burner, I don't know, he was probably *breathing* flames by then—so naturally as soon as he pointed the thing at me again, my skirt ignited, scorched the hair off my legs before I managed to drop it around my feet and kick it away. What *wouldn't* he do? Looks like he'd finally gotten me undressed. It's ironic, isn't it, when you see that news article about him—I taped it to my mirror—and how about that headline, "Pomp and Circumstance Part of the Meal." There sure were some circumstances to consider, all right. Like he could rape me at gunpoint any time he wanted, using that cigarette lighter which looks like a fancy pistol. I wanted something to always remind me what to watch out for, but I didn't take the lighter. Why not? I'll kick myself forever for that. There was so much to choose from. Now one of his red satin cummerbunds hangs over my bed while he still has the lighter and can still use it!

"Tell your dad someone's going to be killed."

During Terence's convalescence, the Imperial Penthouse changed its format and operated without a floor captain, using the standard practice of a hostess who seated the guests and waitresses assigned to tables to take orders and serve meals. The restaurant's menu was also changed and now no longer offered flaming meals. When Terence returned to work he was given a position as a regular waiter, even though by this time most of the male food servers had left the restaurant and were replaced with women. Michelle Rae was given a lunch schedule, ten to three, Wednesday through Sunday. Terence would call the restaurant to make sure she'd clocked out before he arrived for the dinner shift.

During the first week he was back at work, Terence came home and found that his wife had returned to get the children. In a few days she sent a truck for the furniture, and the next communication he had with her was the divorce suit—on grounds of cruel and unusual adultery.

When he said "staff meeting," he didn't mean what he was supposed to mean by it. You know, there was a cartoon on the bulletin board, *staff meeting*, two sticks shaking hands, very funny, right? But long ago someone had changed the drawing, made the two sticks flaming shish-kebabs on skewers. So the announcement of the big meeting was a xerox of that cartoon, but enlarged, tacked to the women's restroom door. *Be There Or Be Square! Yes, You'll Be Paid For Attending!* You bet! It was held at that tavern. Everyone may've been invited, but I'm the one he wanted there. There's no doubt in my mind. What good was I to him merely as an employee? I had to see the real Terence Lovell, had to join the inner-most core of his life. Know what? It was a biker hangout, that bar, a biker gang's headquarters. One or two of them were always there with their leather jackets, chains, black grease under their fingernails (or dried blood), knives eight inches long. They took so many drugs you could get high just lying on the reeking urine-soaked mattress in the back. That's where the initiations were. No one just *lets* you in. Know what he said the first day we started working, the first day of the women food servers, he said, "You don't just work here to earn a salary, you have to *earn* the right to work here!" So maybe I was naive to trust him. To ever set one foot in that bar without a suspicion of what could happen to me. That same ordinary old beer party going on in front—same music, same dancing, same clack of pool balls and whooping laughter—you'd never believe the scene in the back room. It may've looked like a typical orgy at first—sweating bodies moving in rhythm, groaning, changing to new contorted positions, shouts of encouragement, music blaring in the background. But wait, nothing ordinary or healthy like that for the girl who was chosen to be the center of his dark side—she'll have to be both the cause and cure for his violent ache, that's why he's been so relentless, so obsessed, so insane . . . he was driven to it, to the point where he had to paint the tip of his hard-on with 150 proof whisky then use the fancy revolver to ignite it, screaming—not like any sound he ever made before—until he extinguished it in the girl of his unrequited dreams. Tssss.

The only thing left in Terence's living room was the telephone and answering machine. When the phone rang one Monday afternoon, Terence answered and, as instructed by his attorney, turned on the tape recorder:

CALLER: It's me, baby.
LOVELL: Okay. . . .

CALLER: You've been ignoring me
lately.

LOVELL: What do you want now?

CALLER: Come on, now, Terry!

LOVELL: Look, let's level with each
other. How can we end this?
What do I have to do?

CALLER: If it's going to end, the ending has to be *better* than if it continued.

LOVELL: Pardon?

CALLER: A bigger deal. A big bang.
You ever heard of the big bang
theory?

LOVELL: The beginning of the universe?

CALLER: Yeah, but the big bang, if it
started the whole universe, it also
ended something. It may've started
the universe, but what did it end?
What did it *obliterate*?

LOVELL: I still don't know what you
want.

CALLER: What do *you* want, Terry?

LOVELL: I just want my life to get
back to normal.

CALLER: Too late. I've changed your
life, haven't I? Good.

LOVELL: Let's get to the point.

CALLER: You sound anxious. I love
it. You ready?

LOVELL: Ready for what?

CALLER: To see me. To end it. That's
what you wanted, wasn't it? Let's
create the rest of your life out of
our final meeting.

LOVELL: If I agree to meet, it's to
talk, not get married.

CALLER: Once is all it takes, baby.
Bang. The rest of your life will

start. But guess who'll still be there at the center of everything you do. Weren't you going to hang out at the bar tonight?

LOVELL: Is that where you want to meet?

CALLER: Yeah, your turf.

Terence estimated he sat in his empty living room another hour or so, as twilight darkened the windows, holding the elegant cigarette-lighter lookalike gun; and when he tested the trigger once, he half expected to see a little flame pop from the end.

AMEENA MEER

from

Bombay Talkie

SABAH IS WALKING down the street in San Francisco in a miniskirt and guys are yelling out of trucks, making kissing noises or honking. "You look so sweet, baby, so sweet."

She watches her reflection in the shop windows as she passes them. Office equipment store: she can see her face, straight nose (a little wide, but cute and kittenish), shiny brown hair framing the smooth honey-colored skin in not-unflattering waves. She smiles and adjusts her sunglasses. Restaurant furniture: she can see her torso, the jacket looks OK. Pizza parlor: she can only see below the waist because of the counter. She pulls her skirt down, half an inch closer to her knees, and smiles, she knows she has strong legs. Five feet, four inches, of which half are legs, good proportions, she thinks. She's lucky. "Don't pull it down, baby. It looks great." She has to get a mirror. How can a girl live without a full-length mirror?

The dress is a caramel brown, almost the same color as her skin, and she loves the effect. From a distance, it looks as if she's wearing nothing underneath the jacket. It's exciting. Not quite walking down the street in the nude, nothing obviously improper, but—not a business suit, anyway.

She's irritated by all the men yelling at her. It's not for you, she thinks. You think I give a damn whether or not you like it? One of these days, a scorching summer day, when all the men on the street are walking around half-naked, jeans slipping down their waists so she can see the tops of their fat behinds, sweat dripping down their pimply backs, one of these days, she's going to start screaming, screaming insults and obscenities, until even their rough faces turn red with embarrassment. That hot wave of anger, the rage will make her brave enough to do it.

Not today, today it's not worth the effort. She's late for her American Drama class, as usual. On a good day, the shouting doesn't bother her too much, sometimes it even makes her feel good, beautiful, sexy. On a bad day, she wants to wear a burkha. Or carry a machine gun.

One freezing-cold day last winter, she walked out of the door and a guy started hassling her, "Nice legs, woman. Real nice. Come back here and—"

"And what?" Sabah spun around. "What do you want? OK. OK. Drop your pants. Drop 'em now because I don't have much time." All the men outside the building got quiet. The guy talking behind her, she wasn't even sure which one of them it was, didn't say a word. They stared at her.

"It wasn't me," said one of them. They all crowded together.

"It was him," said another one, wiping his eyes on a dirty sleeve. "Sorry."

"Hey, don't pay him no mind, lady."

"Yeah, he don't mean no harm." They all started laughing, and jostling each other.

That was the bravest she'd ever managed to be. She was puffed up with the pride of it all day. She started to tell her mother, on the telephone, but midsentence, she swallowed her words. She knew the response would be sharp, "If you go around looking cheap and accenting your body, you're just inviting all sorts of disgusting behavior."

She could almost hear her mother saying, "Don't you want to get married and live a normal life? I hear Rani's so happy." Rani was her mother's best friend's daughter, once Sabah's best friend, now living in India in nuptial bliss. Sabah's mother promised to send Sabah the wedding pictures.

"Sun treatin' you good today? Mm, like that dress. I like that dress."

Sabah readjusts her bag. She listens to the person behind her and something sounds strange. The footsteps are hard and uneven. Ignore it, she thinks.

"What's wrong? I asked you a question, lady. Don't want to answer me?"

Sabah walks a little faster, but not so fast that he thinks she's running. Calm, stay cool, she tells herself. She can hear his breath between his words and it sounds hoarse and quick.

"Look like you need to learn some manners. Look like I'm going to have to teach you some manners."

Sabah concentrates on her back. Her back is straight and strong. He is talking to her back. She tries to keep walking smoothly, nonchalantly. Even though every nerve in her body feels focused on his breath, his footsteps, she can distract herself. Nothing's happening, she reminds herself. I'm strong. She tries to make every step speak of strength and confidence.

"I'm going to have to take you home and tie you to the bed."

She's panicking now, a wild, nervous clawing in her stomach. She swallows. Down, she tells herself, stay down. She's got it under control. She wonders if she should go into a shop. Her heart is beating like a rabbit's.

"I'll tie you up and then spank your little ass, your tight little ass. You'd like that, wouldn't you?"

There is a crowd around some street musicians. Sabah ducks into the crowd. She stands there for a second, hiding behind a long-haired neohippie with a rainbow backpack, breathing hard. The muscles in her neck twitch. Her eyes dart around the crowd, trying to pick out the body that belonged to the voice. She sees a thick shoulder, a wiry arm in an old T-shirt, the side of an acne-scarred face between a group of students. A bus is pulling up across the street. She'll be later than if she walks, the way buses move in traffic. The scarred face turns toward her. She runs across the street and jumps onto the bus. She gets off in two stops, still trembling. Her breakfast is climbing up her throat. She tries to think about the play they're doing today.

She passes a group of Indians or Pakistanis at the corner. They leer at her and elbow each other as she walks by. Farther down the road, there's a group of their women, in salwar kameezes, their heads covered with scarves. Sabah cringes as they turn to look at her. She's embarrassed. They stare with a mixture of disapproval and discomfort. She knows them too well. She feels like the paper doll who's had the wrong outfit put over her body. The face peeking out is the same as the young Pakistani girl. Sabah can almost hear the mother as she walks by, pulling her daughter close and threatening, "If I ever see you dressed like that—"

What the hell is wrong with her? She can never get it out of her head. Why should she be ashamed of wearing a dress? Why should she feel different from any other American girl?

She walks into the cafe to get an iced cappuccino before class. The Bengali waiters all crowd up to the counter to look at her, their eyes caressing her long hair like their fingers itch to, dancing instead across the counter toward the paper cups. "Are you Italian?" a waiter asks.

"No, Indian," she says.

"That is what I thought," he smiles. "I am from Bangladesh."

Two Asian men watch her as she crosses the street. "Did you see that girl?" one says in Hindi.

"Hey," shouts the other, "Miss America!"

LESLÉA NEWMAN

Women's Rites

"C'MON, JOCELYN. GET WET." Andrea clasps her hands at the surface of the pool and squeezes her palms together, causing a spray of water to smack her best friend's thigh.

"Cut it out, Andrea. You're worse than the boys." Jocelyn, who is perched at the ledge of the shallow end, slaps at the water with a painted toenail. "I don't want to get my hair wet," she says, tossing the coif it has taken her all morning to comb, brush, wash, dry, set and spray.

"Okay, okay." Andrea throws her braid over her shoulder and dog paddles to the deep end where Tommy Battista and his buddies are romping in the chlorine like puppies. She joins them for a rousing game of monkey-in-the-middle, while Jocelyn slides the straps of her two piece down her sweaty shoulders to avoid a dreaded tan line. She leans back on her elbows, lifting her face to the sun, and as if that's some kind of signal, all the boys swim toward Jocelyn, splashing and yelling, pulling on her legs and finally dragging her into the water. Jocelyn screams like she's supposed to; half annoyed and half pleased. "You guys! My hair!" She scrambles out of the pool and grabs a towel. Andrea gets out too, shaking her wet braid at Jocelyn. She laughs at Jocelyn's little shriek, but no one else does. All the boys are staring up at Andrea from the ledge of the pool, which is odd, as they are usually much more interested in Jocelyn.

What gives, Andrea wants to ask, but something in their faces stops her. Finally Tommy Battista speaks. "Kind of nippy out today, huh Andrea?" he asks with a grin.

"What?" Andrea is puzzled. It's at least ninety degrees. She looks at Jocelyn, whose face is all crumpled together in an expression of sheer horror.

"Andrea." Jocelyn puts her arm across her friend's shoulders and turns around so both their backs are toward the boys. "You can see right through your bathing suit," she whispers. *"Everything.* You're supposed to put band-aids over them." She points to her own flat chest. "See?" But Andrea doesn't see a thing. She grabs her towel and races home, leaving her flip-flops behind, not even noticing the hot tar of the road is burning her feet. She dashes up the steps into the bathroom, and shuts the door to study herself in the full length mirror behind it.

It's absolutely true. There, under her brand new, canary-yellow, wet one piece for all the world to see, are her two erect-from-the-cold-water nipples, prominent as two Hershey's kisses atop a golden sponge cake. Andrea stares at her reflection. The two eyes of her nipples stare back. What is she going to do? Andrea wants to die, but she doesn't die. Instead she goes downstairs to show her mother, who decides they will go bra shopping that very afternoon.

"But Ma, I don't need a bra," Andrea tries to protest. "I just need a different bathing suit."

"We'll get you a new suit," Mrs. Greene replies. "But it's time for you to start dressing like a young lady."

"Ma-a," Andrea whines. "Me and the guys were gonna play running bases this afternoon."

"And acting like a young lady," Mrs. Greene continues. "Like your friend, Jocelyn. How come I haven't seen her around for a while? You two have a fight?"

"No." Andrea shakes her head. "Ma, Jocelyn is getting so boring lately. All she ever wants to do is paint her nails and set her hair."

"What's so terrible about that?" Mrs. Greene asks. "Come on, I'll take you out for a sundae after."

"Okay." Andrea gives in, for after today's poolside adventure, she's not terribly anxious to meet up with the boys so soon again anyway.

They drive to the mall, park and head for Macy's, with Andrea lagging behind, pretending great interest in the back-to-school displays, the shoe stores, the record shop, anything to keep a respectable distance between her and her mother, so no one would know she was actually out on a Saturday afternoon with one of her parental units.

Mrs. Greene waits for her daughter at the entrance to Macy's. "We'll start with a training bra," she says.

Training for what, Andrea wants to know, but she doesn't ask. They find the lingerie department and Andrea's mother starts sorting through bins of pastel colored brassieres.

"What's lingerie?" Andrea asks, pronouncing the word with a hard G.

"Lin-ger-ie." Mrs. Greene corrects her. "It means women's underwear."

"Then why don't they just call it the underwear department?" Andrea asks.

"Because," her mother fishes out a pink bra trimmed with lace, "boys wear underwear. Girls wear panties."

"Then why don't they call it the panties department?"

Mrs. Greene pauses, up to her elbows in yellow, white, pink, peach and pale blue polyester. "Andrea, please."

A saleswoman approaches them with a tape measure draped around her neck like a snake. "Can I be of some assistance?" she asks.

"My daughter is here to buy her first bra," Mrs. Greene says. Andrea winces with embarrassment, but her mother sounds pleased, proud even, as if Andrea has done something remarkable.

"Isn't that wonderful?" the saleswoman says, and before Andrea can ask her what's so wonderful about it, she whips the tape measure off her neck and around Andrea's back and across her chest like a lasso. Andrea is very conscious of the slight pressure of the plastic strip against her nipples. "Thirty-two." The saleswoman beams at Andrea's mother as though they are old friends. "Those are over here." She hands Mrs. Greene several bras and leads them to the dressing room.

"I'll come in with you," Mrs. Greene says to her daughter.

"Ma, please." Andrea takes the bras and steps inside a mirrored cubicle, pulling a heavy beige curtain between her mother and herself. Andrea takes off her T-shirt, puts her arms through the straps of the bra, hoists it onto her shoulders and pulls the cups down over her barely budding breasts. Now for the tricky part: hooking the back. Andrea reaches behind herself and tries for several minutes, her arms flapping up and down like two use-less wings.

"How is it?" her mother asks from behind the curtain. "Do you need some help?"

"Just wait a minute," Andrea snaps. She takes the bra off and studies it. Then some ancient, genetic female wisdom springs forth from her body to teach her what women have known forever: how to hook the bra at her waist, swivel it around to the back, put her arms through the straps and pull it onto her shoulders.

"Can I come in?" Without waiting for an answer, Mrs. Greene sweeps open the curtain with one arm, like a stage hand in an old musical. She stops and studies her daughter in the three-way, full length mirror. "Let me see," she says, pulling on Andrea's arms which are crossed in front of her chest.

Slowly Andrea unfolds her arms and drops them to her sides. She stares at her own reflection and at her mother's face floating in the mirror above it. Mrs. Greene looks stunned, then pleased, and then for a quick instant, terribly sad. For a minute Andrea is afraid she's done something wrong, but before she can ask what, Mrs. Greene turns from the mirror and busies herself with the bra, first loosening the straps, then tightening them again. "There," she says, stepping back as though she has just created a masterpiece. "How does that feel?"

"Fine," Andrea lies, for the truth is the elastic band underneath the cups is cutting into her rib cage and the side seams are digging a trench into her flesh.

"Do you want to try the other ones on?" Mrs. Greene asks.

"No, let's just take this." Andrea gets dressed while her mother pays for the bra and two others just like it. They leave the store and walk back through the mall side by side.

"Let's go to Friendly's," Mrs. Greene says, gesturing with the Macy's bag.

"No thanks," Andrea mumbles.

"Are you sure?" Mrs. Greene slows down in front of the ice cream shop. "It's a special day. Don't you want to celebrate?"

Andrea frowns at her mother. "C'mon Ma, let's just go home. I'm not in the mood."

"All right." Mrs. Greene drives home and Andrea takes the Macy's bag upstairs to her room where she cuts the price tags off all the brassieres. Then she puts on one of the bras and slides her favorite light blue tank top over it. It doesn't look any different except her bra strap shows. Andrea moves the strap over to the corner where her arm and shoulder meet, but it soon slides down the smooth flesh of her upper arm. There must be a trick to this, Andrea thinks, and then she remembers seeing Jocelyn pinning her bra straps to the strap of her sundress in the locker room after gym. Andrea goes into her mother's closet where she keeps her sewing box. Two safety pins do the trick all right, but now the silver metal of the pins show. She takes the elastic off the bottom of her braid and combs her hair out over her shoulders with her fingers. There. Now everything is covered.

Andrea stares at herself in the mirror, turning this way and that. She arches her back, places her hands on her hips and puckers up her mouth into a kiss, just as she has seen Jocelyn do. Andrea doesn't recognize the person in the mirror. She doesn't look like someone Andrea would ever want to meet, let alone be. But at the same time, it is hard to turn away from her.

"Andrea, supper," Mrs. Greene calls from downstairs. Andrea snaps out of her daze and changes back into her T-shirt. She opens the top drawer of her dresser where she keeps her underwear and undershirts and puts her new bras away. What should I do with my undershirts now, Andrea wonders. She takes them out of the drawer and sits on the edge of her bed, refolding them one by one. They are clean, fresh-smelling and soft. Andrea lifts the pile onto her lap and strokes the white fabric like some sort of beloved family pet. Her hand moves back and forth over the cool cotton, lulling her, almost hypnotizing her. Then she begins to cry very, very quietly, without knowing why.

FAE MYENNE NG

from

Bone

Aꜰᴛᴇʀ Oɴᴀ ᴅɪᴇᴅ, Leon and Mah acted as if all they heard were their own hearts howling. I felt lost between his noisy loneliness and her endless lament. And I knew Mason wasn't liking that I was staying on Salmon Alley and only visiting him on weekends.

Nina came through for me. She was already living in New York, working as a flight attendant, and she offered to take Mah to Hong Kong. She thought that Leon and Mah just needed a break from each other. It was Mah's first trip back. When she left Hong Kong, everyone called her lucky; to live in America was to have a future.

Secretly I was glad I didn't have to go. I felt for Mah; I felt her shame and regret, to go back for solace and comfort, instead of offering banquets and stories of the good life. Twenty-five years in the land of gold and good fortune, and then she returned to tell her story: the years spent in sweatshops, the prince of the Golden Mountain turned into a toad, and three daughters: one unmarried, another who-cares-where, one dead. I could hear the hushed tone of their questions: "Why? What happened? Too sad!"

The generational contact was a comfort to Mah, and Nina even met a Chinese guy who offered her a job as a tour guide. So they should have come back relieved and renewed. But I don't know what got into Nina, why she had to tell them about the abortion she'd had. I didn't see what good it would do, telling, but Nina did.

Mah and Leon joined forces and ganged up on her, said awful things, made her feel like she was a disgrace. Nina was rotten, doomed, no-good. Good as dead. She'd die in a gutter without rice in her belly, and her spirit—

if she had one—wouldn't be fed. They forecast bad days in this life and the next. They used a word that sounded like *dyeen*. I still can't find an exact translation, but in my mind it's come to mean something lowly, despised.

"I have no eyes for you," Mah said.

"Don't call us," Leon said.

I knew they were using Nina to vent their own frustration and anger about Ona's suicide. I still wonder if there wasn't another way. Everything about that time was steamy and angry. There didn't seem to be any answers.

Of course they hit on me, too: I was the eldest; they thought I was responsible. "You should have known. You should have said something, done something." What could I have said? Don't sleep with him? Find a Chinese guy at least? Like with Ona, I figured it was her own choice.

That's what this trip is about. I want another kind of relationship with Nina. I want an intimacy with her I hadn't had with Ona the last few years.

Nina and I are half-sisters. I have another father and almost eight years over her, but it's not time that separates us, it's temperament. I could endure; I could shut my heart and let Mah and Leon rant. Nina couldn't. She yelled back. She said things. She left.

Being alone and so far away wasn't easy on Nina. She finally quit because flying made her feel like Leon. "Now I understood why he was so out of it. He was always pushing through another time zone."

Nina didn't want to come back to San Francisco. She took a job taking tours to China even though she'd never been to China.

The day Mason and I flew to Kennedy, Nina had just returned from a tour along the Yangtze. Mason knew I had family stuff to talk to her about so he want to Brooklyn to see some guys he knew from mechanic school. Nina was still on China time and she wanted to eat early.

When I suggested Chinatown, Nina said it was too depressing. "The food's good," she said, "but the life's hard down there. I always feel like I should rush through a rice plate and then rush home to sew culottes or assemble radio parts or something."

I agreed. At Chinatown places, you can only talk about the bare issues. In American restaurants, the atmosphere helps me forget. For my reunion with Nina, I wanted nice light, handsome waiters, service. I wanted to forget about Mah and Leon.

"I don't want to eat guilt," Nina said. "Let's splurge. My treat. I made great tips this trip. Besides, I've had Chinese food for twenty-seven days."

We were early and the restaurant wasn't crowded. Our waiter was Spanish and he had that dark island tone Nina likes. I noticed him looking

Nina up and down as we walked in. Nina saw, I'm sure, but it didn't bother her. I watched her hold his look while she ordered two Johnnie Walkers. When he strutted off, she said, "Cute."

"Tight ass."

"The best."

The place was called The Santa Fe and it was done in peach and cactus green. I looked down at the black plates on the pale tablecloth and thought, Ink. I felt strange. I didn't know this tablecloth, this linen, these candles. Everything seemed foreign. It felt like we should be different people. But each time I looked up, she was the same. I knew her. She was my sister. We'd sat with chopsticks, mismatched bowls, braids, and braces, across the Formica tabletop.

Nina picked up her fork and pressed her thumb against the sharp points. "I like three-pronged forks," she said. "It's funny, but you know I hardly ever use chopsticks anymore. At home I eat my rice on a plate, with a fork. I only used chopsticks to hold my hair up." She laughed, tossed her head back. It was Leon's laugh. "Now I have no use for them at all."

I couldn't help it; I rolled my eyes. Who did she think she was talking to, some rich matron lady cruising the Yangtze?

No more braids. In Hong Kong this last trip, she'd cut her hair very short and it showed off her finely shaped head.

I asked if she remembered when Leon gave her a boy's haircut.

Nina looked worried and she touched her head lightly. "Do I look like that, now?"

"No, you look great."

Her hair used to fall down wild to her waist. Nina had Mah's hair: thick and dark and coarse, hair that braids like rope. Now Nina was all features, a brush of brow, long eyes, a slender neck. She looked more vulnerable.

Nina is reed thin and tall. She has a body that clothes look good on. Nina slips something on and it wraps her like skin. Fabric has pulse on her.

In high school, Chinese guys who liked Nina but were afraid to ask her out spread a rumor that she only went out with white guys. When Nina heard about it, she found out which guys and went up to each one of them and told them off.

Nina talked about China, how strange it felt to see only Chinese people. She liked Zhang, the national guide assigned to her group. He spoke Spanish. She was lucky, she said. Zhang was usually assigned to the European tours. She was the first overseas Chinese he'd met. He showed her around Canton; he knew it well; he'd been there during the Cultural Revolution. She was impressed when he brought out his guitar and played Spanish flamenco for the variety show. Nina said, "I like Zhang. He's different."

Everything struck me as strange: Nina saying Guangzhou, Shanghai, Xian, and Chengdu in the northern dialect, Nina in China, Nina with a Chinese guy.

I thought about our different worlds now: Nina had a whole map of China in her head; I had Chinatown, the Mission, the Tenderloin.

Going to China had helped Nina make up with Mah and Leon. When Nina passed through SFO to pick up passengers on her first China trip, Mah and Leon had been too excited to hold on to the grudge. They wanted to go to the airport and see Nina as she changed planes. Mah and Leon and Nina had a reconciliation walking from Domestic to International.

"Are you thinking of marrying this Zhang guy to get him out?" I asked.

Nina said she wasn't stupid and then she turned the question on me, "So, what's your problem with marrying?"

I shrugged. "The banquets. I always hated them."

Nina agreed. "All those people."

We remembered feeling out of place at the huge Leong banquets. Leon and Mah, Ona, Nina, and I, we counted five, one hand, but seated around the banquet table, we barely made a half-circle. We looked for the cute guys, hoping one would be assigned to our table, but we always got the strays: an out-of-town relative, an old man, a white person.

I looked around the restaurant. The waiters were lighting candles. Our waiter brought the drinks. He stopped very close to Nina, seemed to breathe her in. When Nina turned her face toward him I saw the reddish highlights in her hair. We ordered, and the waiter moved off into the dark again.

My scotch tasted good. It reminded me of Leon, Johnnie Walker, or Seagram's 7, that's what they served at Chinese banquets. Nine courses and a bottle. Leon taught us how to drink it from the teacups, without ice. He drank his from a rice bowl, sipping it like hot soup. But by the end of the meal he took it like cool tea, in bold mouthfuls. Nina, Ona, and I, we sat watching, our teacups of scotch in our laps, his three giggly girls.

Relaxed, I thought there was a connection. Johnnie Walker then and Johnnie Walker now. I twirled the glass to make the ice tinkle.

We clinked glasses. Three times for good luck. I relaxed, felt better.

"What's going on with you and Mason?"

"He wants to get married."

"Isn't it about time?"

"I guess so." I wasn't in the mood to talk about it yet. "Here's to Johnnie Walker in shark's fin soup," I said.

"And squab dinners."

"*I Love Lucy.*" I raised my glass, and said again, "To *I Love Lucy,* squab dinners, and brown bags."

"To bones."

"Bones," I repeated. This was a funny that got sad, and knowing it, I kept laughing. I was surprised how much memory there was in one word. Pigeons. Only recently did I learn that the name for them was squab. Our name for them was pigeon—on a plate or flying over Portsmouth Square. A good meal at forty cents a bird. In line by dawn, we waited at the butcher's, listening for the slow, churning motor of the trucks. We watched the live fish flushing out of the tanks into the garbage pails. We smelled the honey-brushed *cha-sui* buns. And when the white laundry truck turned into Wentworth Alley with its puffing trail of feathers, a stench of chicken waste and rotting food filled the alley. Old ladies squeezed in around the truck, reaching into the crates to tug out the plumpest pigeons.

Nina, Ona, and I picked the white ones, those with the most expressive eyes. Dove birds, we called them. We fed them leftover rice in water, and as long as they stayed plump, they were our pets, our baby dove birds.

But then one day we'd come home from school and find them cooked. Mah said they were special, a nutritious treat. She filled our bowls high with little pigeon parts: legs, breasts, and wings. She let us take our dinners out to the front room to watch *I Love Lucy*. Mah opened up a brown bag for the bones. We leaned forward, balanced our bowls on our laps, and crossed our chopsticks in midair and laughed at Lucy. We called out, "Mah! Mah! Come watch! Watch Lucy cry!"

But Mah always sat alone in the kitchen sucking out the sweetness of the lesser parts: the neck, the back, and the head. "Bones are sweeter than you know," she always said. She came out to check the bag. "Clean bones." She shook it. "No waste."

Our dinners came with a warning: "Don't touch. Enjoy." The waiter smiled at Nina but she kept her head down.

I couldn't remember how to say "scallops" in Chinese. Nina shrugged; she didn't know either.

She asked, "What's going on with them? Are they getting along?"

Nina knew I was thinking about Mah and Leon. It's true what Leon says, Nina has radar that way. But I could tell Nina had to work herself up to even mention them, so it's also true what Mah says, that Nina wants the family to be the last thing on her mind. But I didn't hold back, I told her I'd come to New York to get away from their bickering.

"The lights," I said. "At the store. Leon left the job half done. Mah was working in the dark. She called him a useless thing, a stinking corpse. And Leon had an answer. You know that fortune teller's voice he uses when he's on the edge, like he's giving warning? Well, he swore to jump from the Golden Gate, told her not to bother with burying him because even when dead he wouldn't be far enough away. And then he used that stupid thousand-year-old curse of his, you know that one, something about damning the good will that blinded him into taking her as his wife."

Nina speared a scallop and put it on my plate. "Eat," she said. She speared another and ate.

My eyes narrowed; I gave her a serious Big Sister look. "You know what the Baby Store is for Mah . . ."

Something about Nina's expression made me stop: how her eyes flinched, sudden, and how her lips made a contorting line, as if she tasted something bitter.

For a moment, I wanted to force it on her: He's your father.

She couldn't even look at me. She didn't want to hear it. She said I was always telling stories the way she couldn't stand to hear. She thought I had the peace of heart, knowing I'd done my share for Mah and Leon. And I thought she had the courage of heart, doing what she wanted.

I thought about how we were sisters. We ate slowly, chewing like old people; it was a way to fool the stomach, our way of making things last. I speared one of my prawns and put it on her plate. "Try," I said.

The waiter came and asked if everything was all right.

"Everything," Nina said.

I watched him watch Nina. Another time, he might've been lucky. He was definitely her type, a Fa-fa prince, a flower picker, like my father.

She looked up, smiled. The light from the candle made her eyes shimmer. Nina had Mah's eyes. Eyes that made you want to talk.

"I just don't want it," I said.

"Want what?" Nina asked.

"The banquet and stuff."

"You don't have to."

"Mah wants it."

"So?"

"So what am I supposed to say? Mah wants one. She has obligations."

"What are you talking about?"

I put my fork down. "Everybody's always inviting her to their banquets, and she's never had the occasion to invite back."

Nina's voice got harder. "Now you're thinking like her."

"Like what?"

"Do it the way you want."

"It's not that easy."

We didn't say anything for a while. We chewed.

Finally Nina said, "Yes, it is."

I couldn't think of anything to say. I'd already had this argument with Mason too many times. I wanted to say it was easy for her to talk, being three thousand miles away.

But Nina's voice went soft. "Look, you've always been on standby for them. Waiting and doing things their way. Think about it, they have no idea what our lives are about. They don't want to come into our worlds. We keep on having to live in their world. They won't move one bit."

She looked straight at me. "I know about it, too. I helped fill out those forms at the Chinatown employment agencies; I went to the Seaman's Union, too; I listened and hoped for those calls: 'Busboy! Presser! Prep man!' And I know about *should*. I know about *have to*. We should. We want to do more, we want to do everything. But I've learned this: I *can't*."

"Listen." Nina leaned forward. "Marry Mason here. Marry Mason now."

The waiter came by to ask about dessert. Nina shook her head, said she knew a better place.

Nina was right. Mah's and Leon's lives were always on high fire. They both worked too hard; it was as if their marriage was a marriage of toil—of toiling together. The idea was that the next generation would marry for love.

The old way. Matches were made, strangers were wedded, and that was fate. Marriage was for survival. Men were scarce: dead from the wars, or working abroad as sojourners. As such, my father, Lyman Fu, was considered a prince. Mah married my father to escape the war-torn villages, and when he ran off on her, she married Leon to be saved from disgrace.

Saved to work. Mah sat down at her Singer with the dinner rice still in her mouth. When we pulled down the Murphy bed, she was still there, sewing. The hot lamp made all the stitches blur together; the street noises stopped long before she did. And in the morning, long before any of us awoke, she was already there, at work.

Leon worked hard, too. Out at sea, on the ships, Leon worked every room: Engine, Deck, and Navigation. He ran the L. L. Grocery while holding down a night job as a welder at the Bethlehem Steel yard. He talked about a Chinese takeout, a noodle factory, many ideas. Going into the partnership with Luciano, Ong was the first real thing that looked promising, but then it went dangerously the other way.

We remembered how good Mah was to him. How else would we have known him all those years he worked on the ships? Mah always gave him majestic welcomes home, and it was her excitement that made us remember him.

I know Leon, how ugly his words could become. I've heard him. I've listened. And I've always wished for the street noises, as if in the traffic of sound I could escape. I know the hard color of his eyes and the tightness in his jaw. I can almost hear his teeth grind. I know this. Years of it.

Their lives weren't easy. So is their discontent without reason?

What about the first one? You didn't even think to come to the hospital. The first one, I say! Son or daughter, dead or alive, you didn't even come!

What about living or dying? Which did you want for me that time you pushed me back to work before my back brace was off?

Money! Money!! Money to eat with, to buy clothes with, to pass this life with!

Don't start that again! Everything I make at that dead place I hand . . .

How come . . .
What about . . .
So . . .

How many times have Nina, Ona, and I held them apart? The flat *ting!* sound as the blade slapped onto the linoleum floor, the wooden handle of the knife slamming into the corner. Which one of us screamed, repeating all their ugliest words? Who shook them? Who made them stop?

It was obvious. The stories themselves meant little. It was how hot and furious they could become.

Is there no end to it? What makes their ugliness so alive, so thick and impossible to let go of?

We're lucky, not like the bondmaids growing up in service, or the newborn daughters whose mouths were stuffed with ashes. The beardless, soft-shouldered eunuchs, the courtesans with the three-inch feet and the frightened child brides—they're all stories to us. Nina, Ona, and I, we're the lucky generation. Mah and Leon forced themselves to live through the humiliation in this country so that we could have it better. We know so little of the old country. We repeat the names of grandfathers and uncles, but they have always been strangers to us. Family exists only because somebody has a story, and knowing the story connects us to a history. To us, the deformed man is oddly compelling, the forgotten man is a good story, and a beautiful woman suffers.

The waiter stood there, the dark plates balanced on his arm.
"You two Chinese?" he asked.
"No." I let my irritation fill the word. "We're two sisters."
Mason and I only paid five dollars to get married at City Hall. The dark-suited man who married us had the distracted expression of a sweatshop presser. We had just enough time to say I do.

The day was overcast. It was late enough in the afternoon to think about dinner and we decided on Chinatown because it was close enough to walk to. We walked past food carts and I saw the vendors frying dumplings, flipping tofu squares. I liked the urgent, time-pressed feeling on wide Canal Street, the honking cabs, the line of trucks moving like thick ink toward the Manhattan Bridge. Shoppers and sightseers. No strollers, everyone was in a hurry.

We stopped to watch a man pulling threadlike strands between his outstretched hands. Nina said he was counting to a thousand.

"Dragon whiskers," she said. "Candy. A Hong Kong treat."

We bought three. The fine-combed squares melted in our mouths. Sweet. Sticky. A sesame taste.

Nina said she felt rain coming on.

"Great. Rain means good luck."

BETH NUGENT

Locusts

THE CAR IS LONG AND BLACK, with fake wooden sides that are peeling away from the body in thin metallic strips. It honks even before it stops in front of our house, but my parents pay no attention.

The car continues to honk, and finally my mother lifts her head from her book.

—Jesus, she says, then walks to the bathroom and locks the door behind her. My father rises from his chair, dragging his eyes away from the baseball game on the television.

—Helen, he says sharply to her, then notices me by the window. He smiles grimly and wipes his hands across the front of his shirt.

Francine launches herself from the car first; she is splendid in hot pink, blue designer jeans, and breasts, which are clearly distinguishable from the soft bulk of her back and shoulders and stomach. They are a new addition since her last visit here two summers ago when she and I lay on the hot pavement at the pool spreading our hands flat across our chests, searching for even the slightest swelling in the flat bony shapes of our bodies.

This summer we will not go to the pool, since I am still recovering from an unusually severe and inexplicably contracted bout of hepatitis that kept me out of school for the first half of the year. I know that Francine will be uneasy about my hepatitis; she will wonder where I got it and how, but she will decide immediately, looking me over, that its origin could not have been in anything sexual. For the first few nights, I know she will lie awake in the bed across from mine and listen to my breathing, trying to detect germs issuing from my mouth in a thin stream, heading relentlessly toward her. There will be some satisfaction for me in Francine's first few sleepless nights.

Aunt Louise and Uncle Woody follow Francine up the walk, Aunt Louise looking vaguely displeased with the sky and the street and the air, Uncle

Woody rubbing his thick palms together as he comes up the path to the door.

Francine drops her little square night case on the floor and looks me over, then looks outside. —What's that noise? she asks.

—Locusts, I tell her. —Seventeen-year locusts.

The locusts have been here since the beginning of summer; quietly breathing underground for seventeen years, they have emerged to their few months of life, and they are everywhere, eating. It is only the first of August and already the bare branches of trees are beginning to show through; so far, because of my father's constant spraying, only the grape arbor in the back yard has withstood them, but that will go too, eventually. Every tree and bush is covered with the abandoned shells shed by the locusts; transparent brown and intricately limbed, they are far more frightening than the insects themselves, which are slow and pathetically graceless. They seem capable of little other than eating, and don't even bother to fly away when approached, as though survival is not a concern for them; they simply continue to eat until caught or killed.

At lunch one day, I sat at a table across from a boy who ate his entire meal with a brown paper bag quietly buzzing and shifting at his elbow. Every now and then the boy looked at it with a kind of grim satisfaction, but it was only after he'd wadded the remains of his sandwich and its wrapping into a tight little ball that he opened the bag to show me about twenty locusts, their wings torn off, stumbling over and over each other in helpless dumb confusion.

—These bastards won't be eating any more trees, the boy said. —That's for goddamn sure.

They'll be gone by the end of summer, and by next spring the leaves will come back, the bushes will bloom again, and everything will be as it was before. We'll forget they were ever here, my father says, but I think I will never forget the sound they make. It is an incessant humming, a whirr that goes all the time, day and night, and won't stop until the locusts have eaten all the leaves on all the trees and at last laid their eggs and died.

One night my father put his tape recorder on the windowsill and let it record the locusts until the tape ran out.

—That's crazy, my mother said. —Isn't it bad enough we have to listen to them all the time without having them on tape, too?

My father paid no attention to her; he rewound the tape and played it back. Even though it was only a cheap tinny echo of the sound outside, there was something terrible about hearing it like that. For the first time I realized what it was that we were listening to every minute of every day, with no change in pitch or intensity, and for a few hours I could hear nothing else— not the voices of my parents, not the television or the shouts of children outside, only the fevered drone of the locusts inside my head.

I point out a bush covered with locust shells to Francine; she thinks they are ugly and is afraid of them. I tell her not to be, that when one of them flies into her hair, all she has to do is shake it out gently. She quivers delicately. She is disgusted.

—Helen's in the bathroom, my father is saying to Aunt Louise and Uncle Woody. —A bug.

He ignores Aunt Louise's meaningful look, and begins to manage the luggage with Uncle Woody. They make great show of carrying the suitcases inside and upstairs. Women, they are saying, can't go anywhere without a closetful of clothes. Aunt Louise examines me carefully.

—Well, she says, —you've certainly gotten thin.

—Yes, I answer, —I guess so.

—Are you all over that trouble?

I look at the bathroom door and wonder how long my mother can stay in there. I admire her determination; surely she knows there will be consequences.

I nod to my aunt. —All over it, I tell her.

—Still, she says, —it's a shame you had to miss so much of your first year of school. I suppose you didn't get much chance to meet many boys.

She is right, I didn't, but I don't want to talk about it, and I am trying to think of a lie about a handsome tutor, or a hospital intern, when a little bubble of cruelty rises to her surface.

—Francine has lots of boyfriends, she says. —All the boys at Cross want to take her out.

All the boys at Cross fuck her, I would like to say, although I am sure this is not true. But I can see them, crowded around her, darting quick looks at her breasts, while she sends out gracious, smug smiles to the other girls passing by unnoticed. —Where is Francine? I ask.

—In the kitchen. She's hungry. Aunt Louise looks fondly toward the kitchen door. —It was a long drive.

My uncle and my father come downstairs, dusting off their hands. My uncle looks me over while my father stands tentatively in front of the bathroom door, smiling weakly.

—Well, my uncle says, —aren't *you* becoming a little lady here. How old are you now, Susie?

—Almost sixteen.

—Sixteen, he says. —Sweet sixteen. I bet you have a lot of boyfriends.

—No, Uncle Woody, I say, —not yet.

—Oh, he says. —Not yet. Well. He leans forward, with a little smile. —I bet you'd like one, he says. —Wouldn't you? A nice little boyfriend to bring you candy? And take you out in his car?

—Woody, my aunt says.

—Well, he says, —I brought you some candy.

He holds out a bag of candy corns, already opened. He has brought them ever since I snuck into the Halloween candy when I was six or seven; I ate two bags of candy corns and was too sick to go out trick-or-treating the next night. Uncle Woody thinks it is a very funny story. He always brings the candy, but each time he presents it to me as though it is the first time.

I take the candy from him and put it on the table. When I turn back, he is looking at my legs, my knees.

—Woody, my father says, —I want to show you the grape arbor. Maybe you can figure out some way to stop these damn locusts. They're eating everything in sight.

Francine emerges from the kitchen with a strawberry yogurt in one hand and several cookies in the other. A spoon sticks up out of her back pocket.

—Let's go up, she says to me.

As we walk up the stairs, I hear the bathroom door open and my aunt's voice. —Well, Helen, she says, —how are you feeling?

I stop to listen for the answer, but Francine bumps softly into me from behind. —Come *on*, she says, and we walk slowly up to my room, where she sits on the bed cross-legged and lays her cookies out in a neat row in front of her before she opens her yogurt. She is going to tell me about her boyfriends, about the football games and pep rallies, about cruising McDonald's with her friends, about the parties. I cannot hear this, and concentrate instead on the tight painful folds of flesh and denim that blossom when she crosses her legs. So where does everybody hang out? she will want to know. What does everyone *do* around here? she is going to ask me. We will spend a long afternoon, at the end of which she will say, So what are we going to do tonight? There is a carnival just outside town, in the parking lot of the mall; I have driven past it with my father once or twice, and I offer it to Francine.

She looks around my room, which has not changed much since her last visit here, then picks a crumb from her shirt and places it carefully on the tip of her tongue. Boys, her eyes are saying, don't you know any boys? She will want to hang out and find some. She slides her spoon back and forth across her lips and assumes a look of boredom. This is going to be a long summer, she is thinking already.

Like the locusts, they will be here until nearly the end of summer, almost three weeks. When I asked my mother why they were staying so long, she looked up from her book and gazed at me.

—Ask your father, she finally said. —They're his family.

He looked away briefly from the television, just long enough to say, —Helen, then turned back in time to watch the next play.

—Go ahead, she said to me. —Ask him.

My father got up and walked into the kitchen; the icebox door banged open, ice clattered into a glass, and in a few moments my mother put down her book and followed him in. Their voices were just an angry murmur over the ball game, but after a while the back door slammed and the car started. When my mother came back into the living room, she seemed surprised to see me there.

—Susan, she said, —it's late. Why don't you go to bed?

I woke up later to hear voices outside, from the back yard. When I went to the window, I saw my mother and her best friend, Carol, sitting close together in a pool of light on the patio below me. My mother leaned against Carol, and Carol ran her hands smoothly over my mother's hair. It's all right, she was saying over and over; in the half-light of the moon, all the blue suburban lawns stretched out quietly until they blended into the darker blue of whatever lay beyond us.

I went back to bed, and in the morning we were all pleasant at breakfast; there was no sign of the night before, nothing but a neat circle of cigarette butts pressed onto the white concrete of the patio. Later in the afternoon, I watched my father pick them up and scrub at the dark stains they'd left until there were only a few faint smudges, which would wash away in the next rain.

Francine opens her suitcase and stacks her clothes neatly in the space I have left for her in my dresser; her clothes make a bright square of color next to mine in the drawer. Then she opens her little night case and begins pulling out jars of makeup, lipsticks, combs, all of which she lays out on the top of the dresser, humming to herself as she unpacks, as if I am not here.

For dinner there is corn, mashed potatoes, chicken. Usually we do not eat so formally; my mother serves us from pots on the stove and we carry our plates to the table or into the living room to eat, but tonight all the food is piled in dishes and bowls around the table. My mother's third martini sweats by her hand, a cool spot in the middle of the steaming dishes. My uncle looks at me.

—Susie, he says, —I'll take a breast.

I'm not sitting near the chicken, so I pass him an ear of corn instead.

My mother stares at the chicken thigh on her plate and fingers the stem of her glass; when she asks my father to make her another drink, he rises silently, avoiding the look my aunt shoots him across the table.

Uncle Woody is telling us all about the trash masher he just bought, the convenience, the ecology, the sheer beauty of the thing. Bits of corn cling to his lips, and his chin gleams with grease from the butter. I wonder why no one mentions it, but then realize that only my father and I are listening to him. My mother stares at her plate, or at her glass, or out the window; Francine examines her food carefully as she eats, turning it around and around, searching out the perfect marriage of teeth and bite, while Aunt Louise watches my mother with a kind of narrow-eyed curiosity; every move my mother makes provokes my aunt to turn her head sharply and gaze at her for a few long, obvious moments. Only my father and I pay any attention at all to Uncle Woody, and we are too polite to mention the butter. On this, our first night together, someone—perhaps Uncle Woody, perhaps my mother—has lit candles, and we sit here in the hot flickering dusk, knitted together by light and the sound of Uncle Woody's voice. Over all of us is the hum of the locusts, hanging in the air, resting on us like a benediction. After dinner, my father finds a ball game on TV, and Uncle Woody stays at the table to smoke and watch Francine and me carry the dishes into the kitchen. Though we have plenty of ashtrays, he taps his ashes onto his plate, dropping them into the little puddles of melted butter. Aunt Louise seems to be herding my mother around the kitchen; each time we come in, they are in a different corner, until finally my mother is trapped by the stove. When I bring in the bowl with the mashed potatoes, Aunt Louise takes it from me and sets it in the sink.

—You girls go on now, she says. —Ask your Uncle Woody to drive you to the carnival.

I stand just outside the kitchen door, waiting for Francine to change her clothes and Uncle Woody to finish his cigarette.

—Well, my aunt says, inside the kitchen. —You *look* all right.

A match strikes, then a deep breath. —I'm fine, Louise, my mother says. —We're all fine.

Before Aunt Louise replies, my uncle is standing in front of me.

—Ready for the carnival? he asks. He has wiped the butter from his chin, but his skin still glimmers as he smiles down at me. —You can ride up front with me.

At the carnival, my uncle takes my arm and steers me toward the Ferris wheel. He points up at the top car, swinging crazily as the two boys inside pump it back and forth.

—Now that's a ride, he says. —That's the first one we'll go on.

Francine's eyes shine as she gazes around at the bright thumping neon.

—Look, she says, pointing to a group of girls at a concession stand. —Do you know them?

The girls are about my age and probably go to my school, but I shake my head.

—How about them? she says, gesturing toward several boys tossing baseballs at stuffed cats, and I shake my head again.

—Don't you know anyone? she asks. She looks disappointed, but perks up when she spots a display of giant pink stuffed panda bears, and sets off in their direction. My uncle winks at me, then follows behind her, leaving me alone in the middle of this explosion of light and sound, surrounded by roving clumps of boys and girls I don't know.

We fall quickly, after the first few days, into a sort of routine: Francine's eyes open on a day without love and settle hopelessly on mine. Boys, they say, where are all the boys? Then breakfast, then the day, which we all pass separately. Francine covers herself with a glistening coat of tanning oil and sits on the patio, playing solitaire or reading fashion magazines that are too old for her, full of tips on how to meet more men at work, and what kinds of cosmetic surgery can best improve a problem figure. My father, who is taking his vacation from work now, lies on the couch in front of the television, and Aunt Louise sits beside him, knitting, her needles clicking steadily over the noise of the game; I turn the pages of my books without sound, and my mother wanders in and out of the house, trailing smoke and Uncle Woody, who stops every now and then to offer me a handful of candy corns. After dinner, someone takes Francine and me to the carnival, and at night, although it seems we have hardly done anything during the day, we all fall exhausted into bed. Francine plummets immediately into a heavy, resentful sleep, and I lie awake, listening to her gentle snore. Some time before morning, I wake to hear my uncle creeping along the hall. He stops outside my door and listens. Or he does not. His foam soles do not give him away; his bones, his breathing do not give him away. He pauses and listens, then creeps to another door, listening.

As I watch a squirrel run up a tree, my uncle's big laugh comes right in my ear.

—What is that damn squirrel up to anyway? he asks, and suddenly his huge hand comes down on my shoulder. It is like a cement glove, pressing me into the ground and already I have begun to sweat, which Mother warned me against. While this is not something I remember my doctor mentioning, and I'm not entirely sure it's not something my mother made up, since she herself doesn't care for the heat, all the same, I try to stay out of the sun, and the thin trickle of sweat running down my ribs feels alarming and cold.

—Candy, Susie?

When I look up at him, he smiles. I come only to his chest, and I can hear a slight wheeze as he breathes. He holds out his fist and opens it to show me several candy corns, pressed together into a waxy little lump.

—No thank you, Uncle Woody.

—Oh, he says. —You take them. You're a skinny little thing.

He dislodges a few candy corns from the lump in his hand and drops them into mine, then presses my fingers closed over them; the candies are warm and slick and I drop them on the grass. Uncle Woody laughs, then opens his mouth wide and pops his hand over it, throwing the lump of candy in. He winks at me as he chews, and wanders back to the house, shaking his head. I can see him through the windows, moving from the kitchen to the living room, where my father is already watching the doubleheader between Cincinnati and Chicago.

I am in the bathroom taking inventory. Cheekbones: flat; chin: receding; hair: thin; breasts: the same; appearance: problematic.

I have borrowed a few of Francine's cosmetics, and they are spread out on the sink in front of me when she comes in without knocking, wearing a fluffy pink robe. She looks at the makeup on the sink and I begin to offer some explanation, but she moves past me and turns on the water in the bathtub. From the pocket of her robe she takes a little bottle, which she opens and smells; then she pours some of the liquid under the running water. Bright bubbles burst up immediately in the tub, and she smiles as she turns to me.

—Bath oil, she says. —It makes your skin silky and smooth to the touch.

Who is going to touch you, Francine? I think. She lowers herself into the tub and sighs.

Who? I think, and then I say it: —Who?

—What? she says. She lifts a palmful of bubbles to her face and blows them into the air. —I've got a date tonight, she says.

I am mystified. How could she have a date? There are no boys. I look casually into the mirror.

—Oh? I say. —Who with?

—A boy, she says. —A boy I met at the carnival last night.

Last night, I think, and run over the evening in my mind. She must have met the boy when my uncle and I were on the Ferris wheel, or when my uncle was throwing rubber balls at the clown, or when my uncle was buying me candy.

—Where are you going? I ask.

—We're meeting at the carnival, she says, waving her hand over the tops of the hills of bubbles that surround her breasts. I imagine them high up over the lights of the mall parking lot, swaying in the Ferris wheel's artificial ecstasy, an enormous pink fluff of cotton candy in Francine's arms, the boy's hand under her sweater, holding the soft candy of her breast.

We all stand around the front door as Uncle Woody prepares to drive Francine to the carnival. My aunt reaches out with a Kleenex to blot away a little smear of lipstick from Francine's chin.
—Don't you want to go, too, Susie? my uncle asks. —You don't want to stay in all night with us old folks.
—I don't feel well, I tell him. —I'll just read.
—If you want, he says, —we can go to a movie. Just you and me. Like a regular date. I'll buy you popcorn and we can sit in the back row and watch the smoochers.
—Woody, my aunt says, —Francine's going to be late.
Francine turns at the door and tosses me a smile. —I'll see if he has any friends, she says.
Aunt Louise watches them walk out to the car and my father goes back to the living room. I realize that my mother has not been standing with us; she is in the basement, perhaps, or on the patio. When the car pulls out, Aunt Louise turns happily to me.
—Francine is very popular, she says. —Wherever she goes, she seems to make new friends.
I nod, and try to think of something to say, but she turns her head sharply at the suck of the freezer door opening, and heads off toward the sound of an ice tray cracking.

My father stands by the television, tapping absently against the screen. He is torn: either he can watch the game between L.A. and Cincinnati or he can watch the game between Cleveland and Detroit. He looks out the window at the final stretch of evening sun over the grape arbor and wipes his fingers delicately against the front of his shirt, then selects a few candy corns from the bowl on top of the television, put there by my uncle to lure me to the flickering screen while he waits alertly in the shadows. My father finally chooses his game and sits unhappily to watch it, thinking only of the game he is missing, though before long he will be asleep.
Traveling through the house and into my bedroom, the baseball announcer's voice is reassuring: summer, father, home, it says, and its insistent rise and fall blends with the murmur of the locusts. My father lies on the couch, dozing or dreaming, his drink propped on his chest, while beside

him Aunt Louise runs her hand over some model in *Vogue* or *Cosmopolitan*, thinking: I want this, I want this. My mother and my uncle are gone, pursued or pursuing under the dark trees, and somewhere some boy's narrow palm strolls over Francine, charmed by the give of her skin, the resistance of her nipple. Surprised and delighted, he strokes her in the moonlight somewhere. There is no light here but the blue light of the TV and no sound but the sound my uncle does not make, creeping from door to door, the sound not made by the squeaking of his shoes, the protest of his bones.

I go to bed before Francine returns, and when I wake up later, I don't know if she's back yet, but my uncle's shape is dim in the moonlight that comes through my window, and his heavy bulk causes my bed to creak dangerously. The wooden slats underneath are mismatched, and sometimes they slip from the frame, the mattress collapsing right through to the floor.
—Susie, he says. —Susie. He shakes my shoulder. —Susie, wake up.
I feign drowsy confusion and turn away, but he puts his hand on my forehead, turning my face back to him.
—Susie, he says. —I want to tell you a bedtime story. Which one's your favorite?
He brings his face close to mine and shakes my shoulder again. —Which one? he says. —Which one?
He smells of gin, which is what they all drink, and cigarettes, and something else—a sweet, dark, excited smell. I keep my eyes closed. I cannot remember any story except this one.
—Suuusie, he says, his voice rising and falling as if he is calling me from a long distance, and I open my eyes. He smiles. —I knew you were awake, he says.
—I'm tired, Uncle Woody. I want to go to sleep.
—Let me tell you a story first. Look. I brought you some candy.
He opens his hand above me and scatters candy corns on the sheet over my stomach, my breasts.
—I'm sick, I say. —I have to go to the bathroom.
He lies down beside me, pressing himself into the narrow space between my body and the edge of the bed.
—Once upon a time, he begins, —there was a little girl. He moves the hair gently from my face and sighs happily, his breath wet and heavy.
—I'm sick, I say again, and struggle against the sheets to sit.
—Wait, he whispers, and reaches out. —Wait, and then the bed breaks and I am out of it.

Under the bright lights, against the white tile of the bathroom, this is all a dream. The face that stares back at me in the mirror is dreaming. When I come back to my room, everything is as it was before: the bed is neatly on its frame, the candy gone. This is a dream, and I will forget it by morning. In the moment before I fall back asleep, I realize that I have forgotten to check for Francine, but then I remember that this is a dream.

In the morning, all is as usual, and when my English muffin pops up, my aunt hands me the butter.
—Woody says he scared you last night, she says, turning to put another muffin in the toaster.
I carry the butter to the table with my muffin. —Scared me?
—He said he had too much to drink and came into your room by mistake. She watches me carefully as I spread butter on my muffin.
—Oh, I say. —I wasn't scared.
I sit at the table, by the window; outside, my uncle and my father are walking around the yard, examining the bushes carefully. When he sees me watching them, my Uncle Woody waves cheerily and my father looks around to see what he is waving at. A locust hums suddenly past the window, like a tiny dense bird. Somewhere, I've heard, they eat them, fry them up and eat them, a delicacy, like caviar or oysters. My father and Uncle Woody continue their walk around the yard, occasionally plucking locust shells from the leaves.

—Disgusting, my aunt hisses, —disgusting. Her voice cuts through the night like a line of fire burning all that is in its path, straight to my ears.
—You're a disgusting fool, she says, —and don't you think everyone can't see it.
Francine sleeps, or pretends to, though I can hear my aunt's voice clearly, and does not stir when I get up to go to the bathroom. I walk without sound, counting my breaths with each step.
—Listen to me, she says. —You goddamn fool.
I imagine my uncle, next to her in the bed, his jaw working.
—Listen, she says again, and then there is the slap of her palm against his skin, a hideous hurting sound in the night.
—You listen to me.
He must be awake, his skin stinging, staring into the night, surrounded by nothing but her voice. Someday he will kill her. He will come upon her in the laundry room when she thinks he is watching television, and he will

creep up on her in his foam soles and bury her face in the soft sweet-smelling sheets she piles up against tomorrow. He will bury her face in the sheets and he will bury her body in the garden and then he will come upon me like rain. Candy, Susie, candy, he'll say, and I'll come running.

I put my hands over my ears, but Aunt Louise's voice filters through my fingers like smoke, like light through the leaves.

—Disgusting, she says, —disgusting.

My mother is thirty-six years old today. I was born when she was twenty; she has had me all those years. Since she was twenty, there has been me. In four years I will be twenty. For her birthday today, there will be a small dinner with the family and a few of my parents' friends. Uncle Woody has got several bottles of champagne and a big net to play volleyball, or badminton. Carol comes first, early in the day, to help with the dinner. She brings a small present, wrapped in bright blue paper, and a bouquet of flowers, blazing orange and white, like an armful of fire. As Aunt Louise runs for a vase, Carol gives a small flower to me, and the largest and most beautiful flower she puts behind my mother's ear, a flame in her hair.

—There, she says, —now you look like a birthday girl.

My mother almost smiles as she touches the flower, and Carol looks away to where my father and Francine are struggling to put up the net in the back yard. Aunt Louise returns with the flowers in a vase and looks at the flower in my mother's hair.

—Don't you think you'd better put that one in the water, too? she says, and my mother removes the flower and gives it to her. I tuck mine into my top buttonhole.

—Susan, Carol calls from the window. —Come here. Look.

She points to the leaves of a bush that rests against the glass and shows me a large locust, stuck to the leaf with a gummy liquid that comes from its body. It struggles to free itself, but each time one leg comes loose, the locust must put it back down to work loose the other, and so imprisons itself again.

—That means they're going to die soon, Carol says. She smiles. —I'll sort of miss them. I've gotten used to the racket. Imagine how quiet it will be with them gone. We'll be able to hear ourselves think again.

—Well, Aunt Louise says, —that will be a nice change for all of you. She smiles pleasantly as she carries the vase of flowers into the dining room.

I am standing in front of the kitchen window, chopping for the birthday dinner, cutting up carrots and onions and peppers, which will go into the sauce for the lamb, my mother's favorite. Late-afternoon sun glitters from the knife, and I concentrate on the play of my fingers and the blade, my hand moving steadily back along the spine of a carrot, the knife relentlessly pursuing. Everyone has left the house. Francine and Aunt Louise are picking up the birthday cake; Uncle Woody and my father have gone to buy the portable trash masher that will be the family's gift to my mother; my mother and Carol are in the back yard picking grapes, perhaps the last of the season that the locusts will not eat.

I am wondering if, right now, picking up the cake at the bakery, Francine is making new friends, meeting boys who want to date her, and I look up out of the window to see my mother and Carol standing together under the grape arbor; the leaves are still damp from an early shower and they shine in the bright sun as Carol gropes through them looking for grapes. She plucks one out and holds it up, then drops it into the blue-and-white bowl my mother holds. Something she says makes my mother smile—just for a moment, but before the smile is gone, Carol takes my mother's face in her hands and holds it to her own. My mother's face disappears as I watch them kiss under the damp leaves, the grapes hanging above them like ripe flies. The bowl falls from my mother's arms and lands on its side; grapes tumble out over the grass, and as Carol and my mother move together, a shower of rain from the leaves comes down over their heads. Rings are growing around this moment, this sky, this sun, racing over the damp leaves like tiny bullets of light, dazzling my eyes. Uncle Woody will come upon me now like a storm. The sun fades suddenly, blotted out by a cloud, and I look away, back to the counter. Around my hands vegetables lie like piled-up dead. I am amazed I have not cut myself. When I look back at the grape arbor, Carol and my mother are gone; the bowl is no longer on the ground.

At dinner, a little mound of black grapes sits in the middle of the table; they are like cocoons, breathing inarticulately against the blue-and-white pattern of the bowl. I pass rolls to Uncle Woody, next to me; I hand him the salt, the pepper, and I lift my own glass when he raises his in a toast to my mother, who gazes at the trash masher on the floor by her chair. I smile at whatever it is my uncle is saying in his toast, but I saw them kiss, I think, I saw them kiss under the damp leaves, where the grapes stirred above them like sluggish flies. My uncle's words trail over the grapes and around each curve, warming them; my eyes travel the grapes as if on unknown territory, and I follow the trail of my uncle's sentences as if on a map.

—You're going to love this trash masher, Helen, he is saying.

I try to imagine my mother dropping things into the trash masher, cans, napkins, paper plates, but her face disappears into the wide blue sky, the damp leaves, the fat black grapes.

—Ours has saved me plenty—time, effort, money—and let me tell you, that adds up.

Carol cuts her meat up carefully, and my aunt is watching, wondering: What now? What now?

After we have all finished doing whatever we are going to do with our food, my aunt and Francine bring in the birthday cake, a big white thing with my mother's name spelled artlessly across the top and at least three or four too many candles. Carol and my father struggle to light all the candles before the lit ones drip on the frosting, but they are clumsy and too slow, and little blue puddles of wax spread out over my mother's name.

—Make a wish, someone says, and she closes her eyes, then blows out the two or three candles closest to her. Francine stands up and blows out the rest, her eyes closed dreamily, thinking already of the boy she met in the bakery, or in the parking lot of the store. My uncle's hand hovers over the grapes. Do not touch them, I think; do not disturb this. He stops at the grape where I have let my eyes rest, and touches it, catching my eyes on his hand. When he plucks it from the bowl, he smiles.

—Cat got *your* tongue, Susie? he says.

Like hot ash descending, he will come upon me now. My aunt watches him with cat eyes.

Waking, I hear my uncle creep along the hall. He comes to a stop at my door, or he does not, then creeps on.

In my dream, I am sitting in a ring of chairs in a circle of sunlight in the exact center of a long sloping green lawn. In the middle of the circle of chairs is an orange-and-yellow flower, like a flame in the heart; it matches the smaller flower I wear at my breast, in the folds of my dress. Over everything is the sound of the locusts, the soft beat of wings, and in the distance I can hear the voices of men. Behind me is a dark wood, where my mother and Carol stand under the heavy wet leaves. As they kiss, the leaves move and stir and fly away, leaving the branches bare and empty. I run away from them, and behind me my uncle follows, when suddenly the sky is dark with locusts, flying in a huge cloud. My uncle falls back, calling, Candy, Susie, candy, but his voice is obscured by the hum and whirr of the sky.

When I open my eyes, I hear Francine's even breathing coating the night, sliding across the air. I can hear all the different sounds of the house. Disgusting, it breathes; candy, it breathes; carnival, love. I put my hands over my ears, but I can still hear, as if underwater, Francine's slight moan as she dreams a pair of hands worming up out of the sheets to move over her, to push the hair back from her face softly, to touch her lips.

—Francine, I whisper, —Francine. I cannot listen to her.

In the hall at the top of the stairs, it is too dark to see my own hand. My mother sits down beside me before I know she is there, as if the darkness has muffled all my senses. She lights a cigarette and I watch the smoke rise from her face. She smooths back my hair and wipes away my tears with the corner of her robe. Her arm around me, we rock back and forth on the top step; my face is against her neck and she rocks me as if I have awakened from a bad dream, as if we are all alone in the world.

—Susie, she whispers, —Susie, and her voice is like the locusts, a whisper of sound that lies over everything, that lies over the breathing of the house and quiets it. This is all I ever wanted.

She looks at me and her eyes shine in the light cast by her cigarette. There are so many things she could say.

—I'm thirty-six, she finally says, and shakes her head. —Who ever thought everything would be so awful?

I put my face in her hair; the brown is soft and the gray is wiry, and I can hardly hear my own voice. —You'll always have me, I say.

She pulls away and looks at me a moment, then out into the dark room at the bottom of the stairs. They'll be gone soon, I want to tell her; they'll be gone soon and we will be back among ourselves, and everything will be as it was before. Nothing will have happened. There are so many things I could say. Her cigarette is burning down close to the end and I can see the fine white bones of her hands and fingers. There are so many things I could say, but the hum of my heart swallows every word, and when she finally turns her eyes on mine, they are like locusts, moving helplessly against the white of her skin.

SIGRID NUNEZ

from

A Feather on the Breath of God

IT SEEMS TO ME that the room was full of smoke, or smoky light. Or maybe it's the curtains I am remembering. It was summer—that I know. The windows were open, and there were thin curtains—pale but not very clean—slowly shifting in front of the windows, like smoke. Late afternoon of a very warm day. A house somewhere in a neighborhood I didn't know, a house I was driven to and would not have been able to find my way back to. Damp and dark as a cellar when we entered. Who lives here? I do not know. A poor home, shabby, but not wretched. The bed I slipped into moments ago was unmade. My clothes lie on a chair. (For some reason it was important to me to take them off by myself.) There is a big tree outside the window and it is full of birds, singing my disgrace, a song these birds will teach to their young and to other birds, around the world, so that now no matter where I am, in other rooms, in other beds, I sometimes wake to hear them, singing my disgrace.

The man is in the bathroom. I hear the sound of water running, a throat being cleared.

A breeze. Moving curtains. Birds.

He comes into the room and sees me lying in the bed. He unbuttons his shirt as he crosses the floor. His chest is white but his face and hands are brown. Blue eyes. Teeth. Big teeth, one eyetooth pointing out a little: sharp.

Carnivore. Gold chain. Tattoo. Strong. He bends over me smiling, he opens his mouth wide, he covers my mouth with his mouth, my whole mouth. Is he going to swallow me?

Wild heart. Birds.

When he pulls back he is no longer smiling. He is looking the way he looked earlier, in the car, when he was driving us here and thought he had made a wrong turn. As he draws the sheet away from my body, I fight the impulse to curl up.

He says, "You're just a kid, aren't you?"

Sometimes, when you look back at your younger self, you feel as if you are looking not at yourself, but at another person, and that other person still exists somewhere. For many months now I have been living with the image of this girl, thinking about her, not as if she had grown up and become who I am now myself, but as if she were still to be found, just as she was, in that very bed, in that house that she could not have found her way back to.

If I could find my way to that house, I would ask her many questions: What is she doing there? Why did she go with this man? What was she looking for? Mostly I want to know how she of all people—she who is afraid of everything—is not afraid to do this.

An afternoon in June many years later. A brightly lit office in midtown Manhattan. Interview. How long have you been teaching English? What foreign languages do you know? What foreign countries have you visited? Have you ever lived abroad? Do you think you would become homesick, living abroad for two whole years?

The interviewer, a young- and earnest-looking man in his forties, watches my face carefully. The face I choose to show him is young, earnest, a little wonderstruck, unknowing. It is the face he wants to see, the face that will get me this job.

There is an application to fill out. Please use black or blue ink and write clearly. I am shown into another room where other interviewees are sitting at a long table, writing clearly in black or blue ink. A map of the world on the wall. All the same questions I just answered, now asked for in writing. I wish it were permitted to smoke.

On the way home from the interview, I stop and buy some peonies. Later that day I look up from my book and I feel a pang. For they have overbloomed, as peonies do. They have turned themselves practically inside out. All it means is a sooner death for them. There seems to me something almost generous about this. *Straining beauty.* The phrase sticks in my head.

The girl is lying in bed with the man. The man is fast asleep. The girl is not asleep. She is wide awake, she could not be more wide awake, in her whole life she has never been so awake. This is no time to ask her questions. She has to get up, she has to get dressed, she has to get out of there.

Birds. Smoke.

Don't make me say how old I was.

Many times the girl has been told: If a man looks at you, do not look back. Just ignore him. Pretend he's not there.

Her father does not look at her. Her father does not know one daughter from another. But the world is full of fathers, and she can't be invisible to all of them. She cannot remember a time when the temptation did not exist for her. She was forever looking back. Here eyes grew huge with looking back.

As in all things, the girl's mother plays a prominent part. Set on distinguishing *her* child from the "icky little brats" of the projects, she dresses the girl like a dream of a little girl: white tights, short flared skirts with wide starched sashes. Even later, because the mother is the family dressmaker, the girl has little to say about what she wears. Much of what the mother chooses for her is attention-getting, revealing. The daughter quails. "I can't wear that to school!" The mother pooh-poohs her. ("When you are young, you can get away with anything.") Only much later does it occur to the girl to wonder whether her mother would have taken the same risks herself.

Do everything you can to get men to look at you, and when they do, pretend they don't exist. Because only a slut looks back. Is that perfectly clear? Early lesson on the female condition.

Very young, still a child, the girl discovers that she is drawn to men in a way that other children are not. Whatever else there might be in their attention to her, there is also kindness—she is sure she is not mistaken in this. "I wish you were *my* little girl." Reasonable, innocent desire. She is aware of delighting in her ability to make men smile. In general, she prefers the company of adults (women too, but especially men) to that of children. Adults are more appreciative, they are better listeners, and she has so much to say. Men like to touch, to take you on their knees and stroke you as if you were a kitten. She has watched kittens. Roll onto your back, turn up your stomach, tilt your head. As her eyes grew huge, now her face grows more triangular. She knows that there is something off, something unmentionable, that she cannot fathom. Over the whole picture, a wash of sadness. Again, it will occur to her only later: A lot of the men who paid so much attention to her were losers. But from those early days she takes the notion of a masculine love that was kind, furtive, melancholy. Hopeless.

Compared with her father other men are usually bigger, hairier. The neighborhood men are tough, hotheads ever ready with their fists. Some have done time. Often the smell of whiskey on them. Deep rough voices when they speak softly, large rough hands when they caress—this gets to the quick of her. A certain kind of story has a hold on her imagination during this time—the kind of story in which a child is befriended by a wild beast. A movie about a little girl and a lion. The lion is gentle only with the child; no grown-up can get anywhere near him. Another movie, seen many times on television and much loved, about a girl and a gorilla named Joe, supernaturally big and strong. Monstrous when riled, capable of immense destruction, but again, ever gentle with the girl. At the climax of the movie, he rescues children from a burning orphanage. "Joe! Joe! Help, Joe!"

(This is how it was born, I think. This is the root of that dream: He will be loving and tender. He will be strong, fierce, and brute enough to protect me from the world.)

The wish to please, to charm—the desire to provoke desire—runs deep in me and seems to have been there from the beginning. Where I learned how to flirt is a mystery to me. Certainly not from my mother, and not from my sisters, who do not share this trait with me. It was there from the beginning: more a compulsion than a trait. And the conviction—or fantasy—that I could please men, that I knew what men wanted, was always there too.

If a girl is too easy, men will not want her. I was grateful to learn early that this was a lie. But it is hard for a girl, always having to live with the threat of *slut* over her head. And *cocktease*. It was flung at me but it wasn't really true. I almost never withheld.

I do not think it can be possible that I never dreamed of marriage. But if I did, that dream died early and left no trace. What stayed with me was a horror of marriage, and I don't owe this to my parents alone. I saw no happy marriages when I was growing up—at least, not outside of television. (Once, when I complained to my mother about our family life, she shook her head and said, "You've been watching too much television.") The peaceless households of the projects. Wives and husbands forever at each other's throats, and children overwhelmed. Maybe they could fool themselves but they couldn't fool the kids: Mom and Dad wanted to kill each other. I still get anxious when I am around couples. Almost always that tension, the little digs and huffs. A woman who survives being pushed onto the subway tracks by a man from behind says, "The first thing that flashed through my mind was that it was my husband. We'd had a fight that morning."

In high school, a young woman named Miss Perce taught our all-girls' hygiene class. When she showed off her engagement ring, one of the girls asked her how it felt to be getting married. Miss Perce said, "Everything will be different now, and I know I'll have to change. I mean, I won't ever spend five dollars on a lipstick again." Maybe she said more. In fact, she must have said more. But all I remember is that bit about the lipstick and what an odd and disheartening remark it seemed. Twenty-four of the twenty-five girls in that class, I'd bet my ring finger, went on to marry. I often remember Miss Perce when I am buying a lipstick. A good one costs about twenty dollars now.

A big, cheerful family round a well-laid table. A roomy, well-kept house. A dog. A yard. Again, this dream must have been mine too, once upon a time, but it was soon replaced.

A single room. A chair, a table, a bed. Windows on a garden. Music. Books. A cat to teach me how to be alone with dignity. A room where men might come and go but never stay. I began dreaming of this room when I was still in my teens. I saw it waiting for me at the end of a long wavering corridor.

It is not just the heart that has its reasons. Surely in some language of the world there exists a word that means "for reasons of the body." The body: Nothing makes you more aware of it—of its beauty and of its ideal ability to express feeling—than dance. And nothing ennobles the body like ballet. Ballet is all about opening up (turnout: the opening of the crotch and thighs), and the great ballerina roles are full of dancing that is about the opening up, not just of the body, but of the entire being, to love. Go to the ballet, watch Giselle, watch Odette and Juliet and Aurora, and see. The wish to be all body, the dream of a language of movement, pure in a way that speech ("the foe of mystery"—Mann) can never be pure—I would not have been the same lover if I had not danced. And it has been a real ambition of mine, thwarting other ambitions, coming between me and all other goals: to be a woman in love. In love lies the possibility not only of fulfillment but of adventure and risk, and for once I was not afraid—either to suffer or to make suffer. In more than one language the words for *love* and *suffering* are the same, and I have flung myself from cliffs, I have hurled myself at men's hearts like a javelin.

But what will you do when you are old? A woman starts hearing this when she is nowhere near old. In the wink of an eye you go from slut to spinster. But was it so terrible to be an old maid? I saw myself traveling in foreign cities. Bright sun, ancient stones, the endless noon of the streets and the eternal dusk of the churches. Straw hat, sandals, a white blouse, and a skirt flaring gracefully below the knee. Dinner alone: bread, cheese, fruit. Long train rides, rocking, dreaming. *No one knows me.* The unfamiliar peace of a hotel room. The narrow bed with its iron bedstead. Faded wallpaper, original paintings touching in their crudeness. No one knows you, you can make yourself up anew every day. This evening you have written two letters and finished the guidebook. You take a long bath, and when the stranger comes, you make love on the narrow bed, no English, speak with the body. And afterward the bed is too small, good night, my dear, never forget, goodbye, goodbye.

Are there really women like this or only women who write stories about women like this?

Someone has said: To be a woman is always to be hiding something.

A woman, a wife, a mother, sits in a café with me and talks about the man she calls the love of her life. Out of her life now, this love, as he must be, for he was wrong for her in all ways but one. When she left him for good she took one of his shirts, she wanted to have something with his smell in it. It was his smell, she says, that drove her beyond reason, drove her to risk everything that was most important to her. "I keep it in a plastic bag in the bottom drawer of my dresser, and from time to time when I cannot resist I take it out and I bury my face in it."

During the time that I want to tell about now, I had a job teaching English to immigrants. (Broken English: Sometimes I think it is my fate.) Immigrants. Refugees. ("You look like a refugee," my mother used to say, whenever I was not dressed to her liking.)

The students came from all over the world, and it was another teacher who once observed that, in most of their cultures, women who lived as we mostly young and single teachers did would be considered whores. Administrative warnings about provocative clothing and friendly behavior that might be misinterpreted by some of the men.

Just arrived in America, the students speak little or no English, but class is conducted entirely in English. "Another language, another soul." A pretty saying, but not everybody is going to see it this way. The slowness of my class's progress fills me with anxiety. Oh, the stubborn resistance of the adult mind. For every one like my mother there are ten like my father, those who will never know English as a second language.

In the back of the class, by the window, sits the Russian. No better than the others at first, but soon my best student. A seaman from Odessa, but not Ukrainian, and not Jewish, as are most of the other Russian immigrants here. In fact, Vadim would never have left Odessa, he says, were it not for his wife, who is Jewish, and most of whose relatives were already in New York. He is fiercely proud of his Russian blood. The Communists may have destroyed his country, he says, but the Russians will always be a good people. ("Russians have a wide soul.")

Taller than everyone else in class by at least a head. Sharp cheekbones, slanted blue eyes, full lips, large teeth, and a way of smiling that makes you understand why we say to *flash* a smile, because that is just what he does. I think it is the smile that makes me think of a gypsy. (And what makes Vadim smile like that, apropos of nothing, in the middle of class? I find out later, what he had promised himself: "By end this class, I fuck this teacher." And every time he remembered this resolution, he would flash those teeth.)

Teaching the conditional, I ask the students to say what each of us would be if he or she were an animal. I am told that I would be a Siamese cat. And Vadim? "A wolf! A wolf!"

Nothing about him that is not long—long face, long arms and legs, long waist. In youth, a competitive swimmer; at thirty-seven, still long and lithe. An adolescent body, all muscle and bone. But the face is worn, already old, the face of a longtime substance abuser. And the hair is mostly gray. He has the throaty bass voice common to Russian men, and he wears the international uniform: black leather jacket and very tight jeans—the uniform that would not be complete without the knife in one of the pockets. (Walking in the park with him at dusk, I tense at every man who approaches. "You don't have to be afraid," he says. "I am from Odessa. I very good with knife.") When the weather turns warm, I catch a glimpse of the crucifix he wears on a chain around his neck and wonder: What must his wife think of that? In the streets of Brighton Beach, it draws stares and occasional comment. A habit of kissing it when he wants you to believe something he says: not at all convincing.

I am proud (unduly, maybe) of his progress in English—as if he could not have learned so well from any other teacher but me. At a certain point, I have no choice but to recommend that he go to a higher level. When he refuses, I am secretly glad. I give him extra homework, he writes me long letters, which I read and correct, and his progress continues at the same fast rate.

When he asks to see me outside class and I tell him no, he blames his poor English. If I understood Russian, I would not turn him down, he is utterly sure of that. The better his English, the better his chances with me. So he works and works, until he is way ahead of his classmates. Over their heads, he and I hit the ball, our talk full of the double entendres that are the heart of flirtation.

About his own progress he later says: "I did it only for you, because I knew I have only a little time, and I study, study, study, because I want to — to—"

I teach him the word *seduce*.

He laments that he cannot do his seducing in Russian—a richer language than English, he insists, better for making love.

"I like to dream," he writes in one of his letters. "Because in dreams you can have all what you want." He says that he often dreams of going back to Odessa and taking me along as his wife.

In my own dream he stays married, takes me as a lover, and teaches me Russian.

ACHY OBEJAS

We Came All the Way from Cuba So You Could Dress Like This?

for Nena

I'M WEARING A GREEN SWEATER. It's made of some synthetic material, and it's mine. I've been wearing it for two days straight and have no plans to take it off right now.

I'm ten years old. I just got off the boat—or rather, the ship. The actual boat didn't make it: We got picked up halfway from Havana to Miami by a gigantic oil freighter to which they then tied our boat. That's how our boat got smashed to smithereens, its wooden planks breaking off like toothpicks against the ship's big metal hull. Everybody talks about American ingenuity, so I'm not sure why somebody didn't anticipate that would happen. But they didn't. So the boat that brought me and my parents most of the way from Cuba is now just part of the debris that'll wash up on tourist beaches all over the Caribbean.

As I speak, my parents are being interrogated by an official from the office of Immigration and Naturalization Services. It's all a formality because this is 1963, and no Cuban claiming political asylum actually gets turned away. We're evidence that the revolution has failed the middle class and that communism is bad. My parents—my father's an accountant and my mother's a social worker—are living, breathing examples of the suffering Cubans have endured under the tyranny of Fidel Castro.

The immigration officer, a fat Hungarian lady with sparkly hazel eyes and a perpetual smile, asks my parents why they came over, and my father, whose face is bright red from spending two days floating in a little boat on the Atlantic Ocean while secretly terrified, points to me—I'm sitting on a couch across the room, more bored than exhausted—and says, We came for her, so she could have a future.

The immigration officer speaks a halting Spanish, and with it she tells my parents about fleeing the Communists in Hungary. She says they took everything from her family, including a large country estate, with forty-four acres and two lakes, that's now being used as a vocational training center. Can you imagine that, she says. There's an official presidential portrait of John F. Kennedy behind her, which will need to be replaced in a week or so.

I fold my arms in front of my chest and across the green sweater. Tonight the U.S. government will put us up in a noisy transient hotel. We'll be allowed to stay there at taxpayer expense for a couple of days until my godfather—who lives with his mistress somewhere in Miami—comes to get us.

Leaning against the wall at the processing center, I notice a volunteer for Catholic Charities who approaches me with gifts: oatmeal cookies, a plastic doll with blond hair and a blue dress, and a rosary made of white plastic beads. She smiles and talks to me in incomprehensible English, speaking unnaturally loud.

My mother, who's watching while sitting nervously next to my father as we're being processed, will later tell me she remembers this moment as something poignant and good.

All I hold onto is the feel of the doll—cool and hard—and the fact that the Catholic volunteer is trying to get me to exchange my green sweater for a little gray flannel gym jacket with a hood and an American flag logo. I wrap myself up tighter in the sweater, which at this point still smells of salt and Cuban dirt and my grandmother's house, and the Catholic volunteer just squeezes my shoulder and leaves, thinking, I'm sure, that I've been traumatized by the trip across the choppy waters. My mother smiles weakly at me from across the room.

I'm still clutching the doll, a thing I'll never play with but which I'll carry with me all my life, from apartment to apartment, one move after the other. Eventually, her little blond nylon hairs will fall off and, thirty years later, after I'm diagnosed with cancer, she'll sit atop my dresser, scarred and bald like a chemo patient.

Is life destiny or determination?

For all the blond boyfriends I will have, there will be only two yellow-haired lovers. One doesn't really count—a boy in a military academy who subscribes to Republican politics like my parents, and who will try, relatively unsuccessfully, to penetrate me on a south Florida beach. I will squirm away from underneath him, not because his penis hurts me but because the stubble on his face burns my cheek.

The other will be Martha, perceived by the whole lesbian community as a gold digger, but who will love me in spite of my poverty. She'll come to my one-room studio on Saturday mornings when her rich lover is still asleep and rip tee-shirts off my shoulders, brutally and honestly.

One Saturday we'll forget to set the alarm to get her back home in time, and Martha will have to dress in a hurry, the smoky smell of my sex all over her face and her own underwear tangled up in her pants leg. When she gets home, her rich lover will notice the weird bulge at her calf and throw her out, forcing Martha to acknowledge that without a primary relationship for contrast, we can't go on.

It's too dangerous, she'll say, tossing her blond hair away from her face.

Years later, I'll visit Martha, now living seaside in Provincetown with her new lover, a Kennedy cousin still in the closet who has a love of dogs, and freckles sprinkled all over her cheeks.

At the processing center, the Catholic volunteer has found a young Colombian woman to talk to me. I don't know her name, but she's pretty and brown, and she speaks Spanish. She tells me she's not Catholic but that she'd like to offer me Christian comfort anyway. She smells of violet water.

She pulls a Bible from her big purse and asks me, Do you know this, and I say, I'm Catholic, and she says that, well, she was once Catholic, too, but then she was saved and became something else. She says everything will change for me in the United States, as it did for her.

Then she tells me about coming here with her father and how he got sick and died, and she was forced to do all sorts of work, including what she calls sinful work, and how the sinful work taught her so much about life, and then how she got saved. She says there's still a problem, an impulse, which she has to suppress by reading the Bible. She looks at me as if I know what she's talking about.

Across the room, my parents are still talking to the fat Hungarian lady, my father's head bent over the table as he fills out form after form.

Then the Catholic volunteer comes back and asks the Colombian girl something in English, and the girl reaches across me, pats my lap, and starts reading from her Spanish-language Bible: Your breasts are like two fawns, twins of a gazelle that feed upon the lilies. Until the day breathes and the shadows flee, I will hie me to the mountain of myrrh and the hill of frankincense. You are all fair, my love; there is no flaw in you.

Here's what my father dreams I will be in the United States of America: A lawyer, then a judge, in a system of law that is both serious and just. Not that he actually believes in democracy—in fact, he's openly suspicious of the popular will—but he longs for the power and prestige such a career would bring, and which he can't achieve on his own now that we're here, so he projects it all on me. He sees me in courtrooms and lecture halls, at libraries and in elegant restaurants, the object of envy and awe.

My father does not envision me in domestic scenes. He does not imagine me as a wife or mother because to do so would be to imagine someone else closer to me than he is, and he cannot endure that. He will never regret not being a grandfather; it was never part of his plan.

Here's what my mother dreams I will be in the United States of America: The owner of many appliances and a rolling green lawn; mother of two mischievous children; the wife of a boyishly handsome North American man who drinks Pepsi for breakfast; a career woman with a well-paying position in local broadcasting.

My mother pictures me reading the news on TV at four and home at the dinner table by six. She does not propose that I will actually do the cooking, but rather that I'll oversee the undocumented Haitian woman my husband and I have hired for that purpose. She sees me as fulfilled, as she imagines she is.

All I ever think about are kisses, not the deep throaty kind but quick pecks all along my belly just before my lover and I dissolve into warm blankets and tangled sheets in a bed under an open window. I have no view of this scene from a distance, so I don't know if the window frames tall pine trees or tropical bushes permeated with skittering gray lizards.

It's hot and stuffy in the processing center, where I'm sitting under a light that buzzes and clicks. Everything smells of nicotine. I wipe the shine off my face with the sleeve of my sweater. Eventually, I take off the sweater and fold it over my arm.

My father, smoking cigarette after cigarette, mutters about communism and how the Dominican Republic is next and then, possibly, someplace in Central America.

My mother has disappeared to another floor in the building, where the Catholic volunteer insists that she look through boxes filled with clothes donated by generous North Americans. Later, my mother will tell us how the Catholic volunteer pointed to the little gray flannel gym jacket with the hood and the American flag logo, how she plucked a bow tie from a box, then a black synthetic teddy from another and laughed, embarrassed.

My mother will admit she was uncomfortable with the idea of sifting through the boxes, sinking arm-deep into other people's sweat and excretions, but not that she was afraid of offending the Catholic volunteer and that she held her breath, smiled, and fished out a shirt for my father and a light blue cotton dress for me, which we'll never wear.

My parents escaped from Cuba because they did not want me to grow up in a communist state. They are anti-communists, especially my father.

It's because of this that when Martin Luther King, Jr., dies in 1968 and North American cities go up in flames, my father will gloat. King was a Communist, he will say; he studied in Moscow, everybody knows that.

I'll roll my eyes and say nothing. My mother will ask him to please finish his *café con leche* and wipe the milk moustache from the top of his lip.

Later, the morning after Bobby Kennedy's brains are shot all over a California hotel kitchen, my father will greet the news of his death by walking into our kitchen wearing a "Nixon's the One" button.

There's no stopping him now, my father will say; I know, because I was involved with the counterrevolution, and I know he's the one who's going to save us, he's the one who came up with the Bay of Pigs—which would have worked, all the experts agree, if he'd been elected instead of Kennedy, that coward.

My mother will vote for Richard Nixon in 1968, but in spite of his loud support my father will sit out the election, convinced there's no need to become a citizen of the United States (the usual prerequisite for voting) because Nixon will get us back to Cuba in no time, where my father's dormant citizenship will spring to life.

Later that summer, my father, who has resisted getting a television set (too cumbersome to be moved when we go back to Cuba, he will tell us), suddenly buys a huge Zenith color model to watch the Olympics broadcast from Mexico City.

I will sit on the floor, close enough to distinguish the different colored dots, while my father sits a few feet away in a LA-Z-BOY chair and roots for the Cuban boxers, especially Teófilo Stevenson. Every time Stevenson wins one—whether against North Americans or East Germans or whomever—my father will jump up and shout.

Later, when the Cuban flag waves at us during the medal ceremony, and the Cuban national anthem comes through the TV's tinny speakers, my father will stand up in Miami and cover his heart with his palm just like Fidel, watching on his own TV in Havana.

When I get older, I'll tell my father a rumor I heard that Stevenson, for all his heroics, practiced his best boxing moves on his wife, and my father will look at me like I'm crazy and say, Yeah, well, he's a Communist, what did you expect, huh?

In the processing center, my father is visited by a Cuban man with a large camera bag and a steno notebook into which he's constantly scribbling. The man has green Coke-bottle glasses and chews on a pungent Cuban cigar as he nods at everything my father says.

My mother, holding a brown paper bag filled with our new (used) clothes, sits next to me on the couch under the buzzing and clicking lights. She asks me about the Colombian girl, and I tell her she read me parts of the Bible, which makes my mother shudder.

The man with the Coke-bottle glasses and cigar tells my father he's from Santiago de Cuba in Oriente province, near Fidel's hometown, where he claims nobody ever supported the revolution because they knew the real Fidel. Then he tells my father he knew his father, which makes my father very nervous.

The whole northern coast of Havana harbor is mined, my father says to the Cuban man as if to distract him. There are *milicianos* all over the beaches, he goes on; it was a miracle we got out, but we had to do it—for her, and he points my way again.

Then the man with the Coke-bottle glasses and cigar jumps up and pulls a giant camera out of his bag, covering my mother and me with a sudden explosion of light.

In 1971, I'll come home for Thanksgiving from Indiana University where I have a scholarship to study optometry. It'll be the first time in months I'll be without an antiwar demonstration to go to, a consciousness-raising group to attend, or a Gay Liberation meeting to lead.

Alaba'o, I almost didn't recognize you, my mother will say, pulling on the fringes of my suede jacket, promising to mend the holes in my floor-sweeping bell-bottom jeans. My green sweater will be somewhere in the closet of my bedroom in their house.

We left Cuba so you could dress like this? my father will ask over my mother's shoulder.

And for the first and only time in my life, I'll say, Look, you didn't come for me, you came for you; you came because all your rich clients were leaving, and you were going to wind up a cashier in your father's hardware store if you didn't leave, okay?

My father, who works in a bank now, will gasp—*¿Qué qué?*—and step back a bit. And my mother will say, Please, don't talk to your father like that.

And I'll say, It's a free country, I can do anything I want, remember? Christ, he only left because Fidel beat him in that stupid swimming race when they were little.

And then my father will reach over my mother's thin shoulders, grab me by the red bandanna around my neck, and throw me to the floor, where he'll kick me over and over until all I remember is my mother's voice pleading, Please stop, please, please, please stop.

We leave the processing center with the fat Hungarian lady, who drives a large Ford station wagon. My father sits in the front with her, and my mother and I sit in the back, although there is plenty of room for both of us in the front as well. The fat Hungarian lady is taking us to our hotel, where our room will have a kitchenette and a view of an alley from which a tall black transvestite plies her night trade.

Eventually, I'm drawn by the lights of the city, not just the neon streaming by the car windows but also the white globes on the street lamps, and I scamper to the back where I can watch the lights by myself. I close my eyes tight, then open them, loving the tracers and star bursts on my private screen.

Up in front, the fat Hungarian lady and my father are discussing the United States' many betrayals, first of Eastern Europe after World War II, then of Cuba after the Bay of Pigs invasion.

My mother, whom I believe is as beautiful as any of the palm trees fluttering on the median strip as we drive by, leans her head against the car window, tired and bereft. She comes to when the fat Hungarian lady, in a fit of giggles, breaks from the road and into the parking lot of a supermarket so shrouded in light that I'm sure it's a flying saucer docked here in Miami.

We did this when we first came to America, the fat Hungarian lady says, leading us up to the supermarket. And it's something only people like us can appreciate.

My father bobs his head up and down and my mother follows, her feet scraping the ground as she drags me by the hand.

We walk through the front door and then a turnstile, and suddenly we are in the land of plenty—row upon row of cereal boxes, TV dinners, massive displays of fresh pineapple, crate after crate of oranges, shelves of insect repellent, and every kind of broom. The dairy section is jammed with cheese and chocolate milk.

There's a butcher shop in the back, and my father says, Oh my god, look, and points to a slab of bloody red ribs thick with meat. My god my god my god, he says, as if he's never seen such a thing, or as if we're on the verge of starvation.

Calm down, please, my mother says, but he's not listening, choking back tears and hanging off the fat Hungarian lady who's now walking him past the sausages and hot dogs, packaged bologna and chipped beef.

All around us people stare, but then my father says, We just arrived from Cuba, and there's so much here!

The fat Hungarian lady pats his shoulder and says to the gathering crowd, Yes, he came on a little boat with his whole family; look at his beautiful daughter who will now grow up well-fed and free.

I push up against my mother, who feels as smooth and thin as a palm leaf on Good Friday. My father beams at me, tears in his eyes. All the while, complete strangers congratulate him on his wisdom and courage, give him hugs and money, and welcome him to the United States.

There are things that can't be told.

Things like when we couldn't find an apartment, everyone's saying it was because landlords in Miami didn't rent to families with kids, but knowing, always, that it was more than that.

Things like my doing very poorly on an IQ test because I didn't speak English, and getting tossed into a special education track, where it took until high school before somebody realized I didn't belong there.

Things like a North American hairdresser's telling my mother she didn't do her kind of hair.

Like my father, finally realizing he wasn't going to go back to Cuba anytime soon, trying to hang himself with the light cord in the bathroom while my mother cleaned rooms at a nearby luxury hotel, but falling instead and breaking his arm.

Like accepting welfare checks, because there really was no other way.

Like knowing that giving money to exile groups often meant helping somebody buy a private yacht for Caribbean vacations, not for invading Cuba, but also knowing that refusing to donate only invited questions about our own patriotism.

And knowing that Nixon really wasn't the one, and wasn't doing anything, and wouldn't have done anything, even if he'd finished his second term, no matter what a good job the Cuban burglars might have done at the Watergate Hotel.

What if we'd stayed? What if we'd never left Cuba? What if we were there when the last of the counterrevolution was beaten, or when Mariel harbor leaked thousands of Cubans out of the island, or when the Pan-American Games came? What if we'd never left?

All my life, my father will say I would have been a young Communist, falling prey to the revolution's propaganda. According to him, I would have believed ice cream treats came from Fidel, that those hairless Russians were our friends, and that my duty as a revolutionary was to turn him in for his counterrevolutionary activities—which he will swear he'd never have given up if we'd stayed in Cuba.

My mother will shake her head but won't contradict him. She'll say the revolution uses people, and that I, too, would probably have been used, then betrayed, and that we'll never know, but maybe I would have wound up in jail whether I ever believed in the revolution or not, because I would have talked back to the wrong person, me and my big mouth.

I wonder, if we'd stayed then who, if anyone—if not Martha and the boy from the military academy—would have been my blond lovers, or any kind of lovers at all.

And what if we'd stayed, and there had been no revolution?

My parents will never say, as if somehow they know that their lives were meant to exist only in opposition.

I try to imagine who I would have been if Fidel had never come into Havana sitting triumphantly on top of that tank, but I can't. I can only think of variations of who I am, not who I might have been.

In college one day, I'll tell my mother on the phone that I want to go back to Cuba to see, to consider all these questions, and she'll pause, then say, What for? There's nothing there for you, we'll tell you whatever you need to know, don't you trust us?

Over my dead body, my father will say, listening in on the other line.

Years later, when I fly to Washington, D.C., and take a cab straight to the Cuban Interests Section to apply for a visa, a golden-skinned man with the dulled eyes of a bureaucrat will tell me that because I came to the U.S. too young to make the decision to leave for myself—that it was in fact my parents who made it for me—the Cuban government does not recognize my U.S. citizenship.

You need to renew your Cuban passport, he will say. Perhaps your parents have it, or a copy of your birth certificate, or maybe you have a relative or friend who could go through the records in Cuba for you.

I'll remember the passport among my mother's priceless papers, handwritten in blue ink, even the official parts. But when I ask my parents for it, my mother will say nothing, and my father will say, It's not here anymore, but in a bank box, where you'll never see it. Do you think I would let you betray us like that?

The boy from the military academy will say oh baby baby as he grinds his hips into me. And Martha and all the girls before and after her here in the United States will say ooohhh ooooohhhhh oooooooohhhhhhhh as my fingers explore inside them.

But the first time I make love with a Cuban, a politically controversial exile writer of some repute, she will say, *Aaaaaayyyyyyaaaaaayyyyyaaaaay* and lift me by my hair from between her legs, strings of saliva like sea foam between my mouth and her shiny curls. Then she'll drop me onto her mouth where our tongues will poke each other like wily porpoises.

In one swift movement, she'll flip me on my back, pillows falling every which way from the bed, and kiss every part of me, between my breasts and under my arms, and she'll suck my fingertips, and the inside of my elbows. And when she rests her head on my belly, her ear listening not to my heartbeat but to the fluttering of palm trees, she'll sit up, place one hand on my throat, the other on my sex, and kiss me there, under my rib cage, around my navel, where I am softest and palest.

The next morning, listening to her breathing in my arms, I will wonder how this could have happened, and if it would have happened at all if we'd stayed in Cuba. And if so, if it would have been furtive or free, with or without the revolution. And how—knowing now how cataclysmic life really is—I might hold on to her for a little while longer.

When my father dies of a heart attack in 1990 (it will happen while he's driving, yelling at somebody, and the car will just sail over to the sidewalk and stop dead at the curb, where he'll fall to the seat and his arms will somehow fold over his chest, his hands set in prayer), I will come home to Florida from Chicago, where I'll be working as a photographer for the *Tribune*. I won't be taking pictures of murder scenes or politicians then but rather rock stars and local performance artists.

I'll be living in Uptown, in a huge house with a dry darkroom in one of the bedrooms, now converted and sealed black, where I cut up negatives and create photomontages that are exhibited at the Whitney Biennial and hailed by the critics as filled with yearning and hope.

When my father dies, I will feel sadness and a wish that certain things had been said, but I will not want more time with him. I will worry about my mother, just like all the relatives who predict she will die of heartbreak within months (she has diabetes and her vision is failing). But she will instead outlive both him and me.

I'll get to Miami Beach, where they've lived in a little coach house off Collins Avenue since their retirement, and find cousins and aunts helping my mother go through insurance papers and bank records, my father's will, his photographs and mementos: his university degree, a faded list of things to take back to Cuba (including Christmas lights), a jaundiced clipping from *Diario de las Américas* about our arrival which quotes my father as saying that Havana harbor is mined, and a photo of my mother and me, wide-eyed and thin, sitting on the couch in the processing center.

My father's funeral will be simple but well-attended, closed casket at my request, but with a moment reserved for those who want a last look. My mother will stay in the room while the box is pried open (I'll be in the lobby smoking a cigarette, a habit I despised in my father but which I'll pick up at his funeral) and tell me later she stared at the cross above the casket, never registering my father's talcumed and perfumed body beneath it.

I couldn't leave, it wouldn't have looked right, she'll say. But thank god I'm going blind.

Then a minister who we do not know will come and read from the Bible and my mother will reach around my waist and hold onto me as we listen to him say, When all these things come upon you, the blessing and the curse . . . and you call them to mind among all the nations where the Lord your God has driven you, and return to the Lord your God, you and your children, and obey his voice . . . with all your heart and with all your soul; then the Lord your God will return your fortunes, and have compassion upon you, and he will gather you again from all the peoples where the Lord your God has scattered you.

There will be a storm during my father's burial, which means it will end quickly. My mother and several relatives will go back to her house, where a TV will blare from the bedroom filled with bored teenage cousins, the women will talk about how to make *picadillo* with low-fat ground turkey instead of the traditional beef and ham, and the men will sit outside in the yard, drinking beer or small cups of Cuban coffee, and talk about my father's love of Cuba, and how unfortunate it is that he died just as Eastern Europe is breaking free, and Fidel is surely about to fall.

Three days later, after taking my mother to the movies and the mall, church and the local Social Security office, I'll be standing at the front gate with my bags, yelling at the cab driver that I'm coming, when my mother will ask me to wait a minute and run back into the house, emerging minutes later with a box for me that won't fit in any of my bags.

A few things, she'll say, a few things that belong to you that I've been meaning to give you for years and now, well, they're yours.

I'll shake the box, which will emit only a muffled sound, and thank her for whatever it is, hug her and kiss her and tell her I'll call her as soon as I get home. She'll put her chicken bone arms around my neck, kiss the skin there all the way to my shoulders, and get choked up, which will break my heart.

Sleepy and tired in the cab to the airport, I'll lean my head against the window and stare out at the lanky palm trees, their brown and green leaves waving good-bye to me through the still coming drizzle. Everything will be damp, and I'll be hot and stuffy, listening to car horns detonating on every side of me. I'll close my eyes, stare at the blackness, and try to imagine something of yearning and hope, but I'll fall asleep instead, waking only when the driver tells me we've arrived, and that he'll get my bags from the trunk, his hand outstretched for the tip as if it were a condition for the return of my things.

When I get home to Uptown I'll forget all about my mother's box until one day many months later when my memory's fuzzy enough to let me be curious. I'll break it open to find grade school report cards, family pictures of the three of us in Cuba, a love letter to her from my father (in which he talks about wanting to kiss the tender mole by her mouth), Xeroxes of my birth certificate, copies of our requests for political asylum, and my faded blue-ink Cuban passport (expiration date: June 1965), all wrapped up in my old green sweater.

When I call my mother—embarrassed about taking so long to unpack her box, overwhelmed by the treasures within it—her answering machine will pick up and, in a bilingual message, give out her beeper number in case of emergency.

A week after my father's death, my mother will buy a computer with a Braille keyboard and a speaker, start learning how to use it at the community center down the block, and be busy investing in mutual funds at a profit within six months.

But this is all a long way off, of course. Right now, we're in a small hotel room with a kitchenette that U.S. taxpayers have provided for us.

My mother, whose eyes are dark and sunken, sits at a little table eating one of the Royal Castle hamburgers the fat Hungarian lady bought for us. My father munches on another, napkins spread under his hands. Their heads are tilted toward the window which faces an alley. To the far south edge, it offers a view of Biscayne Boulevard and a magically colored thread of night traffic. The air is salty and familiar, the moon brilliant hanging in the sky.

I'm in bed, under sheets that feel heavy with humidity and the smell of cleaning agents. The plastic doll the Catholic volunteer gave me sits on my pillow.

Then my father reaches across the table to my mother and says, We made it, we really made it.

And my mother runs her fingers through his hair and nods, and they both start crying, quietly but heartily, holding and stroking each other as if they are all they have.

And then there's a noise—a screech out in the alley followed by what sounds like a hyena's laughter—and my father leaps up and looks out the window, then starts laughing, too.

Oh my god, come here, look at this, he beckons to my mother, who jumps up and goes to him, positioning herself right under the crook of his arm. Can you believe that, he says.

Only in America, echoes my mother.

And as I lie here wondering about the spectacle outside the window and the new world that awaits us on this and every night of the rest of our lives, even I know we've already come a long way. What none of us can measure yet is how much of the voyage is already behind us.

ESMERALDA SANTIAGO

from

When I Was Puerto Rican

THE FIRST DAY OF SCHOOL Mami walked me to a stone building that
loomed over Graham Avenue, its concrete yard enclosed by an iron fence
with spikes at the top. The front steps were wide but shallow and led up to a
set of heavy double doors that slammed shut behind us as we walked down
the shiny corridor. I clutched my eighth-grade report card filled with A's
and B's, and Mami had my birth certificate. At the front office we were met
by Mr. Grant, a droopy gentleman with thick glasses and a kind smile who
spoke no Spanish. He gave Mami a form to fill out. I knew most of the
words in the squares we were to fill in: NAME, ADDRESS (CITY, STATE),
and OCCUPATION. We gave it to Mr. Grant, who reviewed it, looked at my
birth certificate, studied my report card, then wrote on the top of the form
"7-18."

Don Julio had told me that if students didn't speak English, the schools
in Brooklyn would keep them back one grade until they learned it.

"Seven gray?" I asked Mr. Grant, pointing at his big numbers, and he
nodded.

"I no guan seven gray. I eight gray. I teeneyer."

"You don't speak English," he said. "You have to go to seventh grade while
you're learning."

"I have A's in school Puerto Rico. I lern good. I no seven gray girl."

Mami stared at me, not understanding but knowing I was being rude to
an adult.

"What's going on?" she asked me in Spanish. I told her they wanted to
send me back one grade and I would not have it. This was probably the first

rebellious act she had seen from me outside my usual mouthiness within the family.

"Negi, leave it alone. Those are the rules," she said, a warning in her voice.

"I don't care what their rules say," I answered. "I'm not going back to seventh grade. I can do the work. I'm not stupid."

Mami looked at Mr. Grant, who stared at her as if expecting her to do something about me. She smiled and shrugged her shoulders.

"Meester Grant," I said, seizing the moment. "I go eight gray six mons. Eef I no lern inglish, I go seven gray. Okay?"

"That's not the way we do things here," he said, hesitating.

"I good studen. I lern queek. You see notes." I pointed to the A's in my report card. "I pass seven gray."

So we made a deal.

"You have until Christmas," he said. "I'll be checking on your progress." He scratched out "7-18" and wrote in "8-23." He wrote something on a piece of paper, sealed it inside an envelope, and gave it to me. "Your teacher is Miss Brown. Take this note upstairs to her. Your mother can go," he said and disappeared into his office.

"Wow!" Mami said, "you can speak English!"

I was so proud of myself, I almost burst. In Puerto Rico if I'd been that pushy, I would have been called *mal educada* by the Mr. Grant equivalent and sent home with a note to my mother. But here it was my teacher who was getting the note, I got what I wanted, and my mother was sent home.

"I can find my way after school," I said to Mami. "You don't have to come get me."

"Are you sure?"

"Don't worry," I said. "I'll be all right."

I walked down the black-tiled hallway, past many doors that were half glass, each one labelled with a room number in neat black lettering. Other students stared at me, tried to get my attention, or pointedly ignored me. I kept walking as if I knew where I was going, heading for the sign that said STAIRS with an arrow pointing up. When I reached the end of the hall and looked back, Mami was still standing at the front door watching me, a worried expression on her face. I waved, and she waved back. I started up the stairs, my stomach churning into tight knots. All of a sudden, I was afraid that I was about to make a fool of myself and end up in seventh grade in the middle of the school year. Having to fall back would be worse than just accepting my fate now and hopping forward if I proved to be as good a student as I had convinced Mr. Grant I was. "What have I done?" I kicked myself with the back of my right shoe, much to the surprise of the fellow walking behind me, who laughed uproariously, as if I had meant it as a joke.

Miss Brown's was the learning disabled class, where the administration sent kids with all sorts of problems, none of which, from what I could see, had anything to do with their ability to learn but more with their willingness to do so. They were an unruly group. Those who came to class, anyway. Half of them never showed up, or, when they did, they slept through the lesson or nodded off in the middle of Miss Brown's carefully parsed sentences.

We were outcasts in a school where the smartest eighth graders were in the 8-1 homeroom, each subsequent drop in number indicating one notch less smarts. If your class was in the low double digits, (8-10 for instance), you were smart, but not a pinhead. Once you got into the teens, your intelligence was in question, especially as the numbers rose to the high teens. And then there were the twenties. I was in 8-23, where the dumbest, most undesirable people were placed. My class was, in some ways, the equivalent of seventh grade, perhaps even sixth or fifth.

Miss Brown, the homeroom teacher, who also taught English composition, was a young black woman who wore sweat pads under her arms. The strings holding them in place sometimes slipped outside the short sleeves of her well-pressed white shirts, and she had to turn her back to us in order to adjust them. She was very pretty, with almond eyes and a hairdo that was flat and straight at the top of her head then dipped into tight curls at the ends. Her fingers were well manicured, the nails painted pale pink with white tips. She taught English composition as if everyone cared about it, which I found appealing.

After the first week she moved me from the back of the room to the front seat by her desk, and after that, it felt as if she were teaching me alone. We never spoke, except when I went up to the blackboard.

"Esmeralda," she called in a musical voice, "would you please come up and mark the prepositional phrase?"

In her class, I learned to recognize the structure of the English language, and to draft the parts of a sentence by the position of words relative to pronouns and prepositions without knowing exactly what the whole thing meant.

The school was huge and noisy. There was a social order that, at first, I didn't understand but kept bumping into. Girls and boys who wore matching cardigans walked down the halls hand in hand, sometimes stopping behind lockers to kiss and fondle each other. They were *Americanos* and belonged in the homerooms in the low numbers.

Another group of girls wore heavy makeup, hitched their skirts above their knees, opened one extra button on their blouses, and teased their hair into enormous bouffants held solid with spray. In the morning, they took over the girls' bathroom, where they dragged on cigarettes as they did their hair until the air was unbreathable, thick with smoke and hair spray. The one time I entered the bathroom before classes they chased me out with insults and rough shoves.

Those bold girls with hair and makeup and short skirts, I soon found out, were Italian. The Italians all sat together on one side of the cafeteria, the blacks on another. The two groups hated each other more than they hated Puerto Ricans. At least once a week there was a fight between an Italian and a *moreno,* either in the bathroom, in the school yard, or in an abandoned lot near the school, a no-man's-land that divided their neighborhoods and kept them apart on weekends.

The black girls had their own style. Not for them the big, pouffy hair of the Italians. Their hair was straightened, curled at the tips like Miss Brown's, or pulled up into a twist at the back with wispy curls and straw straight bangs over Cleopatra eyes. Their skirts were also short, except it didn't look like they hitched them up when their mothers weren't looking. They came that way. They had strong, shapely legs and wore knee socks with heavy lace-up shoes that became lethal weapons in fights.

It was rumored that the Italians carried knives, even the girls, and that the *morenos* had brass knuckles in their pockets and steel toes in their heavy shoes. I stayed away from both groups, afraid that if I befriended an Italian, I'd get beat up by a *morena,* or vice versa.

There were two kinds of Puerto Ricans in school: the newly arrived, like myself, and the ones born in Brooklyn of Puerto Rican parents. The two types didn't mix. The Brooklyn Puerto Ricans spoke English, and often no Spanish at all. To them, Puerto Rico was the place where their grandparents lived, a place they visited on school and summer vacations, a place which they complained was backward and mosquito-ridden. Those of us for whom Puerto Rico was still a recent memory were also split into two groups: the ones who longed for the island and the ones who wanted to forget it as soon as possible.

I felt disloyal for wanting to learn English, for liking pizza, for studying the girls with big hair and trying out their styles at home, locked in the bathroom where no one could watch. I practiced walking with the peculiar little hop of the *morenas,* but felt as if I were limping.

I didn't feel comfortable with the newly arrived Puerto Ricans who stuck together in suspicious little groups, criticizing everyone, afraid of everything. And I was not accepted by the Brooklyn Puerto Ricans, who held the secret of coolness. They walked the halls between the Italians and the *morenos,* neither one nor the other, but looking and acting like a combination of both, depending on the texture of their hair, the shade of their skin, their makeup, and the way they walked down the hall.

One day I came home from school to find all our things packed and Mami waiting.

"Your sisters and brothers are coming," she said. "We're moving to a bigger place."

Tata and I helped her drag the stuff out to the sidewalk. After it was all together, Mami walked to Graham Avenue and found a cab. The driver helped us load the trunk, the front seat, and the floor of the rear seat until we were sitting on our bundles for the short ride to Varet Street, on the other side of the projects.

I'd read about but had never seen the projects. Just that weekend a man had taken a nine-year-old girl to the roof of one of the buildings, raped her, and thrown her over the side, down twenty-one stories. *El Diario,* the Spanish newspaper, had covered the story in detail and featured a picture of the building facing Bushwick Avenue, with a dotted line from where the girl was thrown to where she fell.

But Mami didn't talk about that. She said that the new apartment was much bigger, and that Tata would be living with us so she could take care of us while Mami worked. I wouldn't have to change schools.

The air was getting cooler, and before Delsa, Norma, Héctor, and Alicia came, Mami and I went shopping for coats and sweaters in a secondhand store, so that the kids wouldn't get sick their first week in Brooklyn. We also bought a couch and two matching chairs, two big beds, a *chiforobe* with a mirror, and two folding cots. Mami let me pick out the stuff, and I acted like a rich lady, choosing the most ornate pieces I spotted, with gold curlicues painted on the wood, intricate carving, and fancy pulls on the drawers.

Our new place was a railroad-style apartment on the second floor of a three-story house. There were four rooms from front to back, one leading into the other: the living room facing Varet Street, then our bedroom, then Tata's room, then the kitchen. The tub was in the bathroom this time, and the kitchen was big enough for a table and chairs, two folding racks for drying clothes washed by hand in the sink, and a stack of shelves for groceries. The fireplace in the living room, with its plain marble mantel, was blocked off, and we put Tata's television in front of it. The wood floors were dark and difficult to clean because the mop strings caught in splinters and cracks. The ceilings were high, but no cherubs danced around garlands, and no braided molding curled around the borders.

On October 7, 1961, Don Julio, Mami, and I went to the airport to pick up Delsa, Norma, Héctor, and Alicia. Papi had sent them unescorted, with Delsa in charge. The first thing I noticed was that her face was pinched and tired. At eleven years old Delsa looked like a woman, but her tiny body was still that of a little girl.

In the taxi on the way home, I couldn't stop talking, telling Delsa about the broad streets, the big schools, the subway train. I told her about the Italians, the *morenos,* the Jewish. I described how in Brooklyn we didn't have to wear uniforms to school, but on Fridays there was a class called assembly in a big auditorium, and all the kids had to wear white shirts.

Tata prepared a feast: *asopao,* Drake's cakes, Coke, and potato chips. The kids were wide-eyed and scared. I wondered if that's the way I had looked two months earlier and hoped that if I had, it had worn off by now.

SARAH SCHULMAN

The Penis Story

THE NIGHT BEFORE they sat in their usual spots. Jesse's hair was like torrents of black oil plunging into the sea. Ann watched her, remembering standing in the butcher shop looking at smoked meat, smelling the grease, imagining Jesse's tongue on her labia. She was starving.

"I'm just waiting for a man to rescue me," Jesse said.

"Look, Jess," Ann answered. "Why don't we put a timeline on this thing. Let's say, forty. If no man rescues you by the time you're forty, we'll take it from a different angle. What do you say?"

"I say I'll be in a mental hospital by the time I'm forty."

Jesse was thirty-two. This was a realistic possibility.

"Jesse, if instead of being two women, you and I were a woman and a man, would we be lovers by now?"

"Yes." Jesse had to answer yes because it was so obviously true.

"So what's not there for you in us being two women? Is it something concrete about a man, or is it the idea of a man?"

"I don't think it's anything physical. I think it is the idea of a man. I want to know that my lover is a man. I need to be able to say that."

Ann started to shake and covered her legs with a blanket so it wouldn't be so obvious. She felt like a child. She put her head on Jesse's shoulder feeling weak and ridiculous. Then they kissed. It felt so familiar. They'd been doing that for months. Each knew how the other kissed. Ann felt Jesse's hand on her waist and back and chest. Jesse reached her hand to Ann's bra. She'd done this before too. First tentatively, then more directly, she brushed her hands and face against Ann's breasts. Ann kissed her skin and licked it. She sucked her fingers, knowing those nails would have to be cut if Jesse were to ever put her fingers into Ann's body. She looked at Jesse's skin, at her acne scars and blackheads. She wanted to kiss her a hundred times. Then, as always, Jesse became disturbed, agitated. "I'm nervous again," she said. "Like, *oh no—now I'm going to have to fuck.*"

Suddenly Ann remembered that their sexual life together was a piece of glass. She put on her shirt and went home. This was the middle of the night in New York City.

When Ann awoke the next morning from unsettling dreams, she saw that a new attitude had dawned with the new day. She felt accepting, not proud. She felt ready to face adjustment and compromise. She was ready for change. Even though she was fully awake her eyes had not adjusted to the morning. She reached for glasses but found them inadequate. Then she looked down and saw that she had a penis.

Surprisingly, she didn't panic. Ann's mind, even under normal circumstances, worked differently than the minds of many of those around her. She was able to think three thoughts at the same time, and as a result often suffered from headaches, disconnected conversation, and too many ideas. However, at this moment she only had two thoughts: "What is it going to be like to have a penis?" and "I will never be the same again."

It didn't behave the way most penises do. It rather seemed to be trying to find its own way. It swayed a bit as she walked to the bathroom mirror, careful not to let her legs interfere, feeling off balance, as if she had an itch and couldn't scratch it. She tried to sit back on her hips, for she still had hips, and walk pelvis first, for she still had her pelvis. In fact, everything appeared to be the same except that she had no vagina. Except that she had a prick.

"I am a prick," she said to herself.

The first thing she needed to do was piss and that was fun, standing up seeing it hit the water, but it got all over the toilet seat and she had to clean up the yellow drops.

"I am a woman with a penis and I am still cleaning up piss."

This gave her a sense of historical consistency. Now it was time to get dressed.

She knew immediately she didn't want to hide her penis from the world. Ann had never hidden anything else, no matter how controversial. There was nothing wrong with having a penis. Men had them and now she did too. She wasn't going to let her penis keep her from the rest of humanity. She chose a pair of button-up Levis and stuffed her penis into her pants where it bulged pretty obviously. Then she put on a t-shirt that showed off her breasts and her muscles and headed toward the F train to Shelley's house to meet her friends for lunch.

By the time Ann finished riding on the F train she had developed a fairly integrated view of her new self. She was a lesbian with a penis. She was not a man with breasts. She was a woman. This was not androgyny, she'd never liked that word. Women had always been whole to Ann, not half of something waiting to be completed.

They sat in Shelley's living room eating lunch. These were her most attentive friends, the ones who knew best how she lived. They sat around joking until Shelley finally asked, "What's that between your legs?"

"That's my penis," Ann said.

"Oh, so now you have a penis."

"I got it this morning. I woke up and it was there."

They didn't think much of Ann's humor usually, so the conversation moved on to other topics. Judith lit a joint. They got high and said funny things, but they did keep coming back to Ann's penis.

"What are you going to do with it?" Shelley asked.

"I don't know."

"If you really have a penis, why don't you show it to us?" Roberta said. She was always provocative.

Ann remained sitting in her chair but unbuttoned her jeans and pulled her penis out of her panties. She had balls too.

"Is that real?"

Roberta came over and put her face in Ann's crotch. She held Ann's penis in her hand. It just lay there.

"Yup, Ann's got a penis alright."

"Did you eat anything strange yesterday?" Judith asked.

"Maybe it's from masturbating," Roberta suggested, but they all knew that couldn't be true.

"Well, Ann, let me know if you need anything, but I have to say I'm glad we're not lovers anymore because I don't think I could handle this." Judith bit her lip.

"I'm sure you'd do fine," Ann replied in her usual charming way.

Ann put on her flaming electronic lipstick. It smudged accidentally, but she liked the effect. This was preparation for the big event. Ann was ready to have sex. Thanks to her lifelong habit of masturbating before she went to sleep, Ann had sufficiently experimented with erections and come. She'd seen enough men do it and knew how to do it for them, so she had no trouble doing it for herself. Sooner or later she would connect with another person. Now was that time. She wore her t-shirt that said, "Just visiting from another planet." Judith had given it to her and giggled, nervously.

The Central Park Ramble used to be a bird and wildlife sanctuary. Because it's hidden, and therefore foreboding, gay men use it to have sex, and that's where Ann wanted to be. Before she had a penis, Ann used to imagine sometimes while making love that she and her girlfriend were two gay men. Now that she had this penis, she felt open to different kinds of people and new ideas, too.

She saw a gay man walking through the park in his little gym suit. He had a nice tan like Ann did and a gold earring like she did too. His t-shirt also had writing on it. It said, "All-American Boy." His ass stuck out like a mating call.

"Hi," she said.

"Hi," he said.

"Do you want to smoke a joint?" she asked very sweetly.

He looked around suspiciously.

"Don't worry, I'm gay too."

"OK honey, why not. There's nothing much happening anyway."

So, they sat down and smoked a couple of joints and laughed and told about the different boyfriends and girlfriends that they had had, and which ones had gone straight and which ones had broken their hearts. Then Ann produced two beers and they drank those and told about the hearts that they had broken. It was hot and pretty in the park.

Ann mustered up all her courage and said.

"I have a cock."

"You look pretty good for a mid-op," he said.

His name was Mike.

"No, I'm not a transsexual. I'm a lesbian with a penis. I know this is unusual, but would you suck my cock?"

Ann had always wanted to say "suck my cock" because it was one thing a lot of people said to her and she never said to anyone. Once she and her friends made little stickers that said "End Violence in the Lives of Women," which they stuck up all over the subway. Many mornings when she was riding to work, Ann would see that different people had written over them "suck my cock." It seemed like an appropriate response given the world in which we all live.

Mike thought this was out of the ordinary, but he prided himself on taking risks. So he decided "what the hell" and went down on her like an expert.

Well, it did feel nice. It didn't feel like floating in hot water, which is what Ann sometimes thought of when a woman made love to her well with her mouth, but it did feel good. She started thinking about other things. She tried the two-gay-men image but it had lost its magic. Then she remembered Jesse. She saw them together in Jesse's apartment. Each in their usual spots.

"What's the matter, Annie? Your face is giving you away."

"This is such a bastardized version of how I'd like to be relating to you right now."

"Well," said Jesse. "What would it be like?"

"Oh, I'd be sitting here and you'd say 'I'm ready' and I'd say, 'ready for what?' and you'd say, 'I'm ready to make love to you Annie.' Then I'd say 'Why don't we go to your bed?' and we would."

"Yes," Jesse said. "I would smell your smell Annie. I would put my arms on your neck and down over your breasts. I would unbutton your shirt, Annie, and pull it off your shoulders. I would run my fingers down your neck and over your nipples. I would lick your breasts, Annie, I would run my tongue down your neck to your breasts."

Ann could feel Jess's wild hair like the ocean passing over her chest. Jesse's mouth was on her nipples licking, her soft face against Ann's skin. She was licking, licking then sucking harder and faster until Jesse clung to her breasts harder and harder.

"You taste just like my wife," Mike said after she came.

"What?"

Ann's heart was beating. The ocean was crashing in her ears.

"I said, you taste just like my wife, when you come I mean. You don't come sperm, you know, you come women's cum, like pussy."

"Oh thank God."

Ann was relieved.

Another morning Ann woke up and her fingers were all sticky. It was still dark. First she thought she'd had a wet dream, but when she turned on her reading lamp she saw blood all over her hands. Instinctively she put her fingers in her mouth. It was gooey, full of membrane and salty. It was her period. She guessed it had no other place to come out, so it flowed from under her fingernails. She spent the next three and a half days wearing black plastic gloves.

The feeling of her uterine lining coming out of her hands gave Ann some hope. After living with her penis for nearly a month, she was beginning to experience it as a loss, not an acquisition. She was grieving for her former self.

One interesting item was that Ann was suddenly in enormous sexual demand. More women than had ever wanted to make love with her wanted her now. But most of them didn't want anyone to know, so she said no.

There was one woman, though, to whom she said yes. Her name was Muriel. Muriel dreamed that she made love to a woman with a penis and it was called "glancing." So she looked high and low until she found Ann, who she believed had a rare and powerful gift and should be honored.

Ann and Muriel became lovers and Ann learned many new things from this experience. She realized that when you meet a woman, you see the parts of her body that she's going to use to make love to you. You see her mouth and teeth and tongue and fingers. You see her fingers comb her hair, play the piano, wash the dishes, write a letter. You watch her mouth eat and whistle and quiver and scream and kiss. When she makes love to you she brings all this movement and activity with her into your body.

Ann liked this. With her penis, however, it wasn't the same. She had to keep it private. She also didn't like fucking Muriel very much. She missed the old way. Putting her penis into a woman's body was so confusing. Ann knew it wasn't making love "to" Muriel and it certainly wasn't Muriel making love "to" her. It was more like making love "from" Muriel and that just didn't sit right.

One day Ann told Muriel about Jesse.

"I give her everything within my capacity to give and she gives me everything within her capacity to give—only my capacity is larger than hers."

In response Muriel took her to the Museum of Modern Art and pointed to a sculpture by Louise Bourgeois. Ann spent most of the afternoon in front of the large piece, an angry ocean of black penises which rose and crashed, carrying a little box house. The piece was called "Womanhouse." She looked at the penises, their little round heads, their black metal trunks, how they moved together to make waves, and she understood something completely new.

They got together the next day in a bar. As soon as she walked in Ann felt nauseous. She couldn't eat a thing. The smell of grease from Jesse's chicken dinner came in waves to Ann's side of the table. She kept her nose in the beer to cut the stench.

"You're dividing me against myself, Jesse."

Jesse offered her some chicken.

"No thanks, I really don't want any. Look, I can't keep making out with you on a couch because that's as far as you're willing to go before this turns into a lesbian relationship. It makes me feel like nothing."

Ann didn't mention that she had a penis.

"Annie, I can't say I don't love being physical with you because it wouldn't be true."

"I know."

"I feel something ferocious when I smell you. I love kissing you. That's why it's got to stop. I didn't realize when I started this that I was going to want it so much."

"Why is that a problem?"

"Why is that a problem? Why is that a problem?"

Jesse was licking the skin off the bone with her fingers. Slivers of meat stuck out of her long fingernails. She didn't know the answer.

"Jesse, what would happen if someone offered you a woman with a penis?"

Jesse wasn't surprised by this question, because Ann often raised issues from new and interesting perspectives.

"It wouldn't surprise me."

"Why not?"

"Well, Annie, I've never told you this before, actually it's just a secret between me and my therapist, but I feel as though I do have a penis. It's a theoretical penis, in my head. I've got a penis in my head and it's all mine."

"You're right," Ann said. "You do have a penis in your head because you have been totally mind-fucked. You've got an eight-inch cock between your ears."

With that she left the restaurant and left Jesse with the bill.

Soon Ann decided she wanted her clitoris back and she started to consult with doctors who did transsexual surgery. Since Ann had seen, tasted, and touched many clitorises in her short but full life, she knew that each one had its own unique way and wanted her very own cunt back just the way it had always been. So, she called together every woman who had ever made love to her. There was her French professor from college, her brother's girlfriend, her cousin Clarisse, her best friend from high school, Judith, Claudette, Kate, and Jane and assorted others. They all came to a big party at Shelley's house where they got high and drank beer and ate lasagna and when they all felt fine, Ann put a giant piece of white paper on the wall. By committee, they reconstructed Ann's cunt from memory. Some people had been more attentive than others, but they were all willing to make the effort. After a few hours and a couple of arguments as to the exact color tone and how many wrinkles on the left side, they finished the blueprints. "Pussy prints," the figure skater from Iowa City called them.

The following Monday Ann went in for surgery reflecting on the time she had spent with her penis. When you're different, you really have to think about things. You have a lot of information about how the mainstream lives, but they don't know much about you. They also don't know that they don't know, which they don't. Ann wanted one thing, to be a whole woman again. She never wanted to be mutilated by being cut off from herself and she knew that would be a hard thing to overcome, but Ann was willing to try.

ELLEN SHEA

The Dangerous Beauty
of the Open Road

I USUALLY CRUISE at about 70—over the speed limit, but not enough to be conspicuous. Troopers are really after the ones that break 90, the guy who weaves through traffic like a shuttlecock through a loom. Most truckers are happy to hover at 70, an even clip. If you keep up with the flow of the rigs and don't pass too many, you'll do all right.

For safety's sake I have a CB, everybody does, but I don't like all that chatter when I'm driving and I don't like people calling me whenever they feel like it. So I always keep it turned down. Instead I watch for signals that show there's a speed trap up ahead—the sudden choke in traffic like a clogged sink, truckers on the other side coming toward you and flashing their lights in warning. When I pass the trap doing a sedate 55, around the bend I flash my lights in return for the trucks on the other side. Just doing my part.

Driving a car is one of my earliest memories. I held onto the steering wheel and he worked the pedals. I was standing on my father's thighs and he was really steering, else we would have gone right off the road, but still I'll never forget the incredible power I felt. I turned the wheel to the right, and the car (obeying me) swung gently to the right. I was making it go. I didn't think these words; I was too young. But I knew it anyway: I liked controlling this car, forcing it to do my bidding. That was driving. "Fast," I said to my father, which is of course his version of the story, and the speedometer needle jumped from 5 to 10. "Whoosh," my father told me "'Atta girl. You already drive better than your mama." I don't remember my mother being in the car any of the times I was allowed to drive.

My business is legitimate, no secret packages taped underneath the truck or anything, but I don't want to get stopped. Too many speeding tickets will put me right out of commission. And I can't stand having to be polite to those troopers who are, universally, pricks. With their mirror sunglasses and tough guy hats, their jaws working with Wrigley's Spearmint, they live to catch a drug-runner or an escaped convict. Instead they get moving violations and road accidents from here to kingdom come, and lost assholes from Ohio. They want to see your fear when they pull you over and step up to your window, and if you don't trot it out nice for them, they get nasty until you knuckle.

One of them stopped me in Pennsylvania somewhere for doing "19 miles over the speed limit, Ma'am." He saw a girl driving a truck, short hair, muscles on her tan, ropy arms. He wanted to quiz me about who I was and where I was going and why. I got bored with this and told him that last I heard, it was still a free country and did he just want to give me a ticket, or not. His sunglasses hid his eyes, but I could feel their chill.

"What's a dyke like you doing around here?" he said, low and mean, a big grin on his face. "All our girls around here like men, sweetheart, so you're wasting your time." He said this, I swear. Also, he was all of 22 years old.

I kept my mouth shut and took the ticket, then pulled off the shoulder nice and slow. That's what you have to do when you're a stranger, you have to eat this shit right on up, with a pleasant smile on your face. Swallow it down like a good girl. Or you'll be force fed something worse.

I've been a stranger for a while now, and I've learned some valuable things that way.

I inherited the truck from my father. Believe me, there're better legacies you can have. Still and all, somehow I always knew I'd end up taking over his business and motoring that truck down every interstate in the country. She's a small rig and I can handle her fine. She responds to my touch with an amazing eagerness; I can usually get her to do things my father never could. For instance, start up on days when the temperature drops to 20 below. My father called all his trucks Red, like a horse or a dog. Here comes the believable part: of course he showed his Reds more care and attention, maybe even affection, than he ever showed me or my mother.

Driving was my father's life. That and drinking. If you put the two together you can understand a whole lot without my even saying it. How he lived, how he died, what kind of man he was. Even so, my father respected me a lot, or that's what I think. Maybe because I could control the truck, because I'm an ace driver. Because I am as tough and sour as he ever wanted to be.

I tell people I was born in a truck. This isn't true, but it might as well be. It makes for a good story.

It seems that when my mother's time came, my father was out back working on a truck, one of the early Reds. As my mother tells it, she waddled into the yard clutching at her belly and my father asked if couldn't she hang on for five more minutes so's he could finish with the shocks. My mother threw a socket wrench at his head, and missed. Then my father loaded her up in the truck and took her to the hospital where I was born 20 minutes later. My mother likes to tell this story, especially the part about the throwing of the wrench.

"Of course she missed," my father confided in me once, "she could never throw worth a damn. I only took her to the hospital so I wouldn't have to look for my tools all the hell over the place."

"I only missed," my mother would say, "because I was having contractions every two minutes. You almost got born in that truck, and then what would he've done? Run screaming from the place, most likely. Down to the bar to steady his nerves."

So I often tell people that I was born on the road and will probably die on the road, which may well turn out to be true.

Most people do not belong behind the wheel of a car. They don't give IQ tests before they hand out drivers' licenses, and it shows. People who left off school in the third grade, people who can't operate a toaster, people who think New Mexico is in South America—all these people get in their cars every day and drive around for a while. I happen to think that driving requires concentration and skill, deft hand-eye coordination, the ability to think fast on your feet, and instantaneous reaction time. So you see what we're up against.

Truckers must cultivate some rare patience if they're to survive on the job. It's a matter of just going along with it, I tell myself, instead of reacting every time some dim-witted feeble brain cuts you off to do 25 in the left lane of the thruway. The Zen of driving is essential to remember. Certainly, I wish death upon these people, but only in the most benign sort of way, and I will not do anything to facilitate it.

Only, most drivers take such fearsome stupid chances, riding around in their little instruments of death. A two-ton trailer rig can crush a car like it was a cheap beer can, so all that's left is some scrap metal and round pellets of shatter-proof glass scattered across the road. And the bodies. I've seen some accidents, more than I care to remember. You cannot believe what a person looks like when he's been pulled from the wreckage of yet another fiberglass sports car. He will be half-chewed and partially digested and spit out of some demented creature's mouth. State troopers, the young ones, will retch, but the truckers will only turn white because they've usually seen it before, and when they stop to help they know it's almost always too late.

"This is no life for a girl," my mother tells me every time I visit, which isn't too frequently anymore.

"If I was a boy, what would you say?" I asked her once.

My mother laughed. "That it wasn't much of a life for a boy, either." She looked at me hard. "But I guess that's what your father always wanted you to be. A boy. So I shouldn't be too surprised on how you turned out."

That wasn't exactly true, but my mother would naturally see it that way. "I turned out fine," I told her.

"Well," said my mother. She sidestepped this point. "Some day you're gonna want children. Then what?"

Strange that she didn't mention a man. Maybe she knew that wasn't a problem, that I could always have a man, if and when I wanted one.

"No children," I said. "I couldn't take care of a child. I can barely take care of me."

My mother snorted and looked away, out the window and over the hills. "That's what they all say," she told me. "That's what I said. And now look."

Now look, I thought. You only had the one. But before I could say anything more my mother went on.

"You don't want to regret it," she said. "You don't want to wake up one day, old and alone. No children, no family, no real home. I'm not gonna be around forever," she added, though of course she would. My mother was built to last. "Just a truck," she said now. "Is that what you want? Truck's not gonna take care of you when you get sick. Truck's not gonna sleep with you when you're lonesome. Truck's not gonna bury you when you die." Her voice was hard and I knew she was thinking of my father.

There were no guarantees, I told her. "You can't expect happiness," I said. "Just because you do all the right things, what you're supposed to. It doesn't work like that. You can't count on anything, you know that."

"You're wrong," my mother said. She walked to the kitchen sink and leaned on it, gazing into the drain. "You can always count on some things. You can count on ending up with less than you started out with."

I left her standing there, her face to the window hiding tears, or maybe hiding that there were no tears at all. I backed Red down the driveway and tried not to gun the motor as I drove away.

I like to drive fast, yes. Fast and steady. I train myself, but still I have not much patience with the dawdlers, the meek of heart, the older ones who peer over the steering wheel convinced they can still do it, our flaming youth whose greatest thrill is to challenge truckers and play chicken to pass the night away. I never play; they end up buzzing around me like so many harmless gnats. I will sooner pull over than engage them in battle, though many truckers do. Maybe out of boredom, ego, a sense of impending doom.

These are things I hate: break-down, construction, alternate routes, detours, drawbridges, inexplicable slow-ups, heavy beach traffic, rush hour, Friday night exodus during ski and sun seasons, Sunday night returns to the city. I hate driving in the middle of the day, with the general populace. I like those sweet empty hours before dawn. Between three and five in the morning I drive my best, just me and the other truckers. We are terribly courteous to one another, for the most part, as we hurtle through that dead zone finally free of the rest of the driving world.

I used to have a quote written on a piece of paper bag and Scotch-taped to my dashboard. This is what it said:

> The truck devoured the road with high-singing tires, and I rode throned in the lofty, rocking cab, listening to the driver telling me stories about all the people who lived in the places we passed, and what went on in the houses we saw.

It's from a book by Thomas Merton, called *The Seven-Storey Mountain*. I tried to find it in a bookstore once in El Paso, but they'd never even heard of it. I'm sure a better bookstore in a bigger city would have it, except I don't even bother to look for it anymore.

One day I was giving a lift to a trucker I knew slightly, whose rig broke down 20 miles outside of town.

"What's this?" he said, and peeled the quote off the dashboard.

"Nothing," I told him. "Something from a book that I like."

"Something from a book," he said dubiously, and read it. "Sounds like *poetry* or something." He made a gagging noise. When I didn't answer, he said, "You dress kind of funny, too, come to think of it." And laughing, he crumpled up the old brown paper and let the wind snatch it from his hand.

By this time I knew the sentence by heart, so I decided it would be safer to keep it in my head and not on the dashboard. A truck is not a place to fill up with clutter; you can get attached to objects even quicker than to people. That was a good lesson to learn.

Now my truck has very little, but it's complete unto itself. I've got a sleeping bag stashed in the back in case I'm fed up with trucker motels or I want to catch a quick nap somewhere. I have a battery-powered hot plate and three thermoses, a bottle of Jim Beam and one of vodka, a tape deck, plenty of magazines, and a whole medicine cabinet full of stuff, including all the pills that get traded around in truck stops like they were baseball cards for flipping. I have everything I need.

But when I need something more, I stop at a motel or some roadie bar on the outskirts of any town. A place usually with live shit-kicker music and beer for 30 cents a glass.

The sex is almost always very good. Sometimes exceptional. I only take people passing through, like me. I rely on my gift, which I like to think I was given at birth, the way some people have a knack for mathematics or foreign languages. I have a gift for picking the right ones, who will never surprise me, because I don't like surprises. I look for humor and tenderness and passion, and something of grief, since that's what gives people strength and sympathy. As good a combination as you'll ever find.

And then, on those cool motel sheets with the TV turned down low and its blue-white light baptizing our bodies, we go to town, go to town all night sometimes, and my instinct never fails me and I never get hurt. Unless I want to be.

Besides my father's love of driving, his attachment to liquor, and his affection for Red, I've also inherited his intense absorption in food. This is a trait that most truckers share, maybe because a meal breaks up the tedium of a long day and gives you something to look forward to.

I remember my father eating a dinner at home, plowing steadily and silently through his London broil and mashed potatoes with an unwavering focus that fascinated me. My mother and I could talk around him and through him, without expecting a response until he'd wiped his mouth and pushed his plate back, and woke up.

Most of the waitresses at truck stops are named Fran or Adele or Missy and they always seem to wear the same beige and orange polyester uniforms. They'll give pie on the house to the truckers they know, and keep the coffee coming without ever having to be asked for a re-fill. Invariably the older ones feel sorry for me—a lamb lost in wolf territory—and take very good care of me. They bring me choice pieces of pot roast, an extra slab of meat loaf, always the white meat fried chicken, the last slice of chocolate layer cake that's oversized. They can be friendly at times, and so can the men, but the women truckers are a different story.

The other women truckers are a breed apart; they're not like me. Or I'm not like them. They travel with elaborate hair dryers and curling irons and nail polishing kits. They favor matching outfits, pastel sets usually, and tight designer jeans.

I think of them sometimes as I finger-dry my hair in some tiny motel bathroom. I look at my favorite, comfortable clothes in the mirror, grimed and wrinkled, and try to imagine myself working them over with a portable travel iron. I conjure up a picture of filing my plastic press-on nails at night by the glow of the TV. This game never fails to cheer me up, so when I stroll into the coffee shop I almost laugh at the sight of these wondrous creations at their tables, fixing their lipstick in a compact mirror. Their eyes slide right over me. I'm not a man, I'm not a girl, they can't see what I am so they don't see me at all.

Every once in a while, though, one of them will give me careful information on some truckers: who's safe, who I'm to watch out for, who's supposed to be a killer in bed. Or outside bed.

They shouldn't worry. I carry a gun and I know how to use it. I've shot two men because they neither of them believed that I would or could.

Sometimes I think I am a cowboy, sitting high in the saddle as I ride out alone on Red at sunset; my gun not slung low on my hips but strapped to an ankle holster. It chafes and leaves an imprint on my skin, but I no longer feel it except as a comforting presence nestled against my leg.

My gun is illegal. I would carry a knife, except I don't ever want to be that close to danger in order to protect myself.

Driving at night you need your wits about you. The headlights can trick you into a glaze and you're dreaming awake. You don't want to be on cruise control in a truck at night, hugging the wild corners of a two-lane blacktop. You want to be all there, driving, and let the truck know who's boss.

What would happen if I lost my concentration and let Red take over? Then what? Would she turn on the trail for home? Wander off into the underbrush exploring? I keep her on too tight a rein to find out. If I'm done with my delivery quota for the day, I usually stop most nights pretty early. Then I can be on my way before dawn and cover a fair distance before the sun even breaks.

One night or early morning I came home from catting around town to find my father passed out on the stairs, presumably on his way up to bed. As I was used to finding my father in various states of consciousness, this was not too unusual. I only clucked to myself, an angry cluck, and because this time I refused to rouse him and spirit him off to his bed, I kicked him in the side as I went upstairs.

I know how that sounds, but regardless, I did it, and didn't feel too bad for doing it. Maybe it was meant to get him up, or maybe not. When you live with a drunk for a while you learn to exact your revenge in small ways that only you can know about, in ways the drunk cannot possibly retaliate for. It wasn't a kick that would've broken a rib—it would've probably left a bruise, a soreness the next day to add to the general soreness. I was just doing my part, heaping on the guilt, so he'd be forced to wonder the next day: where did that one come from? Did someone sucker punch me in the bar? What door did I go careening off of?

So I kicked him, and as I did, he moaned a little, a small groan that didn't manage to bring him up from whatever depths he was in, and I hesitated, thinking he would wake and then I'd have to help him up. But he didn't wake, and was silent. So I switched off the light and went on up to bed.

Later that morning I was awakened myself by the sound of my mother screaming, over and over. I'd heard my mother scream before, certainly, but not like this. I rolled out of bed and hit the floor running. She was on the stairs next to my father, who hadn't moved a limb since I'd seen him six hours earlier. My mother's eyes were wide and shiny with terror and she was pulling the skin of her cheeks down with both hands, like a parody of some woman in shock. She couldn't form any words, but she didn't have to. I called an ambulance and then I led my mother away from him, into the kitchen, while we waited for it to come. Then I made sure there wasn't anything I could do, and there wasn't.

Like in murder mysteries, I asked the attending doctor to pinpoint the time of death. Unlike murder mysteries, he couldn't really tell me. Some time between three and five in the A.M. is what he'd said. I'd come home about 3:30 that morning.

Once I read an article that mentioned how when a person dies he usually has a little air left in his lungs. If you move the body, the sound of the air escaping creates a small sound, like a moan or a groan. Sometimes this can fool you, the article said, into actually believing the person was still alive when he wasn't.

The fact of the matter remains, there is no way out of this one. I kicked a dead man on the stairs in my house. Or I kicked a man who was engaged in dying. The doctor allowed to me, privately, that my father was not only drunk as the old skunk when he died of a massive coronary, but that his liver was greatly enlarged. "The drink killed him," the doctor told me, shaking his head with a show of sadness. "I'm not telling your mother. But that's what killed him, sure as I'm sitting here."

I didn't care much what killed him, but I cared when. There was another possibility, the one I favor the least. Suppose it hadn't happened yet. Suppose my father was just taking his customary breather after spending seven hours in the bar, and I could've roused him. Gotten him to his feet, maybe even gotten him to yell at me, to maybe take a swing at my head. Then he would've had his heart attack and I could've saved him. In this fantasy, he stayed in the hospital two months, quit drinking and smoking, came home, and was a nice man who liked to shoot pool with his daughter and tinker with his truck and take his wife out to Clam Night at the Holiday Inn.

But this is what I believe in my heart: I kicked my father who was barely cold, half an hour dead, and kicking him, dislodged the last breath he'd ever hold in his lungs.

Because we live in modern times, only hitchhikers I will occasionally pick up are the young girls. Sometimes they just want to get into town, but more often than not they're running away. Running from fathers who beat them or have sex with them, husbands who beat them and rape them when they've had too much to drink. We may live in modern times, but in small towns everywhere girls are still getting married at fifteen.

They are usually surprised and not always pleased to see that I am a woman. They buy into the stereotypes very early and are suspicious of why I have stopped for them. They cannot seem to realize that it is the men they must watch out for. I've heard stories about truckers who'll pick up young girls and boys to see what they can get, take them where they want to go in return for a quick blowjob or a roll around the back of the truck. I don't know if I believe this; most truckers get paid by the load and even a 15 minute break can mean missing a warehouse deadline. Nevertheless, I've met some slimy characters on the road and I wouldn't want to be fresh-faced and fourteen, sitting in the passenger seat.

I stopped for one girl outside Yellow Springs; she claimed to be eighteen but I didn't think she'd see that age for another three years yet.

"I never seen a lady trucker before," she confided to me.

I allowed as how we weren't all that common.

"What made you want to be a trucker when you grew up?" she said.

That made me think. Not having too much ambition herself other than to have babies, she just assumed that's the way it was done. You decided to drive a truck at age three, and then there you were.

It was curious, but no one had ever asked me why. My mother knew why, or thought she knew. My friends shook their heads and secretly enjoyed it—I was someone they were comfortably sorry for, and then they felt better about their own lives. My father's friends, who were all truckers, nodded their heads and told me I'd be sorry. This girl suddenly asked me why and I didn't have an answer.

The pause went on too long for her. "Guess you get to see a lot of places," she decided. "You don't gotta answer to no one, right? Your own boss and all that." She settled my life neatly and moved on to hers, which was much more messy. I left her off in a city that was slightly out of my way. I didn't ask for anything in return.

I've been through all 48 mainland states. While it's true I've seen an awful lot of the country, I haven't seen that many cities. It's not that I don't like people or crowds or noise. Sometimes I do. But those places, they're none of them my home. And I don't belong; I'm not even visiting. It's not like travelling to a place to see friends you know, or to soak up some exotic atmosphere. I'm only passing through. While I'm passing through, I imagine the lives that I never quite see, each one complicated and thorough, with its own history and its own address book filled with other people's names and lives. Sometimes I see a brief flash of people I will never know—I'll pass a lawn party or a wedding letting out of a church, an old man and woman sitting on a porch swing, two children beating each other up with plastic pails and shovels. They never see me. I'm a truck going by. I leave no trace or memory, but I carry them all with me wherever I go.

Mostly I measure how far I've come and how far I'm going by road signs. I chart my progress across the country by hours (how long will it take me to get to Shreveport). Sometimes I picture my truck as a little blip on a huge road map. That's me, traversing all those red and blue lines, skimming past insignificant dots that are towns easy to forget. Forging through the larger congested dots that mean big cities. And there's me and Red, making short work of all those endless lines . . . where do they all go? A grid that stops when you get to the edge of the map. And where do we go from there?

One day my father and I were out in the back working on Red. There was something clearly wrong with her transmission. Though neither of us knew squat about fixing transmissions we were banging away regardless. We were both decked out in our oldest clothes and grimed up; now and then we'd chug from warmish cans of Budweiser. Just like a beer commercial, me and my father. I was working hard, not thinking of anything and not talking much either when suddenly I got that unmistakable feeling when someone's looking at you. I glanced up and it was my father.

He was staring at me as if it were the first time he'd ever laid eyes on me. It came over in such a flash I knew it had to be true—he was looking at me not like a daughter, or even a woman, but as a stranger. Someone who puzzled the hell out of him, someone who didn't belong in his backyard. He stood there, examining me, not a hint of smile on his face. It wasn't a mean look, though, not like he'd decided to hate me. No, because in that instant he didn't know me well enough to hate me. But there was something unpleasant there all the same.

"What," I said, to break the spell.

He shook his head. "Nothing," he said. "Just . . . you're an odd fish, you know? Some kind of odd fish." He dropped his eyes.

"Yeah, and you're a queer duck," I told him, and we both sort of laughed so that the moment was over and we went back to work.

He couldn't understand how this odd fish came to be. He never made the connection that it was him who spawned me.

I've driven in some weather. In wretched Texas heat, where it hit 114 and cars and trucks were littered on the side of the road, steaming, like some freshly killed animals. In rain and snow storms that could make you believe in Jesus, when the back end of Red would go fishtailing down the highway. That sickening skid feeling when the wheels have no grip and no gravity, the weightless suspension of your heart as you steer into the skid, always into the skid, where you don't want to go, teaching your foot not to slam on the brake and send you slithering down an embankment end over end over end.

I've seen tornado weather. I played chicken with a twister, trying to beat it to the next truck stop. There's no more unnatural weather on this earth, though some truckers will claim the Santa Ana winds can make them believe in hell.

The tornado was supposed to be heading away from the direction I was going in, but in its perversity, its fickle black soul, buttonhooked back toward me. I was in South Dakota, next service area 34 miles, when I saw the dark blot on the horizon. It loomed up fast, bouncing on its merry pogo stick way, that eerie howling making my hackles rise like a dog.

The sky was a color that no sky ever had the right to be, a sickly yellow-gray like the end of the world. I pulled Red off onto the shoulder and got out, leaving both windows open. The radio had been bleating warnings every three minutes about what to do if you were unlucky enough to get caught. I was apparently the only one in sight who had. Even though I knew that staying in the truck would only give me the illusion of safety since the twister could toss it like a Matchbox truck, it was still the hardest thing I'd ever done, to climb down out of Red and throw myself into a drainage ditch. When the tornado passed over, screaming, I screamed too.

There was a moment of absolute stillness when all the air seemed to have been sucked up by a huge, invisible pair of lungs. Then dirt and rocks and branches and sod were churning around me, and the twister was gone on its weird, whistling way. I sat up and watched it dance down the highway, touching down lightly here and there, kicking up all manner of things in its wake. I was left behind in my drainage ditch, holding clumps of weeds in my tight fists as if I might fall off the face of the earth.

A while later some people drove by, hailed me as a survivor, and plied me with warm whiskey until I could emerge from my lair shaky but alive, alive-o.

My mother didn't fall apart until after it was all over. Up until then she'd held herself together well enough, for the sake of all the people who'd come to show their respects. She considered it vulgar to break down in front of them. So she was quite the gracious hostess even after the burial, inviting everyone back to the house for a ham and a turkey that she'd cooked herself, the night before. Neighbors had brought in casseroles, candied and glazed and microwaveable, and all manner of pies, including rhubarb, which I hated.

My mother's face was flushed. She darted from one cluster of people to the next, emptying ash trays, re-filling their highballs, urging food. She was giddy with the company, the first successful party she'd ever thrown. She didn't want anyone to leave and when she waved goodbye to each person at the door ("Thanks for coming—safe home now") I expected her to invite them all back to do it again the next weekend. When the last drunk and gorged guest had gone, my mother wandered restless and empty through the house, ending up in the kitchen where I sat with my watery rye.

"What a mess," she said, and sunk into a chair.

"You spent a lot of money," I said.

"And if I did," she said. "Your father deserved a fine send-off. What's money to me now, anyway?"

"Nothing," I said. "Nothing. Only the truck is going to need a few things, if I'm to carry on the business."

"Don't you dare," my mother told me. "Don't you dare mention that truck to me. Tonight." Tears rolled slowly down her face and dripped off her jaw. She seemed too tired or too hopeless to wipe them away. I wanted to get her a tissue but my mother would have interpreted that as pity, something you did for a child or an old person.

"He loved you the best, you know," she said.

"He called me an odd fish," I told her.

"And so you are," she said. "But he loved you the best. Out of the both of us, he loved you the best."

I said, "He had a funny way of showing it."

My mother slapped me full across the face with a ferocious suddenness and my neck cracked. Then she went to bed.

Once I needed some time off so I flew to England for two months and traveled around. I could've rented a car, but I thought that's what I was trying to get away from. Instead I got myself a Britrail pass and spent my time as a passenger. But in my dreams there, I was always driving. Sometimes I was even driving a train, careening down the tracks, hugging a hairpin turn around the edge of a cliff. Always I could feel the pull of the train underneath me, responding to my touch.

In a pub out in the west country, a small trainman's place called The Goat's Head, I sipped the local ale and became the object of some curiosity being as I was American, female, and alone. The natives had a collective accent so thick and fanciful that I could hardly believe we were speaking the same language at times. By the third or fourth round—the local brew being more potent than any beer I'd ever had before—I was floating on the rhythms of their speech. I absorbed most of what they were saying more from the pattern and lilt of their phrasing rather than understand the words themselves.

The fellow next to me, a train engineer, finally found out that I drove a truck back home in the States.

"Cor!" he said. "Lorries. Driving a lorry cross that swaping big country of yours." Never mind that I was a girl, I became his hero. I'd never made anyone's face light up before. It seemed that I'd hit upon his dream—of driving for days and never seeing the ocean, but only the flat and unbreakable expanse of land stretching in front, the sky meeting the earth in a faraway horizon and knowing that you could drive to that point and still keep going. It was the hunger of someone who lives on an island. It was the ancient yearning for the New World, and I discovered with some surprise that I was away from my own land and I was homesick.

We drank and talked of lorries all evening until the barkeep called time. The train engineer offered me a walk to clear our heads and the walk ended in his flat for a nightcap. Contrary to what I'd heard about the British, he was a good and fervent lover. And if he was off exploring some unknown landscape, driving in search of who knows where, I could excuse him for that. Because I found I was off there, too, driving to the edges of some precipice that I couldn't quite see.

My mother has an owl collection. She collects all types of owls without discrimination for quality or craftsmanship: ceramic, glass, wood, plastic, and those hideous ones made out of shells glued together. "Why don't you collect something?" my mother tells me. "It's a good hobby."

I don't have any room for clutter, for collections, for anything that needs preserving and dusting. But one day I realized I'd taken my mother's advice after all. I collect the names of places—towns I've seen and driven by, even towns that were just a sign on the road.

I liked the ones best that had some history to them, history someone in a bar would tell me. Like Baby Head, Texas, which apparently was named when a raiding Comanche captured and killed a white baby and put its head on a pole on the mountain. Or 88, Kentucky, because the postmaster couldn't read or write. I also liked Bill, Wyoming, so called after the first name of most of its citizens.

Then there's the ones I just like the sound of: Cat Mash, Alabama; Slaughter Beach, Delaware; Rough and Ready, California; Experiment, Georgia. West Virginia has towns called War and Mud and Odd. Kentucky has Dwarf and Viper. Texas is the hands-down winner, though. Texas has a love for one-word towns that may or may not be descriptive, like Small and Scurry and Fry, Lawn and Pancake; Necessity, Fairy, Pep, and Goodnight.

I keep the list in my back pocket, not taped to the dashboard. Sometimes at night I take it out and read the names to myself. The names all make a kind of poetry, a lullaby that puts me to sleep.

When I was still pretty small, my father and mother took me to an amusement park. This was fairly unusual, as they weren't that big on family-type outings. Seems like once they had me, they expected me to entertain myself. But we ended up at this amusement park where there was a ride I was wild to try. It involved cars and trucks that you could really drive. The brakes worked, and the steering. They rode gently around a track powered by electricity, like a trolley.

I remember you had to be a certain height to qualify for this ride and I had to strain to reach the line they'd painted for where your head should be. Finally, my turn was up and I climbed into a milk truck. This was much better than bumper cars, where all I wanted to do was drive in peace and all the other kids kept ramming me. The track wound in and out of trees, alongside a small pond, and through a tunnel. I properly observed traffic signals and the flashing railroad crossing sign. I was supremely, thoroughly pleased with myself. I could drive. This was all there was to it—I had always been certain it would be easy and there was no reason to wait until I was grown up to do it.

When I passed my parents waiting at the fence, I tooted the horn and waved like an old pro.

"That's my girl," said my father. His face was split wide with a grin. My mother was looking the other way and didn't see me go by.

It's not just my mother. Other people tell me that it's not much of a life for a girl. Sometimes men will shake their heads in wonderment at me—a woman whose code they cannot crack. Or so they think. A woman who forsakes hearth and home, who does not campaign for bedroom furniture and bassinets. A woman who can change a car tire in twelve minutes flat (if the bolts aren't rusted on), and sleeps many nights in many strange and empty beds, and is not afraid of the dark. A woman who can be alone and not talk to herself.

They watch me pull out of the parking lot after sharing a meal or more than a meal; their eyes follow me as I merge Red smoothly into the flow of traffic. They admire me and yet there is still something underneath that respect, something I once saw in my father's eyes: a puzzlement which can only be resolved in contempt. The women they all know do not do this, do not behave this way. Therefore, what does that make me?

But I've seen some things. I drove through a meteor shower one night and finally stopped along with everyone else who could not keep their eyes on the road. Our faces turned up to the heavens, we watched hundreds of shooting stars trace tails across the sky until we could no longer absorb such a vision and so abandoned it.

I've seen a palace in South Dakota decorated entirely with corn, and a house built with candy, like in Hansel and Gretel. I've driven toward a town that rose up from the desert floor like a citadel, shimmering with heat, that never grew any larger as I approached.

I once saw a trucker hit a deer, a large buck, probably eight points, and we both stopped and helped each other haul him bleeding and unconscious into the back of his truck by way of the electronic ramp. We drove to the city and found the closest veterinarian, who couldn't save the buck's life. Neither the other trucker nor I took the antlers, and the vet charged us fifty dollars for the privilege of making money off the carcass.

I once saw a trucker deliberately swerve to hit a dog who'd run out in the road.

I once saw a topless dancer sit down on her runway and sob after a trucker had thrown a wad of crumpled bills at her feet and yelled to buy herself a good support bra.

I met a man who confessed over too many beers that he was in love with his own mother. "She'll let me take her to the movies, but that's it," he said, "what can I do?"

I've never been visited by aliens from another planet but once saw a UFO. It hovered over a nearby mountain, shimmering with lights, exactly the way it's supposed to do.

I once saw a man killed in a bar, knifed by his best friend over a woman, of course. From that I learned that we have so much blood in us, it is not to be believed. And I learned that no one, no matter how brave, will move to restrain a man driven mad by love.

I once saw a whole field of bats rise up around me from where I scared them from their feasting. I felt the rush of air from the silent flutter of their wings but not a one touched me.

I once saw true love in the face beside me in bed one morning, and I left that same day. I was young and only wanted to jump in my truck, to drive, and it was only several years later that I remembered and understood that look, what it meant.

Some days when I'm tooling down the road, not thinking much of anything, I feel like one of those creatures in Pac-Man. A round head and a big mouth, gobbling up the road, swallowing that white line as fast as I can. It's fun for a while but it can get too hypnotic. Then I get mesmerized by the road and forget where I'm going. You can miss an exit like that. You can lose yourself.

I read an article in a magazine once about the hazards of scuba diving, how a diver can get nitrogen narcosis if he swims down too far. Then he can't tell down from up, and he's so deliriously happy he doesn't care, just keeps swimming further and further toward the bottom of the ocean. Who knows if he ever reaches it. But he never comes back.

Rapture of the deep, it's called.

I've felt it, too, driving late at night. You can follow the pull of your own headlights right off the highway, as you're going round a bend. Lured like a bug to its own senseless, dreamy ecstatic death. That's the dangerous beauty of the open road.

When I'm not on the road, I have a place to stay. I don't always sleep in my truck or in motels. People might expect I live in a small efficiency apartment fully furnished, but no. I live in a large old ramshackle house, hardly furnished at all. I have a phone only because my mother insisted, though no television, no washer and dryer, no microwave, no matching dishes.

"Why don't you buy yourself a comfortable couch?" my mother often says. "Why can't you get yourself a decent set of china, at least?" This is what my mother means by having a home. I don't know, maybe if I had all that I'd be a different person, settle down amongst all the things I'd collected, and never venture forth from such a cozy place.

In back of the house where I live for about 87 days out of the year is a meadow stretching toward the hills and a small copse of trees. When I'm there, I stand at twilight with a drink in my hand and survey all I see. The bats swoop out to search for food, stars begin to spangle the sky, the trees rustle. It's all very pretty. Then I walk around to the front of the house and sit on the steps so I can see the traffic. I watch the cars and trucks go past, their headlights holding them fast to the track.

My heart lifts and I yearn to be one of them driving by. I will only catch a glimpse of that girl sitting on the steps watching the traffic, and wonder who she is, what her life is like, before I turn my eyes away from her and back to the open road.

CHARLOTTE WATSON SHERMAN

BigWater

IT WAS ALMOST TIME to go there. Keta felt it in her bones. Water coming
down and her twelve-year-old frame filling and rounding. Water pushing
past her lungs when she laid on her back in her skinny wooden bed, pushing past and up until her soft brown skin formed small rounded hills on her
chest.

Keta tried to make herself small, tried to hide the secret of her body's
slow unfolding.

"Stop hunching your shoulders, girl."

"Where'd you get those skinny legs?"

Her aunts' smiling litany of questions made Keta blink her eyes and drop
her head.

These were the women—the overflowing thighs and hips of Aunt Sarah,
the softening belly of Aunt Ruth, Aunt Ethel's branchlike limbs, the proud,
wise head of Aunt Josephine. Keta would look at the bodies of these women
when they gathered every Wednesday to sit in a circle in the early evening
light on straight-backed chairs in her mother's living room.

She would stare at the abundant swells of her mother's warm flesh and
then feel the two small lumps on her chest and say, "I'm never going to look
like that."

"You have to start somewhere," Aunt Sarah would smile.

"You have plenty of time to grow, girl."

Aunt Ethel would hide her smile behind her hands and say, "Mine never
did grow."

"They're not what make you a woman," Aunt Ruth would snort. Then,
cigarettes in place, they'd all turn, clicking their heads back into their secret
dark circle.

Keta looked at the shapes and sizes of the women as they laughed and fussed over grown-woman things. She stood at the edge of their laughter, a long black wire, wondering, what does it take to make a real woman?

BigWater. Her mother had gone there. And Aunt Ethel. And Aunt Ruth and Sarah. And Aunt Josephine forced to go, physically forced against her protests.

"It's coming."

"It's coming. She's almost there."

"Doesn't make any sense. Taking me out to that water. Doesn't make any sense."

In the end, though, even Aunt Josephine had gone: out past the edge of town, past a hundred miles of whispering trees, deep into the forest where old stones hold secrets, past walls of chiseled granite, over a silver ribbon bridge into mountains rising like indigo breasts, moving up, into air so blue your bones fill with light.

BigWater. Her mother had gone, and her mother's mother, and her mother before her, and all the way back to the very first. And soon, very soon it would be Keta's turn to listen to the old words of the women.

In the old before time, before the people's spirits were broken, before the many tongues were lost, before the ceremonies were hidden from those who would not understand, women bled together. The moon called out to the water in their bodies, and they bled. One simultaneous stream of blood that carried them from world to world. They were one flesh. One blood. One Mother. The women left the nonbleeding girls, the boys and men, and went into the menstrual huts to wash the moon.

Then one morning, Keta woke to golden light filtering through the curtains, her body slashed with yellow light from her toes to the braids that lay across her head.

It had started as a seed of water planted deep within her brain. With the whisper of a roar, it grew into a stream soaring through her body toward her pubis, moving straight to the heart of her womb where it circled, a liquid burning star, before rushing toward the mouth between her legs. First it paused, then pushed past the brown girlish lips and flowed freely, a soft, strong, shining red river.

BigWater. Keta spent the first hours in bed with thick cotton pads clenched between her legs tight as Aunt Ruth's lips on her menthol cigarettes. She didn't know when the women were coming, but she knew they were all going to come. It was time.

Keta's mother entered a room made new.

"I knew it," her mother said, glancing at Keta's face. "I knew it soon as I smelled that new-woman smell, drifting down the steps like clouds. You feeling alright?" she asked.

Keta nodded. "Feel alright, but kind of funny."

"That's natural. You're changing, baby. Changing from one kind of being into another," her mother said as she rubbed Keta's stomach with lavender oil.

The day after her bleeding stopped, the women brought gifts to Keta's room.

Keta fingered a satin brassiere, a bottle of lavender oil, a photograph of her great-grandmother, a gold robe. She stroked her grandmother's collection of sacred writings.

"Tonight we're going to take you."

"Don't be afraid."

"You're growing up."

"Now, you're one of us."

Aunt Josephine put her hands on Keta's stomach and said, "The blood is the line, Keta. The line passing through all of us. The ceremony marks the line, so you know how special it is. I thought I could be a woman without all that. But I didn't know what being a woman was. I didn't know about the power and the responsibility, until BigWater."

Keta was a bit afraid. Her mother leaned forward, brushing Keta's face with her lips.

"It's important what you are and what you're going to be. I want you to know that I'm proud."

"But I didn't do nothing."

"You're you, aren't you?"

"Yeah, but. . . ."

"That's enough for me," her mother said and each woman hugged Keta fiercely.

As Keta lay in bed she felt herself grow big and small, light and dark, up and down. The blood had changed her, but she didn't know how. When would her breasts start to grow, when would her hips widen? Was she really now a woman?

"Here, drink this," her mother said, holding a cup of black liquid to Keta's lips. "You have to sleep until we get there."

Keta frowned as the warmth moved down her throat.

"We'll get you ready," Keta heard the women say as she began to float inside a deep black silence, warm as her mother's embrace.

"BigWater," breathed Aunt Sarah.

"It seems a hundred years since we've been here," Aunt Josephine said.

"Speak for yourself," growled Aunt Ruth.

"Are you ready?" Keta's mother asked.

Keta nodded, shaking herself fully awake. Her mother squeezed her hand.

"It's time," she said, pulling Keta from the car. "Watch out for the robe."

Keta stroked the softness of the golden robe while her mother covered her head with its hood.

"Queen Mother for a day."

"For an evening."

"For the rest of your life, if that's what you choose."

The sun left an orange light in the sky as shadows twisted and stretched across the ground.

"Do we have everything?" Aunt Josephine asked after they walked a short way into the trees.

Each woman stopped until they formed a dark knot in the path.

"Of course I know we have everything," Josephine said as she started the line moving toward the clearing once again.

Soon, they stepped from the darkness of the trees onto rocks shining like a skin holding water. BigWater, spreading before the women now, a sheet of shimmering blue-green glass.

"There it is, there's the one," Aunt Sarah cried as she pointed to the broad granite stone sitting in the center of a nest of white rocks.

"Here's where we walk."

"Careful, it's slick."

And the group moved slowly into the water across small dark rocks. The women led the way and behind dipped Keta, the hem of the robe floating on the water like a soft yellow flower.

"This is it. This is the one," Aunt Sarah whispered as she sat on the smooth-skinned rock. The others sat too, in a tight dark ring around Keta.

Her mother opened the basket and removed five yellow candles, a cup of white ashes, a spoonful of honey, a packet of bitterroot, a bottle of wine, and a large carved wooden cup.

When the moon's white eye began shining through the trees, Aunt Sarah said, "Let's begin."

Josephine started to hum, an old sound each of the others in turn pushed into the circle until it melted into one long hum rolling over the water.

Keta's mother began:

"This is the place where we come to be women. This is the place we come to be whole. We are following the line of our mothers and their mothers back to the very first one. When the first blood comes and a mother's house fills with its heavy, warm scent, it is time. Are you ready to follow the path of your mothers?"

Keta nodded, though she didn't know yet what her mother meant.

"Don't be afraid, we're going to show you," Aunt Josephine soothed.

The women removed their shoes and eased their bare feet into the water. Then Keta was surrounded by a ring of heavy laughter that held her in a wild embrace before lifting into the air.

Her mother dipped her fingers into the cup of ashes and lightly brushed Keta's face with the soft white powder.

"The bones of the dead. Now you wear the mask of your ancestors, the women who have gone before you and the women yet to come.

"Open your mouth."

Slowly, Keta complied. Her mother placed a drop of the root's bitter, milky sap on the left side of Keta's tongue and a drop of honey on the right.

"One side for the bitterness, one side for the sweetness of Life. Even your body will allow you goodness and sadness. To be a woman means knowing there are two sides to Life."

This was how Keta had felt when she became blood sisters, with her best friend Johnna. They had slit their fingertips with a paring knife, then mixed their blood. She felt safe now, in this circle of women.

"Be still and learn to listen to your body," her mother advised, as her aunts rose from the circle and laughed as they ran barefoot toward the lake's shore. They quickly returned, their long skirts dragging in the water.

"Eat the clay from their hands," her mother said. Each aunt presented a palm holding red clay to Keta.

"Our First Mother's blood poured from the moon into this clay. Her body is in this clay. We take Her body into our bodies so we will gain Her power, Her wisdom. We come here to eat this clay, to be still, to listen to our bodies' prayers. Smell the clay."

Aunt Sarah held the clay to Keta's nose. It smelled like wet dirt.

"This is the smell of our monthly blood, our blood that comes from the moon. People are made of moon-blood and clay. The spirits of our people flow in our blood. It is the blood of Life."

Keta ate some clay from each of her aunts' hands. The women also ate the clay.

"Take off your robe," Keta's mother instructed. Keta removed her robe and handed it to her mother. The women smeared Keta's body with the red clay.

Her mother's fingers gripped the slim bottle of wine and filled the wooden cup.

"This wine is the red water flowing inside you, the liquid cord winding from the women before us, through me to you, connecting us all to our First Mother, the source of all living things. This bloodwine is Her power, now yours. We will all drink from this cup. My mother told me this cup was carved by her mother's mother when she was a girl. You take the first sip, daughter."

Keta held the cup in both hands and raised it to her lips. She dipped her tongue into the pungent red liquid and smiled. This was her first taste of wine. It filled her head with a swirling watery glow.

"We are going to wash you after your first moon," her mother said. "For the last time, you will be bathed as a child. From now on, you will bathe as a woman and will be responsible for your own body."

Keta placed her bare feet in the water. Naked, she stepped from rock to rock as her aunts sat on the old stone laughing, water lapping at the hems of their skirts.

"Always remember how your body feels tonight. This is what happened to me and my mother and her mother before her," her mother said.

Keta watched her mother pass the candles to her aunts. As if looking through water, she saw her mother strike a match. Then Keta felt herself moving, her bones shifting, the candles' glow a fire inside her. She felt something more ancient than memory move through her blood as she moved among the smooth-skinned rocks.

Aunt Ethel leaned forward into the light of her candle and took Keta's right arm. "We're going to wash you like we wash the sacred stones of our dead. We wash them so we can bring them back again, as you will come back. When you were born, the moon was white and had stood up again. It was your beginning."

Keta moved through the water and gave her left arm to Aunt Josephine, who leaned forward, face dancing in the candle's narrow flame. She rubbed the silken water into Keta's arm. "Now the moon is yellow and turning, twisting and turning like a woman trying to get full of herself, trying to become herself, as you will become. It is another beginning."

Keta moved around the circle to Aunt Ruth and put her foot in Aunt Ruth's lap. Aunt Ruth set her glass of wine on the rock and then moved her face from the darkness into her candle's light. As she bathed Keta's foot she said, "Soon, the moon will be full and red. After loving, after battling, the moon will sit down like a woman who has arrived, a woman who belongs, like you will belong. That, too, will be a beginning."

Aunt Sarah grabbed Keta's left leg, let the water drip over her foot. She moved her candle close to Keta's face and looked into the girl's eyes until satisfied with what she saw, then she backed away and said, "This long body is life, girl. Nothing but life. And a woman holds all these moons, all these beginnings inside her body. When the moon is black, it is the dying moon."

Aunt Sarah pressed her fingertips to Keta's forehead, streaking her skin with clay.

"But when the moon is dying," Aunt Sarah continued, "the circle is only half-complete. We must die to be reborn, to complete the circle of Life. That is why we are washing you like we wash the stones to bring back our dead. One part of your life is dying, another being born."

Keta's mother stepped into the water with Keta. She splashed Keta's body, using her hands as cups to pour water over Keta's head, her shoulders, her breasts and buttocks. Keta smiled as the water cascaded over her skin. The water flowed over her body as it had flowed over her mother's body and her mother's before her.

"This will be the only time I will do this," her mother said, kneeling in front of Keta's gleaming body to wash her pubis.

Finally, Keta's mother held her candle to her daughter's face and said, "After tonight, you will be clothed in the knowledge of all these women. This is what makes you a woman. Every month now you'll be reborn and you'll hear a sound like WHOOSHWHOOSHWHOOSHWHOOSH-WHOOSHWHOOSHWHOOSH flowing through the water in your body. It's the old sound of where we all come from."

BigWater. The women were unashamedly drenched with water and wine, and Keta could see the magnificent outlines of their bodies. They talked into the night, their voices inflating Keta's head with notions she had never known until she felt herself swelling, growing larger than the tall black trees, felt her body opening with the sound of words shifting inside water, the bitterroot and honey on her tongue turning to water, her body brimmed with WHOOSHWHOOSHWHOOSHWHOOSH, growing larger, her body rounding with sound, with the women's laughter, and she grew larger still, grew past old granite walls, over indigo mountains, and into the blue-black air so high her body filled with light and the ancient shimmering of water.

APRIL SINCLAIR

from

Coffee Will Make You Black

So this is what it's like to be at Carla's party, I thought, glancing around the basement filled with girls in party dresses and boys in dress shirts and pants. Nobody really looked happy, they just looked cool. Maybe we were having fun and I was just too square to realize it. The boys stood around the food table gulping punch and stuffing themselves with potato chips and hot dogs. I overhead them say, "Man, this" and "Man, that" between bites. The girls were all bunched up on the other side of the room.

I sat next to Patrice and Tanya drinking Hawaiian punch, balancing a paper plate with a half-eaten hot dog and some potato chips on my lap. Carla was standing nearby talking to Joyce and Bernice. Melody and Linda were playing with Carla's little niece and nephew, Malcolm and Lakisha.

"Look, that's her second hot dog," Patrice said.

"Who?" I asked.

"Her," Tanya said pointing to Joyce, a chubby, light-skinned girl. "If Carla had known she was gonna make a pig out of herself she wouldn't have invited her," she added.

"Look, a lot of boys are on their second hot dogs," I pointed out.

Patrice shook her head and sighed. "Stevie, boys are different. They can eat as much as they want and people will think it's cute. If a girl does that, people will talk about her like a dog. Girls can't get away with the things boys can, don't you know that?"

"Yeah, but that doesn't make it right."

"There go Stevie's man, y'all," Tanya teased, pointing to a boy that looked like a groundhog.

"No, it isn't, I don't even know him."

"You know that's your nigger, girl, you ain't got to be shamed." Tanya laughed.

"I never seen him before in my life."

"Well, you better grab him, cause there go you last chance, girl," Tanya insisted.

"Carla, who is that over there? The dufus-looking one with the bifocals," Patrice asked.

"That's Marc's brother, Sherman. I didn't know he was going to bring him," she said, hunching her shoulders.

"I knew that wasn't none of Stevie's man. I knew you was lying." Patrice smiled.

"Well, you shouldn't have let him in." Tanya laughed as Carla walked away.

Patrice elbowed Tanya. "Remember how we used to stick our arms out to see who was the lightest, remember?"

"Yeah, let's do it."

"Put your arm out. Stevie, Tanya, Cassandra, have y'all's palms facing up. Come on, Tessa, Renee, let's see who's the lightest. Peaches, Joyce, Melody, Linda, all y'all come over here. We gonna see who's the lightest!"

"Carla, bring your arm in here, too," Patrice shouted.

I looked at my arm against the bunch of other ones. Mine was in the middle, but closer to the dark ones than the lighter ones.

"Tessa's arm's the lightest. No, check out Peaches' arm."

"Mine is light as Peaches'," Joyce insisted. "Linda's arm is the darkest. Look at her arm next to mine. It looks black!" she added.

Linda looked embarrassed.

"Why are we doing this?" I asked, pulling my arm out of the pile.

"Cause y'all girls! And girls are stupid!" Michael shouted as Tyrone gave him five. The group of boys laughed.

None of the girls answered my question. "Do you think that it makes somebody better 'cause her arm is lighter?" I asked. Everyone was quiet.

"Stevie's right, this game has played out," Carla said, pulling away. "Besides, I ain't gonna let nobody put none of my guests down." Everyone began shaking their arms out and turning away.

I sat in a corner eating my second hot dog, tuning out the chatter of the girls around me. Melody and Linda were dancing with Carla's niece and nephew. They were the only ones who looked to be having any fun. "It's twine time, ooh ahh," Lakisha and Malcolm shouted over and over as they threw their chubby little arms and legs from side to side. I knew that tomorrow everybody would brag about how cool and happening Carla's party had been. And the ones who hadn't been invited would think they'd really missed something. I knew, because I used to be one of them.

Carla turned off the record player and dimmed the lights. She sent Lakisha and Malcolm back outside to play. She stood up waving an empty wine bottle. "It's time! Everybody sit on the rug, make a circle, y'all. We fixin' to play Spin the Bottle!"

The girls moved faster than the boys toward the big piece of gray carpet in the center of the floor. I realized that I didn't want to have any of these boys slobbering on me. What if I got stuck with a boy who had bad breath? I'd never been kissed before and I didn't want my first kiss to be with just anybody. I wanted to save my lips for somebody special.

"Where you goin'?" Carla asked as I slipped out of the room.

"The bathroom."

"Well, hurry back, we're fixin' to play!"

"Okay," I answered happily from the stairs.

You could only hide in the bathroom so long. I headed for the kitchen to talk to Carla's mother. She was frosting Carla's birthday cake while drinking a can of beer and smoking a cigarette.

She wore a tight, black miniskirt and a black and white polka-dot blouse. Mama had said Mrs. Perkins was too dark to have a red tint in her perm and too old and plump to wear miniskirts, after we ran into her shopping at the A&P.

"Stevie, where you at?" Carla's mother asked as I walked into the kitchen.

"Huh? I'm right here."

"It means, how you doing, or how you be, that's what they say in New Orleans."

"Oh, are you from New Orleans?"

"No, I hail from Little Rock."

"Little Rock, Arkansas?"

"That's right. You're so smart."

"Thanks."

"Stevie, I'm so glad you and Carla got to be friends."

"Is it okay if I sit in this chair?"

"Make yourself at home, Stevie, set yourself down."

"Can I help you with anything?"

"Not right now, you can just keep me company. You are so polite. My two other daughters only ran around with riffraff. I tell Carla all the time, Be like Stevie, she's going to amount to something."

"You tell Carla that?"

"Sho do, I preach to her all the time. Carla is my last hope."

"Carla has a good singing voice."

"Stevie, most negroes can carry a tune. I want her to get something in her head. I don't expect my kids to discover the cure for cancer. I just want them to do something with their lives, so my struggle won't have been in vain."

"Well, Carla is really cool. I always looked up to her."

"Cool! Don't make me lose my religion! Cool don't pay the rent! Cool don't pay the bills. The only thing cool do is rhyme with fool! Do you hear me?"

"Yes, ma'm."

"I wish you *would* mention cool to me again, I'll whup you and Carla both! Do you hear me?"

"Yes ma'm." I was having second thoughts about my decision not to play Spin the Bottle.

"Don't get me started," Mrs. Perkins continued. "I have struggled to raise these three girls to the best of my ability, with no help from nobody. Do you hear me?"

I nodded.

"I would shovel shit in a barnyard to feed my children."

I raised my eyebrows. I wasn't used to hearing grown-ups curse.

"I've done damn near everything but steal and sell tail to keep a roof over their heads. Stay in school, I tell them. Education is something that nobody can take away from you," she said, smashing her cigarette out. "Don't end up like me. Look like the only rest I'm gonna get will be in my grave. Stevie, promise me something."

"What?"

"Promise me you'll never put your trust in no man."

I didn't know what to say. I trusted my father and my uncle. Maybe Mrs. Perkins meant other men. Carla's mother didn't wait for me to answer. She just took a drag off her cigarette and threw her head back, and emptied the can of beer into her mouth.

"There is nobody out there for you," Mrs. Perkins shouted and pointed with her knife. "If you make it in this world you're gonna have to make it all by your lonesome. Do you hear me? Cinderella was not written about the negro woman. Do you understand?"

"Yes, I think so," I said, edging back a little from the knife. She was really getting worked up.

"Your Prince Charming ain't never gonna come! Do you hear me?"

"Yes, ma'm," I said. But I still planned to wait and see what would happen.

R E B E C C A   W E L L S

The Elf and the Fairy

(Siddalee, 1963)

Our Lady of Divine Compassion Parochial School is surrounded by sycamore trees. In the fall those big leaves turn yellow and the scorching days of summer are almost over, and you can start breathing again. I walk every school day underneath those trees to the music building, which is between Divine Compassion and Holy Names Academy, where the high school girls walk and talk in their blue-and-white straight skirts and starched blouses. I can hear them at choir practice while I'm walking along with my music folder under my arm. I love the high school girls, especially the ones with bubble hair-dos. But mainly I love getting out of regular classes to take piano. It's the calmest part of my day. I get so tired of everyone—from my classmates to my brothers and sister to my mother—making so much *noise* all the time. I take my quiet wherever I can find it.

On lesson days, I knock on Sister Philomena's frosted-glass door. When she says, Do come in, I open the door and say, Good afternoon, Sister. She is a big nun with a wide face who quotes the Bible a lot. She always seems glad to see me. I'm working on my recital piece, "The Elf and the Fairy," which is considered quite a difficult composition for fourth grade.

At first Sister Philomena asks me, Siddalee, are you certain that you want to choose such an advanced piece for your recital?

Yes Sister, I assure her. I love that piece. I can handle it, I promise you.

This is my big chance to take something hard and do it right.

The first time Sister Philomena plays "The Elf and the Fairy" for me, I close my eyes and go somewhere else. To a place in another state that doesn't have all the hot white light of Louisiana. There are waterfalls there

247

and the air is so sweet and easy to breathe. There are actually fairies darting around, and when you see them you can't tell if they are working or playing—it's all the same thing to them. My grandmother Buggy talks to fairies frequently. She calls me on the phone and tells me about her conversations with them. Fairies aren't strange to me at all. They're sort of like midget guardian angels with a good sense of humor.

I am determined to take myself to that same magic place by learning my recital piece perfectly. I practice for hours and hours, alone in the tiny practice room in the music building. That room is like a monk's cell and I enjoy it—just me, the piano, and one window where the afternoon light comes in and tries to make me sleepy. Sometimes I am tempted just to lie on the floor and take a nap, but Sister Philomena says: God will not allow us to be overwhelmed by temptation, but with it He will provide a way of escape so that we will be able to endure it. I play those notes over and over, until it feels like I can climb up inside them and live there. Piano practice is the best way I know to feel organized.

It's just impossible to practice at home because Little Shep and Lulu do nothing but make fun of me. They run around the piano like wild Indians, screeching out their imitations of opera singers like hyenas. It is kind of a family hobby, to make fun of opera singers. Mama taught Lulu to sing in pidgin Italian, "Ahhh! Spitonya! Ahhh! Pickayaboogers!" and other nasty high-pitched phrases, and that is now Lulu's specialty for our family skits. Playing the piano is right up there with opera singing for Little Shep and Lulu in terms of being something to make fun of.

The other problem with trying to practice at home is that you never know when the place is going to be filled with the Ya-Yas. They roar up in their station wagons and Cadillacs to drink and play *bourrée*. After they play and scream and cheat and drink and smoke, they always start singing songs about men.

They moan out how fish have to swim and birds have to fly and so they have to love one man till they die.

You just cannot concentrate with all their moaning going on. But when I complain to Mama, she says, Don't get dramatic with me, Little Miss Sarah Bernhardt.

So I make a bargain with Baby Jesus: If I play "The Elf and the Fairy" perfectly at my recital, He will forgive me for pinching Lulu in church just to make her cry. If I play the composition flawlessly, Baby Jesus might also forgive me for some other things that I can't quite name but always feel guilty for anyway.

I work harder and harder on the piece, picturing those notes while I try to fall asleep at night. My fingers strike the mattress until it feels like the bed is vibrating. I get all my memory work, fingering, timing, and phrasing down. All I have left to do are the final polishing touches.

But the week before the recital, Mama goes to a big Ya-Ya party out at Little Spring Creek and cuts her foot up something awful on a broken Coke bottle. The other Ya-Yas take her to the nearest emergency room and get the wound sewn up, but the cut is so deep she has to use crutches to get around. We have never seen Mama crippled like this before and it is kind of scary.

The night after Mama's injury, Lulu and I are already in bed. I've sharpened my pencils and laid out my clothes for school the next day. They sit next to my book sack where my books, papers, and art supplies are arranged all neat. I can never fall asleep until everything is organized and ready to go at the foot of my bed.

When I first hear the screaming from my parents' room, I think it's hurt dogs or something. I bolt up and dash down the hall. I can feel my bare feet squeak on the shiny wood floors. When I get to the entrance of Mama's long narrow dressing room, Lulu, Little Shep, and Baylor are already there. How did they get there so fast before me? Daddy is standing next to the chaise longue in his socks and boxer shorts. He has a toothbrush in his hand. Mama has on her pink nightgown with the lace, and the way its gathers fall, you can't hardly tell she's using crutches. I can smell the nightcream on her face. In one hand she has one of the squatty crystal glasses she drinks out of at night, the ones with heavy bottoms that don't tip over.

They are already in the middle of it.

Mama says, You redneck bastard, don't you dare make those kinds of insinuations to me!

Daddy says, Insinuations, hell! I said you're a goddamn drunk and I'll say it again! Why do you think you almost cut your fool foot off?

Even though he hasn't touched her, Mama looks like Daddy has split her up for kindling. Her expression changes and she goes for him, slapping him hard in the face.

They stand there yelling like the four of us are invisible. One closet door is open and I can see Mama's ice-blue crepe sheath hanging with a laundry bag over it.

Daddy lets Mama slap him, then he knocks the glass out of her other hand. The glass falls to the floor and breaks, ice going everywhere, and you can smell bourbon in the dressing room along with Mama's rose sachets that hang in the closet.

Mama braces one of her arms against the wall and raises the fist of her other hand and punches Daddy in the stomach.

As if *you* can talk, you pathetic excuse for a man! she yells. You cowardly dirt-farming loser!

This is not happening, I think. *I am not in this room.*

Then she goes to hit him again, but he pushes her away—not hard, but like she's a duck trying to bite him. It throws her off-balance and she falls down. Those crutches just fly out from under her.

This is the first time in our lives we've ever heard one of them call the other a drunk. It is like dynamite. It's bigger than even seeing her hit him, or the way he pushed her. Just his saying that word "drunk" changes everything, even changes the air in the room.

I don't cry because I can't breathe. Lulu starts eating her hair, like she does whenever she gets upset. Little Shep and Baylor are mute, and Baylor is shaking. He looks so much like a little bird to me.

Daddy looks down at Mama on the floor and then he looks at us. But we won't look at him. He says to Mama, You are not fit to raise these children. Then he turns and walks out of the room.

I help Mama up on her crutches. She is shaking and crying and she says, We are getting out of this hellhole. Yall go get your school clothes.

When we stand there frozen, she yells, Don't just stand there like ignoramuses. Yall heard me, go get your damn school things!

I race to my room where I have my brown-and-gold dress with the drifting leaves laid on the chair. I scoop it up, along with my slip, panties, socks, and cordovan tassel loafers. These loafers are my all-time favorite shoes, hand-me-downs from my teenage cousin and broken-in just right. When I wear them, I feel like a cheerleader who writes poetry, like I have a guaranteed good future.

Lulu says, Sidda, can I bring my turtle?

I say, Shut up, Lulu!

Then I grab my book sack, take my little sister by the hand, and fly down the hall to the kitchen door. As I run, I can see the couch, the TV set, and the piano from the corner of my eye. All our familiar things look foreign to me, and for just a second I can't remember where I am or what I have done in my life before right now.

Mama is already in the car with nothing but her nightgown, crutches, and purse. She's smoking and leaning on the horn, cussing at Daddy, who is nowhere in sight. I'm so frenzied, I drop my book sack, and all my papers fly everywhere. Crayons roll under the car.

One of my loafers falls on the concrete and I reach down to get it, but Mama yells, Sidda, get in the goddamn car!

Then she backs the car out of the long driveway and speeds down the gravel road—away from the house. We are all keyed up. We are quivering with fear and excitement at leaving the house so late on a school night.

We quiz her, Where're we going, Mama? Where're we going?

We're going to Buggy's, she explains and I breathe with relief to hear she has some kind of plan. Maybe this isn't so bad after all, I think. Maybe she's got this all mapped out. Maybe I'm being delivered into the life I was meant for. I love spending the night at my grandmother's old house near City Park. You get to stay up late there and walk to school. It's like a little vacation, if you don't mind her dog and kneeling to pray all the time.

But halfway down the road lined with old pecan trees that leads away from our house, Mama slams on the brakes and turns the car around.

I'm not losing every single thing I deserve because that bastard claims I run out on him! she yells. We're going back! That sonovabitch is not going to get rid of me this goddamn easy!

She squeals the car back under the carport. I walk toward the end of the driveway to catch my breath. But Mama yells at me and I walk back into the house that is all quiet except for the sound of the air conditioner that Mama leaves running till Halloween. I don't let myself look at the furniture like I did on the way out. I go in the bathroom and run cold water on a washrag and put it on my forehead, like you're supposed to do when you're upset. Then I sit in my bed with my flashlight and try to straighten out my school things, which have gotten all messed up in the big getaway.

I don't sleep that night and I keep having a hard time getting my breath. I wish I had a fan blowing straight on me so I could get some air into my body.

The next day at school, my head hurts and the back of my eyes burn. It's Friday, the day for my last piano lesson before my recital. Sister Philomena asks me to rehearse every move—the way I'm supposed to lift my hands to the keyboard before beginning the performance, the exact way I should gracefully rest them in my lap after the piece is over, my perfectly rehearsed curtsy. I try to picture smiling faces applauding for me, but all I can think of is how jumbled up all my school papers are, and how there are some important things missing from the night before that I can't seem to find.

When I play for Sister Philomena, I don't miss any notes, but my timing is way off.

She says, Siddalee, be sure to give yourself some quiet practice time this weekend. And on Sunday, go to Holy Communion. Offer the recital up to the Baby Jesus and everything will be fine. He will give His angels charge concerning you to guard you in all your ways.

But there's no chance to practice on Saturday. The day is devoted to converting our schoolroom into Mama's new bedroom. Daddy is nowhere in sight. Mama and Chaney rip down the blackboards from the walls. They haul out our desks, our toy boxes, and the tall shelves with the set of *World Books*. In their place, Mama moves in a Hollywood bed she gets delivered from Holden's Fine Furniture, along with a matching nightstand and a new portable TV set. Before, no one was even allowed to smoke in that room because it was just for children. It was all ours. But now it is Mama's new bedroom, and she has her silver and crystal ashtray with "Ya-Yas, 1960" engraved on the side right there on her new night table.

On the day of the recital, I'm real tired but still sure of myself. I *really* know "The Elf and the Fairy." Those notes won't abandon me in my powder blue dressy dress and patent leather shoes, with my hair rolled into a French twist, Mama's favorite style. I fast my three hours before Communion. But at Mass, the Sacred Host sticks to the roof of my mouth and makes me nauseated. I feel like spitting up on the floor, but a mortal sin like that could easily take away my power of speech and make me grow a harelip to boot.

That Sunday afternoon the Divine Compassion auditorium is filled with mothers and fathers and aunts and grandmothers and the smell of floral arrangements and floor varnish.

Mama hugs me tightly and whispers, I adore you!

I join the music students in the front row. I perch on my folding chair with my feet crossed at the ankles and off to one side like we're supposed to do. I watch the other students, one by one, rise from their seats, climb the steps to the high stage, and plunk out their recital pieces. Each one of them looks so afraid. I almost pity them. They're so insecure, so ill-composed. I feel utterly calm; I do not even feel like a child.

When it's my turn, I sit down at the piano. My hands are steady, my hair is clean, my heart is true. But the moment I hit the first note, somebody else's hands—wild, shaking, and ignorant—take over. At first I'm only kind of curious and dizzy. It takes me eight entire measures to realize that I am the one producing the crazy frantic noise. I am confused, because part of me can actually hear myself playing the music impeccably. But the other part of me knows that the only thing left of "The Elf and the Fairy" is the phrasing. The rest is ugly, unrelated notes that crash through the thick air in that gymnasium. Inside myself, I can hear all the beauty, but my body can't respond. *And I don't even consider just giving up.* I keep on playing because I *have* to. And because I truly believe that I will finally discover the right notes and lead the audience into my elf and fairy world, where peaceful out-of-state light glimmers and cleanses and redeems.

I cannot stop myself. I attack the keyboard for the exact length of time it would've taken me to perform the piece like it's written. But not once do I manage to hit a note that sounds anything like the music I have spent months rehearsing.

When I finish, I am sweating all over. I stand up from the piano in a trance and curtsy like I've practiced a hundred times in front of the mirror. I look out into the audience. Even the other children are silent and wide-eyed. All the mothers are wiping tears from their eyes. I hate them all. Afterward they walk by me and stare at me. Later that afternoon, some of the mothers call Mama to see how I am "taking it."

The next day at school nobody makes fun of me. In fact, they are nicer than usual, which feels worse. I don't want anything to do with them. That afternoon, instead of going to my music lesson, I sneak out behind the parish hall where nobody can see me. I take one of Mama's cigarette lighters out of my uniform pocket and I light the sheet music of "The Elf and the Fairy" on fire. I just flip open that little lighter and hold the flame under the notes. I think about setting all the grass back there on fire as well, but that would cause more trouble than I feel up to. I just burn up all those elf and fairy chords and stomp on the runaway sparks.

Just as I'm finishing up, I hear somebody over by the walkway calling out my name. It's Sister Philomena. She sounds like she is scared that I'm lost. I remember how clean and neat her music room is, how when she plays the piano it makes me feel like everything is in the right place for at least a while. I think about running to her and burying my head in her rustling black habit. For some reason I think that if I do that, she will reach down and touch my face with her long cool fingers that know how to move across a keyboard with total control.

I don't run to her, though. I hide behind the concrete steps until she stops calling out my name and finally goes away.

All I think then is, Don't you dare call out my name ever again. *You don't even know who I am.*

S. L. WISENBERG

The Sweetheart Is In

What the Boys Were Like

They were all over Ceci Rubin's house, swarming like bees around her sister Ellen. Though her sister was not the kind of flower you might think; even though Ellen was Sweetheart of the Senesch boys' group, she was a Nice Girl. She needed to be met two-thirds of the way in order to flirt. Had to be coached. Did not bat her eyes with frequency or naturalness. Did not laugh with the requisite ease; it was always a nervous giggle, an internal clattering of the throat muscles.

But this is about Ceci. And the boys. The boys did not swarm to the playroom, lean over the pool table, twist the handles controlling the little men on the Foosball game, in order to see Ceci Rubin. She was another accoutrement of the house, like the playroom itself. For them, finding a perky extra girl in the home of their Sweetheart was like any other pleasant surprise—like finding someone has a wonderful dog so friendly and shaggy it bridges all conversations, or a mother who listens to problems and sings bawdy songs (only an example; no mother like that existed in Houston in 1970, in that neighborhood at least), or a father who gives advice about something useful—not as personal as sex but, for instance, about car insurance, or avoiding the draft. Ceci's father was in the bubble bath business, and handed out samples to all the boys each time they came over. He'd shake their hands first.

The boys fascinated Ceci. They leaned and lounged like cats, and were just as mysterious to her and to Ellen, who had always had as pets beagles and sea monkeys, nothing in between. The boys would sprawl on the love seats (everything had a name; there was not simply furniture in that house but buffets, davenports, credenzas, and islands), talk one moment about the rubbers in their wallets, the next about ways to avoid the draft—both suggesting realms that were equally strange to Ceci. Ricky Bogen was seventeen and a half and was already thinking of joining the Coast Guard. He'd called the office once for brochures. Dan Cook knew a guy who'd drunk ten cups of coffee in two days, swallowing five tablets of No Doz with each, and been so jittery and nervous and produced such contaminated piss that they got him out of the recruitment center fast, almost calling an ambulance, and speaking of piss, Sam Frederickson's older brother had bought some from a diabetic hanging out in front of the center. Rob Chazin was thinking of the seminary, even at this early date, and Joe Amos was reading everything from Maimonides to St. Augustine (even though Peter Griswold said Augustine was irrelevant to Jews) in order to fill out conscientious objector forms. He'd already had an appointment with his rabbi. Who'd Been in Korea, so that didn't help much.

Ceci, listening as she looked for some string in the drawers of the nearby built-in buffet, didn't quite understand this Being in Korea, thought maybe it was a metaphor, as she'd learned in English, maybe for venereal disease? She tested it on her tongue, and in a few minutes, said to Sam: Korea like in the Korean War? Yeah, Babe, he'd said, and that Babe was enough to give her tingles up until the time she brushed her teeth and fell asleep.

How the Boys Sounded

The boys were noisy in their machines, no matter what the machine was. Even if it was a bicycle. They scraped the kickstands against the cement of the driveway, scraped it up to the front door (bikes, even European ten-speeds, were not allowed indoors on the highly polished and buffed terrazzo). And cars—! They zoomed in doing something with the exhaust or the muffler, Ceci wasn't sure what it was called, to make their presence known. Then the honks. Each boys' group had a certain honk pattern which the members pounded out while passing by the home of a member or a Sweetheart. The one for Senesch was Come-out-come-out-you-son-of-a-bitch, but for the sake of appearances and parents, it was Come-out-come-out-wherever-you-are. The cars were crucial. In Ellen's scrapbook was a photograph of an unidentified odometer showing 1803.00 miles, which was the Senesch chapter number. Ceci was unsure how the chapters were assigned these numbers; this whole boys' club business, she was apt to say, is beyond me. Ceci had elements of an old lady to her. She stopped just short of being fussy. She was serious and studious and fancied herself deep but laughed often, mostly to herself. But since the boys had been coming around, she was beginning to laugh more in public. With the boys, she didn't have to play dumb, which she'd been doing since fourth grade. The boys of Senesch really wanted to know what she thought. They saw her as some artifact, encouraged her to be devil's advocate, praised her when she asked: If I killed my sister—or you—while you were standing right here, it would be wrong, so how could any war be justified? Someone left behind a copy of St. Augustine's just-war theory, and she read it in one night. Sam mentioned Thomas Merton, and she went to the Meyer branch library to check out his books.

They encouraged her, called her St. Cecilia, and Joe sang the Simon and Garfunkel song to her: *Cecilia, you're breakin' my heart, you're shaking my confidence daily—*. Other times he would call her Dorothy Parker and require a pun before they could have a normal conversation.

I am truly changed, Ceci would think to herself. I am no longer shy. But Ellen still called her The Pain. When Ellen wanted Ceci to leave the room, she would say, Ceci, go breathe.

What This Breathing Business Was

It began when Ceci was born and she was taken right away into a special room called I See You—This is how she had heard the story, ever since she was a little girl.

She was in ICU for two days, deprived of mother's milk and mother's love though the nurses were quite attentive and one even sang songs to her. Christmas songs, it turned out, but the family was not that particular, no worry about imprinting. Just as long as she was kept company by another warm human voice, they said. They prided themselves on their rationality. Though Ceci's parents kept kosher and went to shul whenever they knew the family of the bar or bat mitzvah. They were modern Jews, followed the mitzvot that made sense. Though there was behind everything—so faint you could barely feel it—a strong belief in God the primitive goat-bearded deity of the Old Testament. He hovered. He took note of their Sh'mas they said every night before going to sleep.

As she grew older, Ceci's lungs cleared, but they never really cleared up. She would breathe fine then it would start up—never an attack, she hated that word, but more like an advancing case of the flu. So she couldn't run very hard or jump rope, because that would bring on the wheezing. In her childhood, as she said, she stayed inside, read, painted at the easel in her room. Mixed colors again and again, watched them swirl in the blue enamel pot of water. Like cream disappearing into coffee, changing it to cream and coffee. Coffee with cream.

When Ceci was eleven, two years before Ellen was made Sweetheart, she'd had pneumonia so bad she'd had to spend four days in the hospital. She came home with a breathing machine the size of an old-fashioned radio. She filled it with distilled water and liquid bronchodilators morning and night, breathing in the mist for twenty minutes, as she said, at a stretch. It made what she'd just heard called white noise. Drowned everything out.

With hand-held sprays and pills and the machine, though, everything was A-OK, under control. Next semester, said her doctor, she could take gym for the first time in two years. Partly she dreaded this because she'd never properly learned the games the teachers expected her to know: softball, volleyball, and badminton. She'd never quite got the hang of team lines.

In the meantime, no one could tell anything was wrong. Couldn't (usually) hear her wheezing. Under control. Like anybody else.

What Ceci Did with the Boys

Once one of them stayed even after Ceci told him at the door that Ellen wasn't in. They played a round of pool and he won handily. He taught her wrist action in Foosball. He told her about his application for Harvard, the grueling half-day of SAT testing, told her that he thought he might become a conscientious objector. Oh I know about that, she said; CO. She'd read about Quakers being COs in World War I. Nowadays you had to get a draft board to approve it. She knew some people Up North had poured their blood over the draft board file folders. But not in Houston.

The boy's name was Jerry Schwartz. His brother was at Stanford, living in a co-ed dormitory and being part of The Movement. Ceci imagined him there among palm trees, studying, shouting, learning about Europe.

When Jerry left that afternoon, he said, Fair Lady, I doff my hat to you (though he wasn't wearing one), and shook her hand, lingering over it so long she thought he was about to take it to his lips. But he didn't.

What the Parents Thought of This Sweetheart Business

They were proud but befuddled. They'd always said it was important for their girls to have friends in the Jewish community. But they were not quite used to these long, loud boys. The Rubins didn't have norms for boys. Their directives boiled down to geography. The boys couldn't smoke in the house.

The backyard was OK, as long as they put out the butts in the ashtrays of their own cars. They weren't supposed to step one foot into Ellen's bedroom. Though they did troop there sometimes, in a group. It was there that Ellen kept the large brown-spotted stuffed salamander that the boys of Senesch had special-ordered for her. There was another salamander, made of plywood, which stood in the windowsill in the den and faced the circle driveway. It stood on its tail and wore a sly grin. On its stomach were the words *The Sweetheart Is*. Screwed into its joined front paws was a hook which held a cardboard square. On one side the square said *In*; and on the other, *Out*.

Ellen always forgot to change it. Ceci thought of making it say *In* all the time so the boys would come to her. Hadn't she read in *Little Women* that Mozart or Shakespeare had tried for one sister, and gotten the other one? There was also Jacob in the Bible, wasn't there? She remembered something about a wedding, and Jacob (or Isaac?) hadn't been allowed to lift up the heavy veil and see who was under there until after the rabbi had already pronounced the words. And then it was too late.

How Ellen Was Crowned and Chosen

It was at the Sweetheart Dance. It was a surprise but Ceci and her parents had been alerted and stood there in the back, sneakily, hiding in shadow. The name was announced and Ellen fainted. Ceci, hardy in all parts of her body except the lungs, envied Ellen her ability to faint at crucial moments, a coda to underscore the specialness of events. After the dance, Ellen and the boys and their dates went to the IHOP (Ceci heard later) and ordered breakfast to go, drove to Galveston, and ate soggy pancakes on the beach. Someone brought a bedspread to sit on.

At dinner the next Friday night, Ceci's grandmother said she did not like this at all. For twenty years she'd been a guest in that house for the Sabbath meal. She could not imagine anyone finding the sunrise something to go to, like a movie or symphony. She told Ceci's mother: A waste, a waste it sounds to me. Ceci's mother worried but found it impolite to worry in front of other people, and her mother-in-law was still other people. Of course the thing that no one said but everyone thought about was the impropriety of boys and girls of a certain age traveling unsupervised to another town, another county, the untamed ocean overnight. The overnight part. That's what they're doing now, Ceci's father said mildly. He was modern and trusted the mores of the age and therefore individuals because he could not conceive of them violating the norms. After all, this wasn't Chicago or New

York and these boys and girls Ellen was friendly with were honors students, not hippies or zippies or whatever. Ceci's mother didn't trust anything but convention. And not even that. But she was afraid to say so.

What Ceci Knew

In writing, in cold hard facts in Ellen's diary, Ceci had read that Ellen's best friend Naomi had swum naked with not one but three boys. The diary was kept locked, but easily opened, in an oversized photo album on a bookshelf. Ceci wondered if like the character in the book *1984* Ellen kept a hair or something equally minute between the pages to determine whether the diary had been tampered with. But it was Ceci's firm belief that Ellen secretly wanted her to read it—even if only for the challenge of catching Ceci give herself away by releasing a bit of information in conversation that could have been obtained from the diary alone.

Ellen was rather reserved in what she revealed about herself in the diary—as taciturn as she was in person. Once Ceci had asked her if she'd ever French kissed, and Ellen, embarrassed, an edge of incredulity to her voice, responded: Yeess! She would not elucidate.

This sex business was something Ceci didn't think about concretely, except figured it was something like New York City—big and confusing and exciting. The mystery at hand was smaller and closer—periods. There were tantalizing light blue boxes under the sink in her parents' bathroom and pink ones in the bathroom she shared with Ellen. Ceci had not yet begun. She waited for it, mistaking stomach cramps for those kind. She would see Ellen's sanitary belt hanging on the towel rack, and twice in the school bathroom she had unwrapped the cotton and blood jelly rolls in the steel basket attached to the wall and smelled the rust-iron personal foreign blood.

At night, Ceci had her own more than dimly related secret habit. She rocked quietly in bed, thumb against that ridge of flesh, until she felt a turnaround unwinding feeling. She'd been doing this for years and thought it was something little girls did, something like holding on to your baby blanket too long. Next time, she'd think, I'll stop.

What Ceci Worried About

She was afraid that she wouldn't do the exciting things life owed her. Afraid a boy wouldn't love her and kiss her. Afraid she'd be too tall all her life. Afraid she wouldn't be famous. Afraid her feet would never stop growing.

Afraid she'd be ugly forever. (She didn't believe her mother when she called her beautiful.) She was confident she'd get into a good college Up North. She did well on standardized tests. She hadn't told Jerry Schwartz that, he with his reports of grueling APs and SATs.

She was afraid her best friend Sheryl Lefkowitz didn't really like her as much as she liked another girl, Annie Kaplan, who went to another junior high. She was afraid of being abandoned. She feared and anticipated returning to gym classes. She imagined that her return would mark an opening in her life—she would pick up everything she had missed and forge unbreakable bonds. Because surely it was in the locker room that these alliances were formed: the invitations to walk home after school, to go shopping for shoes and purses at Palais Royal, to go get haircuts, to look up *Everything You Always Wanted to Know About Sex* at the Meyer library, to spend the night.

She felt both older and younger than her friends. Sheryl Lefkowitz, for example, was already ahead of Ceci in some departments. She had let a boy feel her breasts. She told Ceci about a girl giving what was called a hand job. Ceci wondered how these girls knew what to do. She would have no idea. She'd heard that once you started they wouldn't let you stop until the sperm came out of there and some of them made you drink it.

How Ceci Was with the Boys After a While

Ceci began to feel adopted by them. They took her bowling and one night got her drunk on André Cold Duck at Joe Felts's house (his parents gone) and she sang songs with them, making up the words. Ellen got mad. Ceci didn't care. The boys were very careful with her. They did not, for example, have her sit on anybody's lap, the way they had girls their own age do. They made a joke: Sit on my lap and we'll see what comes up. She didn't get it, but knew it was not something her mother would want her to laugh at. Just like jokes they made about the pool table balls.

She helped Jerry Schwartz make up the creative services for Senesch Sabbath Morning with Herzl girls' group. They chose works, as Jerry called them, by Eugene O'Neill and Leonard Cohen and the Beatles. This excited Ceci. She had not known that Jews could pray by reciting *Blackbird singing in the dead of night.* He showed her a poem by W. H. Auden: *But poetry makes nothing happen.* He explained to her that people have to do things in the world. He talked about the Chicago Seven; all she'd remembered about it was a TV screen full of hippies with long dark hair making peace signs. He explained the difference between hippies and Yippies. (No such thing as zippies, he said.) He told her about his underground paper at St. Mark's, a private school in River Oaks. His family lived just outside River Oaks, near Rice University. He told her how Jews couldn't even live in River Oaks unless they were very very rich. He brought her a copy of his paper with reports about Vietnam and protest and editorials with cusswords. The typing was poor and so was the reproduction. He told her she could keep a copy. The mimeographing ink came off on her hands.

How Ellen Felt About All These Developments

She was mad. Said the same thing she said when she was seven and Ceci was three: Maa, tell Ceci to play with her own friends.

How Ceci Entertained Another Boy

Tom Hessler rang the bell even though the brown-spotted plywood salamander in the window said *Out,* and he and Ceci made Tollhouse mint brownies even though her mother had told her not to do any baking because she needed the kitchen at five. Her mother was mad but only for a few minutes. Tom took half of the batch home (that had always been the house rule—share with the guest baker), wrapped in foil, pecans sprinkled on top.

Late that night he fed it into his girlfriend's mouth, lightly flicking the dark crumbs from the corners of her lips. The girlfriend said, Mmmm, mmm, my favorite, chocolate! And he said, Oh you, you're mi señorita favorita.

Tom didn't tell this part to Ceci when he played Foosball with her a week later. All he said was that his girlfriend would only eat one brownie because of her *dy*-et. Ellen was standing next to him as he was saying this, and he turned to put his arm around her lazily. For some reason he was thinking of Bogart at this moment and turned to Ceci and said, Game's over, get lost, kid. The next time Ceci saw him he put his arm around her that same way. She tried to bite his hand and was embarrassed at how desperate it seemed, not at all playful.

How Ellen the Nice Girl Got to Be Sweetheart in the First Place

Ellen was not a tart. When she was just a civilian, back in tenth grade, she'd had one good friend who was a boy; he'd moved to town from Dallas the end of the semester, and she'd been nice to him because she was nice to everyone, especially new boys in her homeroom. He was popular and persuasive with other males. He joined Senesch that summer. The other boys in Senesch wanted to elect one of two girls who were Class A Number One flirts, supreme gigglers and hairtossers. Ellen was the dark horse, the spoiler, the one who upset the established power-mongers. She won the election. She was pretty so it didn't matter. She was like a sleeper movie. By the time people have seen it, they feel bad that but for a quirk, they might have missed it. And so they feel doubly grateful.

What Ellen's Manner Was

She would say, Hello, how are you, making a reference, as the girl-gets-boy guidebooks suggest, to something the boy had mentioned the day before. She began to read the sports pages, to talk about the Astros' chances on the pennant. The boys were nonplussed. They'd never heard of girls who knew about sports. They'd say, like indignant fathers, Now what do we have here? Secretly they were pleased. They congratulated themselves on their choice. They began to say, Hay as in horses, we sure know how to pick 'em.

Ellen was the supreme democrat. No one boy got more attention than the other. She regulated her inflections. She became all things to everyone. A queen. Dabbing the foreheads of the dying teeming poor camped at her gates. Unwashed. Each time she descended she became more and more aloof. And therefore more and more disinterested. Which is not the same as *un*interested. And thus more and more fair.

What Ellen Did to Herself

She took hair from the top of her head and rolled it around two empty orange juice cans, wrapped the rest with oversized bobby pins and oversized clips, and sat under the dryer for two hours (so adept at this, folded this into her life, that she could hold telephone conversations while under the hood with other girls similarly encumbered). She shaved her armpit hair, her leg hair, plucked her eyebrows, curled her lashes, applied a silver or blue silver or gold Yardley face mask once a week, and used all manner of potions and astringents and henna hair lighteners and straighteners at various intervals.

Ceci tried to emulate, hoping for her underarm and leg hairs to darken and lengthen so she could rid herself of them. She bought her own Clearasil tube (cherishing that pasty smell), awaiting pimples, was elated when Ellen showed her the hiding place of blackheads: the crease between lip and chin.

What Ceci Learned from Ellen and Others

The Surfer Stomp. That she was supposed to be afraid of boys. That you didn't go to second base until the fourth or fifth date at the earliest. That you were always supposed to say No at least twice to new ventures of the flesh. That no one wore tampons.

Also: Don't call boys (her mother said), boys don't like to be chased. Study their interests. Plan your makeup color scheme to coincide with and complement your clothing scheme, which means planning ahead on the little charts provided by the teen magazines.

What Happened When Mr. and Mrs. Rubin
Went Away for a Marketing Convention

The boys were like an occupying army. They ate Granny Smith apples from the drawer in the refrigerator and picked tangelos from the backyard and poured themselves mixed drinks. They tracked in mud and seemed to have no homes of their own. They were dark and alive and loud.

Sam Frederick and Joe Amos left behind on the antique davenport a tape cassette from their legendary Sam and Joe I Won't Go Show. Ellen left with them to go to a meeting. As they were shutting the door, Joe said, Don't wait up for her. They all three laughed. Ceci made herself a tuna melt, loaded the dishwasher. Her homework was finished. She had no one to call. Her hair wasn't dirty enough to wash. She took her parents' old copy of *The Group* (She can read anything she wants, her father would say. If she doesn't understand it, it won't hurt her.) and leafed through it while she breathed on her machine. She wanted to be with people. She wanted talking.

Don't wait up for her, Joe had said. Ceci took the boys' tape and rewound it to the beginning and brought it to the bathroom. She turned on the bath water.

Sam and Joe were singing the anti-war song they'd made up: *Ain't no use to wonder why, I think I'm gonna die—and it's 5–6–7, open up them pearly gates—*. Then they trailed off to advertise an upcoming interview with the Ass-tit Jewish-American Indian princess who showed off her wares for the poor boys in boot camp in Butt Butte, Wyoming. The field of Ceci's mind was an expanse of far-reaching cities and villages, but she had not thought of that. Ass-tit, Butt Butte, had not been in her vocabulary. Though she had had those kinds of images while she was in her bed, rubbing with her thumb. Or in the tub.

She ran more warm water over a handful of Barnston's bubble powder and imagined the Ass-tit Princess, greeted by the cheering invading army of Salamanders, boys touching her nut-brown breasts shed of their loincloth just for them, large nut-brown maiden, the eye of her tit warmed in someone's eyeless hand. Someone's brown cheek and lips, and she was the princess and the hand and the hands.

Ellen had never mentioned to Ceci any nut-brown maidens or princesses or do-it-yourself thumb projects of her own. Ellen wouldn't, Ceci thought. She was the Sweetheart and she was four years older. Besides, she hadn't mentioned it in her diary. The juiciest thing Ceci had read in Ellen's diary was about Ellen's friend Naomi.

Ceci thought of Naomi, naked, water streaming over her shoulders and swishing her pubic hair. Like seaweed. Mermaids. She wondered if Ellen did that too. That overnight in Galveston with the boys and pancakes—.

(Always the baby, the one it doesn't matter if she's wearing her robe and two orange juice cans on her head, she's the baby, the one who doesn't count, the one too young to go out with. You, Ceci, go and get the door and tell them I'm almost ready, Ellen would say. Entertain them. But not too much. Make them laugh *once*.)

Ceci in her tub filled with bubble bath from her father's factory imagined a dance hall hostess knocking and not noticing Ceci, and lying on top of her, still not feeling her, then a man coming in the door and soaping the lady on top of Ceci. Ceci would stay so so quiet because she finally would learn something, here was her chance. She began to hum. Quick—she thought she heard Ellen unlock the back door and Ceci reached over and stopped the tape (thinking: Thomas Merton was electrocuted in his bathtub) and jumped out to turn on the radio real loud, KPRC, news and talk.

What Ceci Knew About the War

That it was wrong. The government was wrong but mostly only the Jews and Northerners and Catholics and students in California knew it. Jerry's underground paper was against it from the word Go, and it also editorialized about, as he called it, concerns of its constituency. It editorialized against the uniforms they had to wear in his private school. One day he organized almost everyone not to wear their ties. They won. Now every Friday they could leave the ties at home. It was a great victory. But he said he felt uneasy about it. The principal had given in too easily.

How the News Came to Ceci's Class

There was some sort of murmuring, the sort of buzz that precedes a big announcement. The history teacher, Mrs. Simpson, was late to class. She said there would not be a quiz but to prepare for a discussion on the League of Nations. Then she left. While she was gone Joel Arner and Jimmy Buxbaum covered the entire two boards with ticktacktoe graphs. Mrs. Simpson returned and said, All right, class. There will be a pop quiz. Then she whispered and looked furtive. She told them: Four students in Ohio were killed in a protest against the war. They were wild, she said. They burned down a building.

Did they have weapons? asked Joey.

I think so, she said. Yes definitely. They attacked officers of the National Guard.

Ceci wondered if that was what Ricky Bogen was going to join. She imagined him lying dead. But those weren't the ones that died. The ones that died were college students. Up North.

She imagined herself a college girl, lots of dates, boys carrying her books, boys running fingers through her hair, which had somehow changed to blonde and straight (you could accomplish great transformations in college), laughing, maybe a little lipstick, long lashbuilding mascara with those little hairs in the wand, blue eyeshadow, laughing and talking about philosophy. My philosophy of life, the college Ceci would be saying, is helping people. Get to know everyone. She would be walking on a campus green, by old-fashioned Old English buildings. And then the boy on her right, call him for the sake of argument Barry or Jerry, would be shot. Blood on his lumberjack shirt. Jerry Schwartz, blood on his salamander tee shirt, coming out of the paw.

The report I heard in the teachers' lounge, said Mrs. Simpson, is there were two boys and two girls.

A college girl, Ceci thought, putting her hand to her heart, and could almost feel the wet blood trickling. She wondered if she would have her period by then. Of course of course. By then it would be old hat. She thought of the Xs she would make on a wall calendar. But for nothing. Blood all over the nut-brown maiden, down her seaweed hairs. She, Ceci, fallen on the grass in front of three-story stone college buildings that looked like Steak and Ales.

It wasn't my fault, she said to herself. It wasn't the students' fault, she said in a whisper. They didn't do anything wrong, she said loudly and evenly, loud as a boy.

Then she ducked her head and wrote her name, shakily, and Pop Quiz #5 on the looseleaf sheet.

What Happened at Home

The phone was ringing. Right off the hook, Ceci thought to herself. Jerry Schwartz said, Hello, did you hear? She said, This is Ceci, this is me, not Ellen. He said, I know. Did you hear? Did you hear?

Yes, she said, yes, the college students. Ellen's not here.

He said, I have the car. I can come by—

Out of some instinct, some sense of propriety, she said, I'll meet you at the JCC.

She knew it took ten minutes to walk there. It would take him at least that long to drive. Walk slowly and carry a big stick, she thought. Walk slowly and your lungs will be friends with you forever. No flare-ups.

How They Were at the JCC and in the Car

He was on the steps waiting. Eyes kind of red. You need Murine, she thought. Once at Bruce Gottschalk's house, Bill Somebody had splashed Murine up and down his face, turned off the lights, and shined a black light on his face. The Murine tracks were purple. Everyone said, Psy-cho-del-ic.

At the JCC Jerry said, I'll take you to my house.

Some alarm started to go off in a far reach of her mind but Ceci had not been properly trained. No boys in her bedroom. But could she be in a boy's living room?

Maybe the front steps.

The car radio was full of music and bulletins, and *Open up the pearly gates*—That's Sam and Joe's song, Ceci said, except I don't think the words are the same, exactly. How did that get on the radio? Jerry laughed, not turning to her. That's Country Joe McDonald. He sang that at Woodstock. You thought those two clowns wrote it? They couldn't write their way out of a paper bag. They couldn't even get the lyrics down in that stupid tape they made.

She absorbed this.

How They Were at His House

The TV was on, and the radio, on KILT, old music—"Dead Man's Curve." It was dark, the glow of the TV on a braided or brocaded couch. Kleenex in a wad. Tennis shoes in a corner. Newspapers awry. I wanted to tell you this, he said. He sat her down on the sofa. His finger brushed past her ear. She felt it, felt it more right afterwards. One two three four seconds later. Still. Two four six eight. Why don't we defoliate. Like a shadow touch. Look at this, she thought. He's angry about the students at Kent State but there are tears in his eyes. She was afraid he was going to sob. He took an envelope from his back pocket. He was wearing jeans. Must have changed from his school clothes, she thought. She'd never seen him in his St. Mark's High School private uniform. She saw some dark material bunched in a corner. Maybe the uniform. Ceci wondered if this was one of the days they wore ties. Every day but one. Which? Friday? He was saying something about a moratorium. Sounded like natatorium. Auditorium. Black armbands, he said. The TV was saying, Allison said she wanted peace; she said this to her mother on the phone yesterday. Tears on faces. Weeping. Gasps. Tear gas, said a man.

She wondered what the burn of tear gas was like. Pneumonia was a cold, rattly feeling. Did tear gas burn your bronchial tubes forever, down to the alveoli, something no machine could fix, would it give you emphysema? She took a deep breath to remind herself that she was in good shape. I'm in good shape, she said to herself. My lungs are my friends. She listened to her breath, she felt the little bruise of pain at the end of each long breath, as always.

Look, he said, unfolding a letter from the envelope. Harvard wrote me and said, Fuck off.

For a moment she believed him and wondered at this disregard. Didn't they expect parents to read it? He unfolded the letter and read: Dear Mr. Schwartz, Unfortunately we cannot accept you for admission into Harvard. We had many qualified candidates and we regret that we could not accept all of them. Our waiting list is full also, but we wish you success and achievement in your academic life and in the world beyond.

There's nothing I can do, he said. Nothing. He was down now, head on her shoulder like a baby, like a puppy. She touched his hair. She had never touched a boy's hair. Her father's hair was thinning, wet with Vitalis. This was poodle hair, like her own. She massaged his head, and with her other hand rubbed her own scalp, to feel what it felt like.

A kind of tickle. More exciting when it's two.

But not the kind of tickle that made her feel like laughing.

Then he was rocking his body against hers. My ribs, she thought. His ribs. Tackling. I'm a football player. My lungs are strong and fine. Maybe I will outgrow this asthma business after all. He held her in a bear hug. She had danced the bear hug three times at two different dances at the JCC and at Westwood Country Club. She pressed her lips against his face. Her mouth. Little scratchiness: he shaves! She wondered if he'd been crying, inched out her tongue. Salt.

He tongued her ear.

She tongued his. More like dirt than wax.

He cupped her chin.

Sweet nut-brown Indian maiden.

She clamped her thighs. For no reason. And again. Again. She could feel his fingers all up and down her back almost like a massage. Or how she'd imagined a massage.

She clamped her thighs.

He moved his hands back to her face, made circles on her cheeks with his hands.

She rocked and rocked, the nut-brown Indian maiden. He was a puppy and so was she. Boys weren't like cats at all. I am not thinking, she was thinking. This is what it is like not to be thinking. Though if she was thinking this, she must be . . .

Puppy hair puppy tail, knobs, elbows, salt. The boys didn't want to go, Allison said, the people were telling the microphone on TV. The boys didn't want to go. Poor poor thing, she was thinking. Poor thing, poor little puppyface, poor boy but so old he can drive, *2–4–6–8, don't give a damn, next stop—*

My poor poor little beagle, she thought. Ceci, he whispered, Ceci honey, he whispered.

Ceci honey, she thought. I'm a honey. I'm Ceci honey. God please, she was praying rocking crying too, please God don't let him call me sweetheart . . .

BANANA YOSHIMOTO

from

Kitchen

THE PLACE I LIKE BEST in this world is the kitchen. No matter where it is, no matter what kind, if it's a kitchen, if it's a place where they make food, it's fine with me. Ideally it should be well broken in. Lots of tea towels, dry and immaculate. White tile catching the light (ting! ting!).

I love even incredibly dirty kitchens to distraction—vegetable droppings all over the floor, so dirty your slippers turn black on the bottom. Strangely, it's better if this kind of kitchen is large. I lean up against the silver door of a towering, giant refrigerator stocked with enough food to get through a winter. When I raise my eyes from the oil-spattered gas burner and the rusty kitchen knife, outside the window stars are glittering, lonely.

Now only the kitchen and I are left. It's just a little nicer than being all alone.

When I'm dead worn out, in a reverie, I often think that when it comes time to die, I want to breathe my last in a kitchen. Whether it's cold and I'm all alone, or somebody's there and it's warm, I'll stare death fearlessly in the eye. If it's a kitchen, I'll think, "How good."

Before the Tanabe family took me in, I spent every night in the kitchen. After my grandmother died, I couldn't sleep. One morning at dawn I trundled out of my room in search of comfort and found that the one place I *could* sleep was beside the refrigerator.

My parents—my name is Mikage Sakurai—both died when they were young. After that my grandparents brought me up. I was going into junior high when my grandfather died. From then on, it was just my grandmother and me.

When my grandmother died the other day, I was taken by surprise. My family had steadily decreased one by one as the years went by, but when it suddenly dawned on me that I was all alone, everything before my eyes seemed false. The fact that time continued to pass in the usual way in this apartment where I grew up, even though now I was here all alone, amazed me. It was total science fiction. The blackness of the cosmos.

Three days after the funeral I was still in a daze. Steeped in a sadness so great I could barely cry, shuffling softly in gentle drowsiness, I pulled my futon into the deathly silent, gleaming kitchen. Wrapped in a blanket, like Linus, I slept. The hum of the refrigerator kept me from thinking of my loneliness. There, the long night came on in perfect peace, and morning came.

But . . . I just wanted to sleep under the stars.

I wanted to wake up in the morning light.

Aside from that, I just drifted, listless.

However! I couldn't exist like that. Reality is wonderful.

I thought of the money my grandmother had left me—just enough. The place was too big, too expensive, for one person. I had to look for another apartment. There was no way around it. I thumbed through the listings, but when I saw so many places all the same lined up like that, it made my head swim. Moving takes a lot of time and trouble. It takes energy.

I had no strength; my joints ached from sleeping in the kitchen day and night. When I realized how much effort moving would require—I'd have to pull myself together and go look at places. Move my stuff. Get a phone installed—I lay around instead, sleeping, in despair. It was then that a miracle, a godsend, came calling one afternoon. I remember it well.

Dingdong. Suddenly the doorbell rang.

It was a somewhat cloudy spring afternoon. I was intently involved in tying up old magazines with string while glancing at the apartment listings with half an eye but no interest, wondering how I was going to move. Flustered, looking like I'd just gotten out of bed, I ran out and without thinking undid the latch and opened the door. Thank god it wasn't a robber. There stood Yuichi Tanabe.

"Thank you for your help the other day," I said. He was a nice young man, a year younger than me, who had helped out a lot at the funeral. I think he'd said he went to the same university I did. I was taking time off.

"Not at all," he said. "Did you decide on a place to live yet?"

"Not even close." I smiled.

"I see."

"Would you like to come in for some tea?"

"No. I'm on my way somewhere and I'm kind of in a hurry." He grinned. "I just stopped by to ask you something. I was talking to my mother, and we were thinking you ought to come to our house for a while."

"Huh?" I said.

"In any case, why don't you come over tonight around seven? Here's the directions."

"Okay . . ." I said vacantly, taking the slip of paper.

"All right, then, good. Mom and I are both looking forward to your coming." His smile was so bright as he stood in my doorway that I zoomed in for a closeup on his pupils. I couldn't take my eyes off him. I think I heard a spirit call my name.

"Okay," I said. "I'll be there."

Bad as it sounds, it was like I was possessed. His attitude was so totally "cool," though, I felt I could trust him. In the black gloom before my eyes (as it always is in cases of bewitchment), I saw a straight road leading from me to him. He seemed to glow with white light. That was the effect he had on me.

"Okay, see you later," he said, smiling, and left.

Before my grandmother's funeral I had barely known him. On the day itself, when Yuichi Tanabe showed up all of a sudden, I actually wondered if he had been her lover. His hands trembled as he lit the incense; his eyes were swollen from crying. When he saw my grandmother's picture on the altar, again his tears fell like rain. My first thought when I saw that was that my love for my own grandmother was nothing compared to this boy's, whoever he was. He looked that sad.

Then, mopping his face with a handkerchief, he said, "Let me help with something." After that, he helped me a lot.

Yuichi Tanabe . . . I must have been quite confused if I took that long to remember when I'd heard grandmother mention his name.

He was the boy who worked part-time at my grandmother's favorite flower shop. I remembered hearing her say, any number of times, things like, "What a nice boy they have working there. . . . That Tanabe boy . . . today, again . . ." Grandmother loved cut flowers. Because the ones in our kitchen were not allowed to wilt, she'd go to the flower shop a couple of times a week. When I thought of that, I remembered him walking behind my grandmother, a large potted plant in his arms.

He was a long-limbed young man with pretty features. I didn't know anything more about him, but I might have seen him hard at work in the flower shop. Even after I got to know him a little I still had an impression of aloofness. No matter how nice his manner and expression, he seemed like a loner. I barely knew him, really.

It was raining that hazy spring night. A gentle, warm rain enveloped the neighborhood as I walked with directions in hand.

My apartment building and the one where the Tanabes lived were separated by Chuo Park. As I crossed through, I was inundated with the green smell of the night. I walked, sloshing down the shiny wet path that glittered with the colors of the rainbow.

To be frank, I was only going because they'd asked me. I didn't think about it beyond that. I looked up at the towering apartment building and thought, their apartment on the tenth floor is so high, the view must be beautiful at night. . . .

Getting off the elevator, I was alarmed by the sound of my own footsteps in the hall. I rang the bell, and abruptly, Yuichi opened the door. "Come in."

"Thanks." I stepped inside. The room was truly strange.

First thing, as I looked toward the kitchen, my gaze landed with a thud on the enormous sofa in the living room. Against the backdrop of the large kitchen with its shelves of pots and pans—no table, no carpet, just "it." Covered in beige fabric, it looked like something out of a commercial. An entire family could watch TV on it. A dog too big to keep in Japan could stretch out across it—sideways. It was really a marvelous sofa.

In front of the large window leading onto the terrace was a jungle of plants growing in bowls, planters, and all kinds of pots. Looking around, I saw that the whole house was filled with flowers; there were vases full of spring blooms everywhere.

"My mother says she'll get away from work soon. Take a look around if you'd like. Should I give you the tour? Or pick a room, then I'll know what kind of person you are," said Yuichi, making tea.

"What kind? . . . " I seated myself on the deep, comfy sofa.

"I mean, what you want to know about a house and the people who live there, their tastes. A lot of people would say you learn a lot from the toilet," he said, smiling, unconcerned. He had a very relaxed way of talking.

"The kitchen," I said.

"Well, here it is. Look at whatever you want."

While he made tea, I explored the kitchen. I took everything in: the good quality of the mat on the wood floor and of Yuichi's slippers; a practical minimum of well-worn kitchen things, precisely arranged. A Silverstone frying pan and a delightful German-made vegetable peeler—a peeler to make even the laziest grandmother enjoy slip, slipping those skins off.

Lit by a small fluorescent lamp, all kinds of plates silently awaited their turns; glasses sparkled. It was clear that in spite of the disorder everything was of the finest quality. There were things with special uses, like . . . porcelain bowls, *gratin* dishes, gigantic platters, two beer steins. Somehow it was all very satisfying. I even opened the small refrigerator (Yuichi said it was okay)—everything was neatly organized, nothing just "left."

I looked around, nodding and murmuring approvingly, "Mmm, mmm." It was a good kitchen. I fell in love with it at first sight.

I went back and sat on the sofa, and out came hot tea.

Usually, the first time I go to a house, face to face with people I barely know, I feel an immense loneliness. I saw myself reflected in the glass of the large terrace window while black gloom spread over the rain-hounded night panorama. I was tied by blood to no creature in this world. I could go anywhere, do anything. It was dizzying.

Suddenly, to see that the world was so large, the cosmos so black. The unbounded fascination of it, the unbounded loneliness . . . For the first time, these days, I was touching it with these hands, these eyes. I've been looking at the world half-blind, I thought.

"Why did you invite me here?" I asked.

"We thought you might be having a hard time," Yuichi said, peering kindly at me. "Your grandmother was always so sweet to me, and look at this house, we have all this room. Shouldn't you be moving?"

"Yes. Although the landlord's been nice enough to give me extra time."

"So why not move in with us?" he said, as though it were the most natural thing in the world.

He struck just the right note, neither cold nor oppressively kind. It made me warm to him; my heart welled up to the point of tears. Just then, with the scratch of a key in the door, an incredibly beautiful woman came running in, all out of breath.

I was so stunned, I gaped. Though she didn't seem young, she was truly beautiful. From her outfit and dramatic makeup, which really wouldn't do for daytime, I understood that hers was night work.

Yuichi introduced me: "This is Mikage Sakurai."

"How do you do," she said in a slightly husky voice, still panting, with a smile. "I'm Yuichi's mother. My name is Eriko."

This was his mother? Dumbfounded, I couldn't take my eyes off her. Hair that rustled like silk to her shoulders; the deep sparkle of her long, narrow eyes; well-formed lips, a nose with a high, straight bridge—the whole of her gave off a marvelous light that seemed to vibrate with life force. She didn't look human. I had never seen anyone like her.

I was staring to the point of rudeness. "How do you do," I replied at last, smiling back at her.

"We're so pleased to have you here," she said to me warmly, and then, turning to Yuichi, "I'm sorry, Yuichi. I just can't get away tonight. I dashed out for a second saying that I was off to the bathroom. But I'll have plenty of time in the morning. I hope Mikage will agree to spend the night." She was in a rush and ran to the door, red dress flying.

"I'll drive you," said Yuichi.

"Sorry to put you to so much trouble," I said.

"Not at all. Who ever would have thought the club would be so busy tonight? It's me who should apologize. Well! See you in the morning!"

She ran out in her high heels, and Yuichi called back to me, "Wait here! Watch TV or something!" then ran after her, leaving me alone in a daze.

I felt certain that if you looked really closely you would see a few normal signs of age—crow's feet, less-than-perfect teeth—some part of her that looked like a real human being. Still, she was stunning. She made me want to be with her again. There was a warm light, like her afterimage, softly glowing in my heart. That must be what they mean by "charm." Like Helen Keller when she understood "water" for the first time, the word burst into reality for me, its living example before my eyes. It's no exaggeration; the encounter was that overwhelming.

Yuichi returned, jingling the car keys. "If she could only get away for ten minutes, she should have just called," he said, taking off his shoes in the entryway.

I stayed where I was on the sofa and answered "Mmm," noncommittally.

"Mikage," he said, "were you a little bit intimidated by my mother?"

"Yes," I told him frankly. "I've never seen a woman that beautiful."

"Yes. But . . ." Smiling, he sat down on the floor right in front of me. "She's had plastic surgery."

"Oh?" I said, feigning nonchalance. "I wondered why she didn't look anything like you."

"And that's not all. Guess what else—she's a man." He could barely contain his amusement.

This was too much. I just stared at him in wide-eyed silence. I expected any second he would say, "Just kidding." Those tapered fingers, those mannerisms, the way she carried herself . . . I held my breath remembering that beautiful face; he, on the other hand, was enjoying this.

"Yes, but . . ." My mouth hung open. "You've been saying all along, 'my mother' this, and 'my mother' that. . . . "

"Yes, but. Could *you* call someone who looked like that 'Dad'?" he asked calmly. He has a point, I thought. An extremely good answer.

"What about the name Eriko?"

"It's actually Yuji."

It was as though there were a haze in front of my eyes. When I was finally ready to hear the story, I said, "So, who gave birth to you?"

"Eriko was a man a long time ago. He married very young. The person he married was my mother."

"Wow . . . I wonder what she was like." I couldn't imagine.

"I don't remember her myself. She died when I was little. I have a picture, though. Want to see it?"

"Yes." I nodded. Without getting up, he dragged his bag across the floor, then took an old photograph out of his wallet and handed it to me.

She was someone whose face told you nothing about her. Short hair, small eyes and nose. The impression was of a very odd woman of indeterminate age. When I didn't say anything, Yuichi said, "She looks strange, doesn't she?"

I smiled uncomfortably.

"As a child Eriko was taken in by her family. I don't know why. They grew up together. Even as a man he was good-looking, and apparently he was very popular with women. Why he would marry such a strange . . ." he said smiling, looking at the photo. "He must have been pretty attached to my mother. So much so he turned his back on the debt of gratitude he owed his foster parents and eloped with her."

I nodded.

"After my real mother died, Eriko quit her job, gathered me up, and asked herself, 'What do I want to do now?' What she decided was, 'Become a woman.' She knew she'd never love anybody else. She says that before she became a woman she was very shy. Because she hates to do things halfway, she had everything 'done,' from her face to her whatever, and with the money she had left over she bought that nightclub. She raised me a woman alone, as it were." He smiled.

"What an *amazing* life story!"

"She's not dead yet," said Yuichi.

Whether I could trust him or whether he still had something up his sleeve . . . the more I found out about these people, the more I didn't know what to expect.

But I trusted their kitchen. Even though they didn't look alike, there were certain traits they shared. Their faces shone like buddhas when they smiled. I like that, I thought.

"I'll be out of here early in the morning, so just help yourself to whatever you want."

A sleepy-looking Yuichi, his arms full of blankets, pillows, and pajamas for me, showed me how the shower worked and pointed out the towels.

Unable to think of much of anything after hearing such a (fantastic!) life story, I had watched a video with Yuichi. We had chatted about things like the flower shop and my grandmother, and time passed quickly. Now it was one in the morning. That sofa was delectable. It was so big, so soft, so deep, I felt that once I surrendered to it I'd never get up again.

"Your mother," I said after a while. "I bet the first time she sat on this sofa in the furniture store, she just had to have it and bought it right then and there."

"You got it," he said. "As soon as she gets an idea in her head she does it, you know? I just stand back in amazement at her way of making things happen."

"No kidding."

"So that sofa is yours for the time being. It's your bed. It's great for us to be able to put it to good use."

"Is it," I ventured softly, "is it really okay for me to sleep here?"

"Sure," he said, without a hint of hesitation.

"I'm very grateful."

After the usual instructions on how to make myself at home, he said good night and went to his room.

I was sleepy, too.

Showering at someone else's house, I thought about what was happening to me, and my exhaustions washed away under the hot water.

I put on the borrowed pajamas and, barefoot, went into the silent living room. I just had to go back for one more look at the kitchen. It was really a good kitchen.

Then I stumbled over to the sofa that was to be my bed for the night and turned out the lamp. Suspended in the dim light before the window overlooking the magnificent tenth-floor view, the plants breathed softly, resting. By now the rain had stopped, and the atmosphere, sparkling, replete with moisture, refracted the glittering night splendidly.

Wrapped in blankets, I thought how funny it was that tonight, too, here I was sleeping next to the kitchen. I smiled to myself. But this time I wasn't lonely. Maybe I had been waiting for this. Maybe all I had been hoping for was a bed in which to be able to stop thinking, just for a little while, about what happened before and what would happen in the future. I was too sad to be able to sleep in the same bed with anyone; that would only make the sadness worse. But here was a kitchen, some plants, someone sleeping in the next room, perfect quiet . . . this was the best. This place was . . . the best.

At peace, I slept.

SHAY YOUNGBLOOD

Blood Oranges

IT IS SUMMER, I am fourteen years old. Instead of going to church on Sundays I begin to go to Golden Gate Park by myself to watch baseball games. Aunt Merleen always said, "God gives you two eyes, one to keep on what you have, and one to keep on what you want." The whole month of July I keep both my eyes on the back gate at Golden Park looking for number twenty-two, my lucky number according to the psychic who sits in the window on Fourth Street. I don't know what I am thinking. Maybe I hope that he will notice me out of all the other girls waiting around after the baseball game looking for a number. Dark hair, dark eyes in a beautiful face. Lips that speak Spanish. I imagine that he will teach me things, give me things, take me away from it all. He is the one to stain me with passion.

Four o'clock P.M., Saturday, July thirteenth, Jesus de la Rosa, number twenty-two, outfielder for the Rick City Astros, looks me dead in the eye and smiles. He throws a baseball at me, underhand. I catch it and I throw it back in a high arc that makes us both stretch our necks. In midair the baseball turns into a perfect orange which he gives to me along with a single word, *naranja*, orange.

I watched the other girls catch baseballs for four weeks and I know that he is choosing me. I have never seen a baseball turn into an orange before. I am told not to speak to strangers, but when Jesus takes me by the hand I follow him to the steak house across the street. He eats hunched over the food like a starving animal. Wolfing down a huge steak and french fries like he hasn't eaten in days. I sip on sour chianti and nibble at the cold french fries at the edge of his plate like I'm not hungry. I'm not sure he'll buy me dinner so I drink the water the waitress plops down in front of each of us and refill the glass with chianti every chance I get, trying to look eighteen.

I find out from the baseball program the ladies' room attendant lets me read, that he is from the Dominican Republic. I don't speak Spanish and he only speaks a few words of English so we spend a lot of time looking into each other's eyes, smiling shyly at each other. Somehow we understand each other. I keep one eye on Jesus and the other one on my left hand which he is using to dance with under the table. He is doing a merengue with my hand on the red vinyl space between us. I can't breathe and my breasts seem to grow when he touches me.

When we get to the hotel where he lives during baseball season, the desk clerk stares at us, but he doesn't say anything. In the elevator I can hear my heart beating. I wonder if he can hear it too. Inside Jesus' room there are two twin beds neatly made up with light blue bedspreads. The dresser is cluttered with loose change, sports magazines and two-for-one coupons from local restaurants. There is a glass of water on the bedside table next to a phone next to a photograph of the Virgin Mary. My head starts spinning so I sit down on one of the beds. Jesus takes a shower while I flip through the channels on the color tv. I am strangely calm. I eat the orange, a deep burgundy color inside. The juice drips down my arm and onto the bed staining it like blood, *sangre*. I even eat the peel which tastes like flowers, *flores*. He comes out of the bathroom wearing a white T-shirt and boxer shorts. He stands there in the doorway looking at me for a long time and then he starts to cry. I turn off the tv and we lie down together in one of the tiny beds in the dark, looking out of the window counting stars. Estrella de Noche, he calls me, Night Star. He puts his arms around me and starts singing the sweetest song I've ever heard. I don't understand the words, they are all in Spanish, but the meaning is clear, *claro*. I close my eyes and he kisses me, softly, sweetly on my left cheek. In his big, strong arms I feel safe, wanted, wise to choose him. I kiss him on the lips and feel a slow shock of electricity snake through our bodies. I clench my thighs to hold this feeling. With my tongue I paint his neck and hairless chest. He separates my legs with his large, smooth hands feeling how wet I am. He seduces me slowly, touches me as if I am something fragile and very precious. He puts my hand inside his shorts. He is hard. I am afraid he won't fit inside me. I mime this idea with my hands and he laughs and says something in Spanish then eases a finger inside me dipping it back and forth. It feels good and I'm not scared anymore. When he finally enters me I bite into the thick muscle of his shoulder and cry a little. I hold him inside me long after he has come, hoping that this small pain will turn into a perfect little girl who will love me. We fall asleep and dream the same dreams.

We live in a pale blue house with a red tiled roof next to an orchard of blooming lemon trees. Our children are stars that glow in a navy blue sky. Jesus rubs my feet with mint leaves. With my tongue I tattoo his back with a bouquet of red and or-

ange flowers. Our children sing like angels above the trees. They sing to us in Spanish. Only dreams, solo sueños.

My eyes can still find his features in the dark. He seemed to me then everything beautiful and magic and good. I never saw him again, but I always listened for the music of his voice in my dreams. *Que sueñes con los ángelitos.* I hope Jesus is dreaming with the angels.

About the Contributors

DOROTHY ALLISON is the author of *Trash*, a short story collection; *Bastard Out of Carolina*, a novel; *Skin: Writing About Sex, Class and Literature*; and *The Women Who Hate Me: Poetry, 1980–1990*.

KAREN E. BENDER has had fiction published in *The Iowa Review, The Kenyon Review* and *Pushcart Prize XVIII*. She is currently completing a novel.

JULIE BLACKWOMON has had work published in the anthologies *Women's Glib* and *Riding Desire*; some of her fiction was collected in *Voyages Out II*. She is currently working on two new books: *All the Way Home* and *Marching for Boobie*.

AMY BLOOM's books include *Come to Me* and *Just One Look*.

MARUSYA BOCIURKIW is a Canadian writer and filmmaker of Ukrainian descent. Her stories and articles have appeared in *QueerLooks, Canadian Women's Studies Journal*, and *By, For & About: Feminist Cultural Criticism*. She is the author of *The Woman Who Loved Airports: Stories & Narratives*.

REBECCA BROWN is the author of the short story collections *The Terrible Girls* and *Annie Oakley's Girl*; her novels include *The Children's Crusade* and *The Gifts of the Body*.

SANDRA CISNEROS is the author of *The House on Mango Street, Woman Hollering Creek, My Wicked Wicked Ways*, and *Loose Woman*.

EDWIDGE DANTICAT was born in Haiti. Her short stories have been published in over twenty periodicals. She is the author of the story collection *Krik? Krak!* and the novel *Breath, Eyes, Memory*.

LISA HARRIS has published fiction and poetry in numerous anthologies and journals, including: *Word of Mouth, Puerto del Sol, Fennel Stalk*, and *Slipstream*. Her novella *Flights* and a novel *Resurrecting the Quick* are forthcoming.

SUSAN HAWTHORNE, an Australian writer, is the author of *The Falling Woman* (a novel), as well as the editor of *The Exploding Frangipani: Lesbian Writing from Australia and New Zealand* and *Australia for Women: Travel and Culture*.

PAM HOUSTON is the author of the short story collection *Cowboys Are My Weakness*.

GISH JEN is the author of the novel *Typical American*. Her stories have been widely anthologized.

PAGAN KENNEDY's books include *Stripping & Other Stories, Platforms: A Microwaved Cultural Chronicle of the 1970s,* and *Spinsters* (a novel).

BINNIE KIRSHENBAUM is a short story writer and novelist. Her books include *History on a Personal Note, A Disturbance in One Place,* and *On Mermaid Avenue*.

CRIS MAZZA is the author of the novels *Your Name Here: _____, Exposed,* and *How to Leave a Country*. Her short story collections include *Is It Sexual Harassment Yet?* and *Revelation Countdown*.

AMEENA MEER is the author of *Bombay Talkie*.

LESLÉA NEWMAN has published numerous novels, short story and poetry collections, nonfiction titles, and children's books. Her most recent books include *In Every Laugh a Tear, Every Woman's Dream, Writing from the Heart,* and *Fat Chance*.

FAE MYENNE NG is the author of the novel *Bone*. Her short stories have been published in many journals and anthologies.

BETH NUGENT is the author of the short story collection *City of Boys*.

SIGRID NUNEZ is the author of the novel *A Feather on the Breath of God* and is currently working on a new novel.

ACHY OBEJAS is a poet, fiction writer, and journalist. She is the author of the short story collection *We Came All the Way from Cuba So You Could Dress Like This?*

ESMERALDA SANTIAGO is the author of the novel *When I Was Puerto Rican*.

SARAH SCHULMAN is the author of six novels, including *Empathy, People in Trouble,* and *Rat Bohemia,* as well as the nonfiction book *My American History: Lesbian and Gay Life During the Reagan/Bush Years*.

ELLEN SHEA's fiction has appeared in several journals and anthologies, including *My Father's Daughter* and *Word of Mouth*.

CHARLOTTE WATSON SHERMAN is the author of a short story collection, *Killing Color,* and a novel, *One Dark Body*.

APRIL SINCLAIR is the author of *Coffee Will Make You Black*. She is currently working on the sequel to this novel.

REBECCA WELLS is the author of *Little Altars Everywhere* and is completing a new book.

S. L. WISENBERG has had work published in numerous magazines and anthologies, including: *The New Yorker, Michigan Quarterly Review, Another Chicago Magazine* and *My Mother's Daughter*.

BANANA YOSHIMOTO is the author of *Kitchen, N.P.,* and *Lizard*.

SHAY YOUNGBLOOD is the author of *The Big Mama Stories* and is currently working on a novel.